Brother, Can You Spare a Billion?

Brother, Can You Spare a Billion?

The United States, the IMF, and the International Lender of Last Resort

Daniel McDowell

Maxwell School of Citizenship and
Public Affairs
Syracuse University

Oxford University Press is a department of the University of Oxford. It furthers
the University's objective of excellence in research, scholarship, and education
by publishing worldwide. Oxford is a registered trade mark of Oxford University
Press in the UK and certain other countries.

Published in the United States of America by Oxford University Press
198 Madison Avenue, New York, NY 10016, United States of America.

CIP data is on file at the Library of Congress.
ISBN 978–0–19–060576–6

For Sara Lu. We did it.

CONTENTS

FIGURES

TABLES

PREFACE

March of 2008 was a big month for my wife, Sara, and I. At the time, we were in our mid-twenties. Sara was a public school teacher in Culpeper, Virginia. I was a graduate student at the University of Virginia. That month, after weeks of searching and deliberation, we bought a house. It was by far the largest investment of our young marriage. Our new place was a modest townhouse in Culpeper, but it was everything we wanted at that time. Our excitement and sense of accomplishment, however, were quickly replaced by anxiety and regret. On the morning of September 15, 2008—the day after my twenty-sixth birthday—I started my day with a drive to Charlottesville. It turned out to be the most memorable commute of my life. As usual, I tuned into National Public Radio as I hit the road. For the next hour, I listened to reports of Lehman Brothers' bankruptcy and the financial chaos that was unfolding. In the weeks and months that followed, we watched helplessly as the equity in our home was quickly turned upside down. As a new homeowner, I felt helpless. Yet, as a young scholar interested in global financial and monetary affairs, I was also enamored with the international financial crisis that was unfolding.

One day, I happened upon a news article that changed the direction of my research. The report explained that the US Federal Reserve was providing hundreds of billions of dollars in emergency financing to more than a dozen foreign central banks. Global dollar funding markets had seized and the Fed, it seemed, had stepped in to provide an unprecedented amount of global liquidity to stabilize the global financial system. This floored me. Most of what I had read in my graduate seminars implied that the International Monetary Fund (IMF) had, for several decades, assumed the role of an international lender of last resort (ILLR) for the world economy. The Fed's actions seemed more consistent with the work of Charles Kindleberger. In the 1970s and 1980s, Kindleberger and others argued that, throughout history, the world's leading economy tended to provide international liquidity in times of crisis. The more I researched this topic, the more I learned about the role of the United States as an ILLR dating back as far as the 1960s. Moreover, it struck me as odd that so little had been written about this topic. With little research to build on, I set off to explain—first to myself, then to others—why the United States had for decades regularly chosen to unilaterally bail out foreign economies in times of crisis.

This book is the culmination of more than eight years of work answering that question. Its realization would not have been possible were it not for the support of many family members, friends, and colleagues. I began working on this project while I was at the University of Virginia. During and after my time in Charlottesville, Benjamin (Jerry) Cohen, David Leblang, and Herman Schwartz regularly provided invaluable scholarly and professional advice. It is safe to say that most of what I know about the international monetary system, I learned from conversations and email correspondence with Jerry from his home base in Santa Barbara, California. His patience with me in those early days is beyond my own comprehension. David was both the source of great optimism as well as my first contact when I was looking for data or in need of methodological advice. Herman instilled ambition in my work by consistently challenging me to think big about my research. Together, these three scholars greatly shaped and nurtured this project in its earliest days. I am deeply indebted to each of them. While at Virginia, my research also benefited from the advice of Michelle Claiborne, Dale Copeland, Jeffrey Legro, John Echeverri-Gent, and Sonal Pandya. Each of these scholars provided guidance that helped get my ideas off of the ground and I owe each of them my gratitude.

At Syracuse University, I received helpful comments on my manuscript from Kristy Buzard, Matt Cleary, Margarita Estevez-Abe, Chris Faricy, Shana Gadarian, Dimitar Gueorguiev, Seth Jolly, Audie Klotz, Quinn Mulroy, Tom Ogorzalek, Abbey Steele, Seiki Tanaka, and Brian Taylor. Among this group, Audie, Matt, Margarita, Seth, and Shana deserve special mention. As my office neighbor, Audie became my de facto scholarly mentor as I worked to revise the manuscript. On too many occasions to count, she selflessly opened her door (and her ears) to her junior colleague and provided me with invaluable advice. Matt and Margarita graciously read several chapters of this project and provided insightful and valuable commentary. Seth and Shana freely shared their own experiences—both ups and downs—as young scholars that had recently published their first books. I cannot thank these colleagues enough for their help. I am indebted to James Steinberg for his time and efforts on my behalf. I would also like to thank Rani Kusumadewi for her excellent research assistance on this project. In general, I am thankful for my department's commitment to creating a very supportive environment that enables junior faculty to thrive.

This book benefited greatly from many other colleagues. First and foremost, Lawrence Broz and Jeffry Frieden deserve special mention for participating in a book manuscript workshop at Syracuse University in October 2013. Both Lawrence and Jeff read the entire manuscript and provided painstaking, detailed, critical commentary that significantly shaped the final draft presented here. The impact of their advice cannot be overstated. I also owe a debt of gratitude to Eric Helleiner who, all the way back in 2009, strongly encouraged me to move forward on this project at a time when I was very close to walking away from it. I am very thankful for my good friend and coauthor Steven Liao who regularly offered methodological and technical help as well as lighthearted conversation over that last two years. Three friends and colleagues from my time at the University of Virginia—Christopher Ferrero, Jon Shoup, and Joel Voss—each provided valuable input in the early stages of the project and, more important, regularly provided camaraderie and needed distraction from work over the last eight years. I appreciate comments received on this work from Stephen Kaplan, Jonathan Kirshner, Stephen Nelson, Tom Pepinsky, and David Steinberg. Patrick McGraw did excellent copy editing work on the book for which I am grateful. I thank David McBride, my editor at Oxford University Press, for his guidance as well as two anonymous reviewers for their incredibly detailed, constructive comments that greatly improved the book.

I owe my largest debt of gratitude to my family for their unyielding love and support. I thank my in-laws, Bill and Vicki, for always supporting me and my scholarly aspirations, even when this took their daughter hundreds of miles away from them. My brother, David, is also my oldest friend and has chipped in these past few years to help me through some tough times. As a child, my parents, John and Kathy, instilled in me an intellectual curiosity that has propelled me to this point. The confidence I drew from their enduring love and belief in my abilities cannot be overstated. My children—Luella, Eileen, and William—are my greatest accomplishment as well as my greatest motivation. On bad days, when working on this book felt like drudgery, my kids reminded me of what really matters most in life. Finally, I am most thankful for my wife and partner of ten years, Sara. Words cannot express her contributions to this project. She has been there each and every day throughout this process. She walked away from her dream job of seven years so I could accept a position at Syracuse University. She selflessly took on the role of lead parent so I could focus on achieving this goal. She endured countless moments of her husband's exasperation as I wrestled with my research. She picked me up when I failed and she was the loudest cheerleader when I achieved success. Put succinctly, Sara deserves coauthorship on this book. It would not have been written without her. For all she has done, this book is dedicated to her.

ABBREVIATIONS

ABCP	asset-backed commercial paper
ACBPH	Annual Cross-US Border Portfolio Holdings
ARM	adjustable-rate mortgage
BIS	Bank for International Settlements
CD	certificate of deposit
CELS	Country Exposure Lending Survey
EBM	Executive Board Minutes
ECB	European Central Bank
EEC	European Economic Community
EFF	Extended Fund Facility
EME	emerging market economy
ESF	Exchange Stabilization Fund
FCS	Foreign Currency Subcommittee
FDI	foreign direct investment
FOMC	Federal Open Market Committee
FRBNY	Federal Reserve Bank of New York
G-7, [10], [20]	Group of Seven, [Ten], [20]
GAB	General Arrangements to Borrow
GATT	General Agreement on Tariffs and Trade
ILLR	international lender of last resort
IMF	International Monetary Fund
LIBOR	London Interbank Offered Rate
MBS	mortgage-backed securities
NAB	New Arrangements to Borrow
NSC	National Security Council
SBA	Stand-By Arrangement
SIFI	systemically important financial institution
SNB	Swiss National Bank
TAF	Term Auction Facility
TSLF	Term Securities Lending Facility

CHAPTER 1

Introduction

For the world economy to be stable, it needs a stabilizer, some country that would undertake
to provide . . . a rediscount mechanism for providing liquidity when the monetary system is
frozen in panic.

Charles P. Kindleberger (1981, p. 247)

There is a scene in Frank Capra's classic film *It's a Wonderful Life* in which the protagonist George Bailey and his new bride, Mary, are waiting in a cab to be whisked away on their honeymoon. Their plans are suddenly interrupted when the driver notices an angry crowd forming in front of the savings and loan, which was founded by George's father. Despite Mary's pleas to the contrary, George steps out of the cab into the rain and rushes over to investigate the situation. George is greeted by his Uncle Billy, who, stammering, pronounces, "This is a pickle, George . . . . The bank called our loan." Billy proceeds to explain that the savings and loan had to hand over all its cash to the bank and, in a panic, he closed the doors. Determined not to allow his father's life's work to collapse, George reopens the doors and invites the crowd inside. When one angry depositor demands his entire investment on the spot, George enters into one of the more memorable soliloquies of the film: "No, but you . . . you . . . you're thinking of this place all wrong. As if I had the money back in a safe. The, the money's not here. Well, your money's in Joe's house . . . . That's right next to yours. And in the Kennedy house, and Mrs. Macklin's house, and a hundred others." Although many depositors seem sympathetic to George, they insist that they desperately need some cash to get through the week. In a sacrificial gesture, Mary instructs George to use the money they had set aside for their honeymoon to make payments to the depositors, calming the panic. At 6:00 p.m., George closes the bank for the night while he, Mary, and Billy celebrate knowing that, with two dollars left, the savings and loan has survived.

What the fictitious savings and loan in Bedford Falls had just survived was a liquidity crisis. As George explained to the crowd, the institution held considerable assets, primarily in the form of mortgages. However, these assets were relatively illiquid. That is, although they were quite valuable, they could not easily be turned into cash. Their full value was realized over time as individual homeowners made interest and principal payments to the savings and loan. Under normal circumstances, the savings and loan would have held a sizable amount of cash on the premises in order to meet standard daily liabilities, typically cash withdrawals at the counter from depositors. However, because another lender had called in a loan, the savings and loan no longer had that cushion. When depositors got word that they might be running out of cash, they panicked and demanded their money on the spot. This confluence of events meant that the Bedford Falls savings and loan was illiquid (the cash it had on hand was less than that of its counter liabilities) yet not insolvent (its total assets were greater than those liabilities).

Were it not for George and Mary Bailey's injection of liquidity and George's personal charisma, which helped him to calm the crowd, the savings and loan would have likely collapsed under the panic. That is unless some *other* lender were willing to provide emergency financing to the small-town bank. In economic parlance, that lender is fittingly referred to as the "lender of last resort." Walter Bagehot is generally recognized as the originator of this concept.[1] During the nineteenth century, financial crises were fairly common occurrences. Bank runs would lead to drains on central bank gold reserves, often prompting monetary authorities to contract credit. Although this response intuitively seemed the proper course of action, it invariably served to worsen the crisis.[2] Recognizing the self-fulfilling nature of financial crises, Bagehot argued that the central bank should do just the opposite. The only way to end such a mania is to immediately assure the public that there is no shortage of liquidity. Thus, when faced with panics, the monetary authority should provide *unlimited* and *automatic* credit to any party with good collateral.[3] Bagehot's lender of last resort was not simply doing the banks a favor, however. He understood that allowing a solvent bank to collapse, perhaps because of a rumor

---

1. Bagehot 1873. In truth, Bagehot's work represented the full maturation of ideas that had been brewing in Britain for decades.

2. Goodhart and Illing 2002.

3. However, he added that this lending should take place at a high rate of interest relative to the precrisis period. Bagehot called this lending at a "penalty rate." Any institution that was unable to present good collateral was to be deemed insolvent and should be allowed to fail.

or speculation about its health, was bad not just for the bank but for the public good as well. Panics—Bagehot recognized—often spread quickly from one institution to another, threatening the stability of the broader, national financial system.

Of course, today national economies are integrated into a global economy. Financial crises are now rarely confined to one country. In most cases, their effects spill across national borders, inhibiting the market's ability to distribute capital internationally as well as domestically. For years, scholars have recognized that a stable global economy requires sufficient liquidity, especially during financial panics.[4] Yet, because the world economy lacks the equivalent of a global central bank, there is no formal *international* lender of last resort (ILLR). In such circumstances, the question naturally arises: Who will provide global liquidity?

1. THE PUZZLE

The most obvious choice for the job of providing global liquidity is the International Monetary Fund (IMF), also simply known as the Fund. Indeed, scholars writing on this subject often refer to the Fund as the world's de facto ILLR.[5] The IMF's role in this regard is undeniable. The multilateral institution was designed for the very purpose of smoothing out temporary imbalances in member countries' balance of payments.[6] However, the scholarly emphasis on the role of the IMF has left us with an incomplete picture of how international financial crises are actually managed. As this book will show, the Fund is often not the only—or even the primary—source of liquidity during crises. For instance, when global credit markets seized after the major US investment bank Lehman Brothers filed for Chapter 11 bankruptcy protection in September 2008, financial institutions in Europe, Asia, and beyond faced a Bedford Falls–style liquidity crisis (albeit on a much larger scale). Amid the panic, their outstanding loans were being "called" by US-based lenders. Without sufficient dollar reserves to cover these debts, these foreign institutions faced the very real prospect of defaulting on substantial obligations to their major US creditors. What these institutions needed was a liquidity injection à la George and Mary Bailey. What the global financial system

---

4. Kindleberger 1973, 1981; Lake 1993.

5. Wallich (1977), Sachs (1995), Vreeland (1999), Boughton (2000), and Copelovitch (2010) all refer to the Fund as an ILLR. These are just a few examples of many.

6. While the IMF was not designed to be a true ILLR, as I discuss in chapter 2, the institution has evolved to fill this role over time.

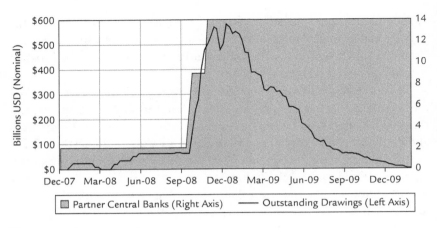

Figure 1.1
Federal Reserve Swap Line Credits, 2007–2009

needed was an ILLR: *an actor that is prepared to respond to international financial crises by providing credit to illiquid institutions in foreign jurisdictions when no other actor is willing or able.* In the fall of 2008, that liquidity came from the United States. As global credit markets froze following the collapse of Lehman Brothers on September 15, 2008, the Federal Reserve (the Fed) stepped in to provide an unprecedented amount of dollars to 14 foreign central banks until market strains began to ease in the second half of 2009. Figure 1.1 presents outstanding foreign central bank drawings on the Federal Reserve's emergency credit lines (formally, these credit lines are called currency swap agreements, discussed in detail in the following chapter) during the 2008 global financial crisis. The figure also reports the total number of partner central banks that had access to a credit line.[7] At the peak of their use, the US monetary authority provided almost $600 billion in emergency liquidity to a global economy starved for dollars.

Although this instance is without question the most consequential example of the United States acting as an ILLR, it is by no means an exception. In fact, following World War II, the United States has made a pretty regular habit of providing liquidity to foreign governments in an effort to manage foreign financial and monetary crises. The United States' first significant foray into such activities began in the early 1960s. At that time, the Federal Reserve provided hundreds of millions of dollars in bilateral financial assistance to the "Paris Club" economies to help them deal with short-term balance-of-payments problems and to protect the stability of

7. Data were obtained by the author from the Federal Reserve's website at http://www.ny.frb.org/markets/ quar_reports.html.

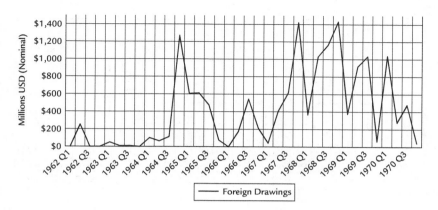

Figure 1.2
Federal Reserve Swap Line Credits, 1962–1970

the Bretton Woods monetary order.[8] In the 1980s and 1990s, as financial crises erupted and spread throughout Latin America, East Asia, and beyond, the United States repeatedly acted as an ILLR by providing direct bailout packages on roughly 40 different occasions to more than 20 countries facing financial ruin. These actions included, most famously, a $20 billion rescue package for an embattled Mexico in 1995. In such cases, the US Treasury generally provided the emergency liquidity by tapping a Depression-era funding source known as the Exchange Stabilization Fund (ESF). Nonetheless, the aim was the same: emergency, short-term liquidity provision to foreign jurisdictions in crisis. Figure 1.2 presents total foreign drawings from the Fed by quarter from 1962 through 1970.[9] Figure 1.3 plots the net total of new ESF commitments by year as well as the total number of recipient countries to which those commitments were made from 1978 through 2007.[10]

Although scholars of international financial crisis management have rightfully focused on the role of the IMF as an international financial crisis manager, they have largely overlooked the important role of ad hoc, emergency credits among states *outside* of the Fund. Following World War II, the United States has been the primary source of such funds. And yet it is puzzling why US economic policymakers would ever choose to put national resources at risk in order to "bail out" foreign governments and citizens to whom they are not beholden when they could convince the IMF to do

8. The Paris Club is also referred to as the Group of Ten (G-10).
9. Data were collected by the author from relevant historic Federal Reserve *Monthly Review* publications available at http://www.ny.frb.org/research/monthly_review/1963.html.
10. Data were obtained by the author from a document on ESF credits obtained by request from the US Treasury.

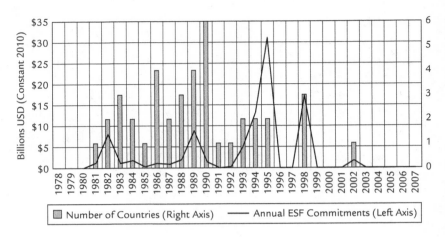

Figure 1.3
ESF Credits, 1978–2007

so. Neither the Federal Reserve nor the US Treasury has a mandate to stabilize foreign financial and monetary systems during times of crisis—yet, over and over again, they choose to do so. On the other hand, the IMF does have such a mandate and was created, in part, to manage just such problems. Indeed, there are at least three reasons why the United States should prefer multilateral lending via the Fund over providing bailouts on its own.

First, *the United States holds considerable sway over IMF lending.* It is true that the United States does not have direct control over IMF decisions and may have to compromise when its interests are not aligned with other powerful members within the Fund.[11] Nonetheless, its status as a top shareholder gives it a considerable amount of influence over the decisions the IMF makes. Research has shown time and again that US economic and strategic interests are highly correlated with Fund lending decisions.[12] Second, delegating the "dirty work" of financial rescues to a supranational institution like the Fund *provides political cover* for US policymakers. Conversely, providing bailouts directly can leave US economic policymakers vulnerable to domestic political backlashes and resentment.[13] Third, IMF lending *reduces the direct costs and risks* of providing liquidity during times of crisis by distributing these across the Fund membership.[14] The Fund is an institution built on the concept of burden sharing. By design, it prevents

---

11. Copelovitch 2010.
12. Broz and Hawes 2006; Dreher and Jensen 2007; Dreher, Sturm, and Vreeland 2009; Dreher and Vaubel 2004; Oatley and Yackee 2004; Stone 2004; Thacker 1999; Vreeland 2003.
13. Abbot and Snidal 1998; Dreher et al. 2009; Vaubel 1986, 1996.
14. Dreher et al. 2009; Eldar 2008.

the rest of the world from free-riding on larger economies, like the United States, that may be compelled to act as an ILLR in its absence. Given the benefits of relying on multilateral action to manage international financial crises, US actions as an ILLR outside of the IMF appear all the more puzzling. Why not sit back and let the IMF manage crises? Put differently, why does the United States ever provide bailouts *unilaterally* when the IMF was designed (largely by the United States) to provide bailouts *multilaterally*?

2. THE ARGUMENT

Scholars of international relations have asked similar questions about the use of US power in security affairs: Why does the United States sometimes choose to use military force unilaterally as opposed to relying on multilateral action? A common answer in the security studies literature is that "powerful states go it alone because they *can*."[15] Unipolarity, it is argued, breeds unilateralism.[16] Yet this answer is not very satisfying. Although the *ability* to act alone is without question a prerequisite for US actions as an ILLR, it does not explain the decision to actually *employ* this capability. In fact, I contend the United States has never really wanted to be in the international bailout business. For all of the reasons cited above, its general preference is for the IMF to assume this role. However, despite the fact that acting through an established multilateral process provides numerous benefits to the United States, situations can arise where it has incentives to "go it alone" outside of existing institutions. Stated broadly, my argument is that *the United States will act independently as an ILLR when it believes a multilateral response via the IMF is either too slow or too small to protect vital US economic and financial interests.*

Multilateralism, as defined by John Ruggie, demands that states surrender decision-making flexibility and resist short-term gains in exchange for benefits over the long run.[17] During times of "normal politics" states operate with lengthy time horizons and should be more willing to think long-term and give up some flexibility. However, when faced with extraordinary and unforeseen circumstances, multilateralism "will entail higher transactions costs than centralized mechanisms" and can "create problems for an organization attempting . . . to respond quickly to some exogenous crisis."[18] Similarly, Stewart Patrick notes that multilateral action

---

15. Kreps 2011, p. 4.
16. Boot 2002; Brooks and Wohlforth 2005; Jervis 2009.
17. Ruggie 1992.
18. Martin 1992, p. 772.

"can slow decisions, dilute objectives, constrain instruments, and culminate in policies of the lowest common denominator."[19] Elsewhere, Robert Keohane admits that even staunch advocates of multilateral institutions have trouble arguing they are "more efficient than states" and notes they tend to "respond *slowly* and often *partially* to rapidly changing events."[20] Echoing Keohane, Sarah Kreps adds that despite the benefit of burden sharing, multilateral actions are "more time-consuming, less reliable, and more limiting" than going it alone.[21] In sum, despite the very real benefits of multilateralism, scholars of international relations have long recognized that it also brings with it some risks. This is particularly the case during unforeseen crises when policy responses need to be fast, flexible, and forceful. Thus, under certain conditions, states may prefer the freedom of action that is associated with policymaking outside of existing multilateral forums. If a state cares enough about a particular policy outcome and believes that multilateralism will fail to adequately protect its interests, then the expected value of unilateral action can be greater than the expected value of relying on an existing multilateral solution—even if it must bear all the costs of action.

I argue that US international bailouts are a direct response to two chronic weaknesses of the IMF that limit its effectiveness as an ILLR. Both of these shortcomings derive directly from Bagehot's classic conception of the lender of last resort that lends automatically and freely. The first of these I call the *problem of unresponsiveness*. Because of the bureaucratic and multilateral process by which IMF loans are negotiated and approved, the institution has rarely lived up to Bagehot's classical conception of a crisis lender that provides credit automatically to stem panics. What good is a fire truck if it arrives after the house has already burned to the ground? The second weakness plaguing the Fund I refer to as the *problem of resource insufficiency*. Because IMF resources are finite (limited by the amount its members pay in) and because member countries are limited in the amount of funds they can draw at a given time (called an "access limit," based on their quota) situations can emerge where the institution simply does not have the resources necessary to stem a crisis on its own. Because the IMF cannot create money like a central bank, the institution does not live up to Bagehot's classical conception of an LLR that lends without limit during panics. What good is a fire truck if it runs out of water? I contend that when vital US economic interests are threatened by

19. Patrick 2002, p. 10.
20. Keohane 2006, p. 4. Emphasis added.
21. Kreps 2011, p. 6.

foreign financial conflagrations and US officials fear that the IMF is incapable of effectively protecting these interests on its own, they will pursue actions *outside of the Fund* that will. To paraphrase a William J. Clinton administration axiom, the United States opts for multilateralism when it can but acts unilaterally when it must.

What are these vital interests that US policymakers are protecting? The answer depends on historical context. In some respects, this book is as much a historical narrative as it is an empirical investigation. Although the primary subject—the role of America as an ILLR—is a constant, the context wherein these actions take place varies greatly over time. Consequently, the specific threats to US interests that motivated US policymakers to act as an ILLR depend on the circumstances unique to the context within which a particular crisis occurred. During the 1960s, policymakers acted to protect the country's gold reserves and the dollar's exchange rate—the linchpin of the Bretton Woods monetary system. In the 1980s and 1990s, policymakers acted to protect the US financial system from sovereign debt and currency crises throughout the developing world. In 2008, policymakers acted to protect the US financial system from foreign bank defaults and the domestic housing market from rising interest rates. In every case, what motivated policymakers to act was a desire to protect *US* economic interests from a gathering threat. Still, even as its actions have been without exception self-interested, indirectly they help produce the global public good of stability in the international financial and monetary systems. Thus, the outcome of American ILLR actions resembles a joint product: when two (or more) outputs are generated by a single production process.

Although the specific interests that prompt policymakers to intervene in order to protect change over time, the process through which these interests are revealed to be threatened is consistent. The process begins with some transformation in the global financial system. Far from being static, over the past half century the global financial system has undergone a series of changes as national economies have become increasingly integrated with each other.[22] Each period of change has brought with it new economic possibilities but also new risks and attendant challenges for managing these risks. Often, policymakers are unaware of the full scale of such risks until the risks reveal themselves in the form of a crisis. When an unforeseen international crisis finally erupts, it poses unique challenges to maintaining global financial stability. Typically, a crisis reveals the Fund to be incapable of effectively acting as the ILLR due to the problem of

22. Helleiner 1994.

Figure 1.4
Stages of the Argument

unresponsiveness, resource insufficiency, or a combination of the two. In many cases, the IMF has worked to implement reforms aimed at addressing these problems once they have been made apparent. For example, the Fund may increase member quotas to expand its resources. Or it may introduce a new lending mechanism designed to provide financing more swiftly. However, implementation of these reforms tends to be difficult and necessarily takes time. Reforms like these tend to come too late to address the immediate crisis. With the Fund ill equipped to manage the situation multilaterally, states will look for a solution outside of the IMF. If policymakers believe vital US economic interests are threatened by a crisis, the United States will step in and provide international liquidity. Figure 1.4 presents the order of these stages visually.[23]

The argument ultimately rests on two key testable claims: (1) the belief among US economic policymakers that a particular international crisis poses a serious threat to vital US economic and financial interests, and (2) an inability of the IMF to protect those interests on its own due to the problem of resource insufficiency or unresponsiveness (or both). This book assesses the veracity of both assertions by employing a combination of methods. First, and most important, I look at what policymakers actually said when facing a particular crisis. How grave did they perceive the threat to US interests to be? Could the Fund be trusted to protect these interests on its own? I accomplish this through a careful review of primary historical documents, including congressional testimony, Federal Open Market Committee (FOMC) transcripts, Federal Reserve and Treasury quarterly reviews, and IMF executive board transcripts, as well as interview data. These sources are also supported by secondary historical sources to further uncover what policymakers were thinking and to reconstruct the risks facing the US economy when they made their decisions. The core of the book rests on these detailed historical accounts. In addition to the historical case-study analysis, I also develop and test multiple empirical models of the bailout selection criteria employed by the Treasury and Fed. I do this by exploiting geographic and temporal

---

23. To be clear, this is not intended to suggest causality, only the temporal order of these stages. For example, a financial crisis does not *cause* the IMF to be inadequate. Rather, it simply reveals the underlying inadequacies of the institution.

variation in the recipients of US rescues. To accomplish this, I constructed two unique datasets. The first includes all requests for IMF assistance between 1983 and 1999. The empirical results shed light on why only a small fraction of these countries received an additional bailout from the US Treasury. The second dataset, focusing on the 2008 crisis, includes all countries that had signed the IMF's Article VIII (the Fed's informal requirement for a swap agreement). Analysis of these data helps to unpack why the Fed selected 14 foreign central banks for liquidity lines but passed over others. These statistical analyses enable me to further uncover the motives of policymakers by determining whether their observed actions are consistent with the public and private justifications I discuss in my case studies.

3. PLAN OF THE BOOK AND FINDINGS

The following chapter opens with a brief intellectual history of the ILLR concept. In large part due to the work of the US economist Charles P. Kindleberger, scholars initially attributed the role of global financial stabilizer to the world's leading economy, generally referred to as the "hegemon." For years, the concept was largely subsumed by theories of hegemonic stability. However, the analytical focus of scholars shifted in the 1980s and 1990s as the IMF took on a more prominent role in international financial crisis management. As economists and political economists alike became increasingly focused on the IMF as the ILLR, analysis of direct lending between states outside of that institution fell by the wayside even though such actions continued. Meanwhile, the Fund's efforts were not without critics. Several scholars highlighted the institution's shortcomings as international financial stabilizer. After further considering the IMF's weaknesses as an ILLR, the chapter ends with a brief overview of the key US ILLR mechanism employed by the Federal Reserve and Treasury: emergency loans via reciprocal currency swaps with foreign central banks. In addition to discussing how this works in practice, I consider why the provision of liquidity via these channels more closely approximates Bagehot's ideal-type LLR for the global economy. First, I point to the independence of the Fed's swap lines and the Treasury's ESF from Congress. This autonomy enables swift action. Second, I draw attention to the ability of the Fed to create dollars—the closest thing the world economy has to truly global currency. Thus, it has the capability to provide virtually unlimited global liquidity.

The remainder of the book comprises empirical chapters structured around the history of change in the global financial system. Although the system's need for an ILLR is a constant, the specific challenges facing the world economy vary across time. Thus, in order to uncover the particular motivations behind US efforts to provide international liquidity, I focus on four distinct historical periods. Table 1.1 lists these periods and summarizes the basic findings of my analysis including (1) the changes in the international financial system that generated an opening for a new kind of crisis, (2) the problems that an ILLR was needed to address, (3) the shortcoming(s) that inhibited the IMF from effectively managing the crisis on its own, and (4) the specific US interests that US policymakers sought to protect via the provision of international liquidity. The arguments and findings of each chapter are summarized below.

Chapter 3: By the early 1960s the Bretton Woods monetary order, still only in its teens, was showing premature signs of age in the face of easing restrictions on international capital flows. As newly freed private capital was flowing out of the United States to new offshore financial markets in Europe, the stability of the system's linchpin currency—the dollar—became jointly threatened by the "gold drain" and the threat of a speculative

Table 1.1 OUTLINE OF THE BOOK

	Chapter 3	Chapters 4, 5, and 6		Chapter 7
	1960s	1980s	1990s	2008
System change	relaxation of capital controls; shift from dollar shortage to dollar glut	globalization of commercial bank lending	globalization of portfolio investing	foreign banks build up massive dollar-denominated assets/liabilities
ILLR needed to	stabilize Bretton Woods monetary regime	prevent sovereign defaults	stabilize emerging market currencies	stabilize global financial system
IMF weakness	resource insufficiency and unresponsiveness	unresponsiveness	resource insufficiency	resource insufficiency
US interests	prevent gold drain; protect dollar from potential speculative attack	protect US banking system from foreign shocks	protect US financial system from foreign shocks	protect US financial system from foreign shocks; prevent interest rates from rising for US homeowners

attack against its fixed exchange rate. It was in this context that the Federal Reserve, led by Chairman William McChesney Martin, pushed for the construction of a central bank currency swap system through which short-term liquidity could be provided directly between the United States and the Paris Club countries. Although these arrangements ultimately resulted in the United States' first foray into the provision of international liquidity following World War II, the impetus for the creation of this system was quite self-interested. US economic policymakers were motivated to create these alternative financing arrangements due to emergent US preferences for a more effective ILLR mechanism. In particular, for the first time since the IMF was created, policymakers were fearful that the United States itself might need to draw on the Fund's resources.

A growing glut of dollars in the global economy was draining the country's gold stock as countries increasingly looked to convert their expanding dollar reserves into bullion before the greenback was devalued. These conversions, in turn, increased the odds of a speculative attack against the dollar, which would have forced just such a devaluation. The United States needed access to foreign exchange if it was to protect itself from both threats. However, at the time, the Fund was chiefly a lender of dollars and could not provide the United States with the sufficient foreign exchange it would need in the event of a serious crisis. A new international agreement would soon be reached—the General Arrangements to Borrow (GAB)—that increased the Fund's access to foreign exchange and hence its ability to provide credit to the United States. Yet it also added a lengthy, cumbersome, and risky negotiation process. The problem of resource insufficiency was replaced with the problem of unresponsiveness. Because US officials viewed the IMF as too unresponsive to effectively react to a crisis, they responded by developing a program to provide the United States access to substantial, flexible, on-demand emergency financing directly between central banks. Paradoxically, the initial impetus for the swap deals was the *United States' need* for an ILLR. However, the Fed soon emerged as the primary lender in the swap system. Foreign central banks quickly made use of the reciprocal nature of the swap lines for their own short-term liquidity needs. This chapter explains why the motivation behind the Fed's ILLR activities was not an interest in meeting its partners' needs, but rather in meeting its own.

Chapters 4, 5, and 6: Chapter 4 documents how the international financial system began to change during the 1970s. The end of the Bretton Woods regime in 1971 and the continued removal of barriers to international capital flows paved the way for the globalization of finance. Leading the globalization charge were US banks, which dramatically expanded their foreign balance sheets during the 1970s and early 1980s. Billions of dollars in lending went to developing countries. For the first time in decades, the US financial system was no longer confined within national borders. Banks were now directly exposed to foreign financial shocks. When a wave of developing-country debt crises hit in the early 1980s, the IMF adopted a crisis-management strategy known as "concerted lending" that further inhibited the institution's ability to provide speedy loans. By refusing to release funds until commercial banks increased their exposures, the IMF was trying to keep the banks "in the game." However, for many countries in dire need of credit, this meant historically long waits for emergency financing as negotiations with the banks dragged on. Within this context Treasury stepped in to provide "bridge loans" to a select group of economies in crisis by tapping the ESF—a 50-year-old fund that provided Treasury with resources, independent of congressional appropriation, which it could deploy to bail out foreign governments.

By the late 1980s, the IMF moved away from the concerted lending strategy. In the 1990s, it implemented several reforms designed to increase the institution's ability to respond swiftly to rapidly developing crises. Yet, even as the Fund was working to become a more responsive ILLR, continued changes in the global financial system undermined these efforts. After retrenching throughout the 1980s, US banks again began to rapidly expand their foreign portfolios during the following decade. Additionally, portfolio capital flows from the United States to select emerging markets expanded significantly. The result was that the financial exposures and spillover channels into the US economy from foreign crises grew even more complex. By the time a slew of currency crises spread across developing countries in the mid- to late 1990s, the IMF's effectiveness as an ILLR remained limited. The complexity and herdlike behavior of financial markets required immense rescue packages that the Fund could not provide on its own. Again, Treasury stepped in and provided funds via the ESF on several occasions—this time supplementing IMF credits.

Between 1982 and 1999, the ESF provided emergency loans to more than 20 different countries on more than 50 separate occasions. Chapters 5 and 6 aim to answer the following question: What motivated the United States to act as the ILLR during these years? More precisely, why did some countries in crisis receive US assistance while others facing similar circumstances were passed over? Treasury repeatedly defended its actions as being necessary to preserve the stability and integrity of the US financial system. Because the US financial system now expanded beyond US borders, LLR actions had to follow suit. Yet, many members of Congress disagreed, charging that Treasury was "bailing out" irresponsible countries and, even worse, the big Wall Street banks. Theoretically, defensive financial considerations could motivate the United States to provide bailouts through either causal pathway: special interests or the national interest. Because commercial banks are clear beneficiaries of international bailouts, they have incentives to lobby their government for such policies. Thus, Treasury's actions might represent the influence of powerful financial interests on the United States' foreign economic policy. Without ignoring the impact of private interests on policy outcomes, I contend that it is too simplistic to view economic policymakers as mere agents of the private financial sector. They are also individuals operating inside state institutions with their own interests in policy. Although Treasury and the Fed have missions encompassing a number of roles, each is charged with providing a key public good for the US economy: protecting and providing for the stability of the US financial system, broadly construed. I expect that policymakers prefer policy choices that increase the likelihood their institution will live up to this mandate. Thus, via the national interest pathway, ESF credits may also represent economic policymakers' efforts to defend the stability of the US financial system, broadly defined, which extends beyond Wall Street banks to "Main Street" as well.

In order to assess the validity of these two competing views, I develop and test an empirical model of ESF bailout selection in chapter 5. Central to my analysis is newly collected data from decades of Federal Reserve reports on the foreign lending activities of major US banks that allow me to model (1) where the institutions were exposed as well as (2) how their stock of capital has varied over time. This is important because financial system exposure to foreign crises is not simply a function of outstanding foreign loans but also of the capital that financial institutions hold in reserve. Ultimately, my statistical analysis finds that as the exposure of major US banks to a foreign country in financial distress increases, the United States was far more likely to intervene on the foreign country's behalf and provide a bailout. However, this effect is strongest when systemic risk facing the US financial system is elevated. In other words, my analysis shows that the context within which specific financial crises occur influences the likelihood that Treasury will provide an emergency rescue to a country in distress. The results support the assertion that US economic policymakers intervene where major banks are exposed in order to protect the *national* financial and economic interest rather than just the private financial interests of banks. Chapter 6 builds on this argument by presenting data from carefully selected case studies from the 1980s and 1990s. These include cases where Treasury provided bailouts as well as cases where it did not. The cases further support the argument that policymakers decided to act as an ILLR because they believed that

IMF actions alone would not protect the US financial system from grave harm due to spillovers from foreign financial shocks.

Chapter 7: The final empirical chapter puts the spotlight on the most recent example of US ILLR actions during the global financial crisis of 2008. No other moment in history so laid bare the inability of the IMF to act effectively to stabilize the global financial system in the face of a systemic crisis. Beginning in the summer of 2007 and culminating in the fall of 2008, the freezing of global credit markets on fears of exposure to toxic subprime mortgages in the United States led to an acute shortage of dollars in international financial markets. This development was a consequence of yet another change in the global financial system that began at the end of the twentieth century: the massive growth in foreign (primarily European) banks' dollar-denominated assets, which were concentrated in US mortgage-backed securities. The inability to access the short-term dollar financing they needed to roll over debts in 2008 meant that many foreign institutions could be forced to default on their obligations to predominantly US financial institutions. After nearly a decade of remarkable global financial stability, the IMF had not significantly increased its lendable resources since 1999—despite the dramatic growth of the global financial system. Consequently, when the crisis hit, the Fund was not prepared to respond and, thus, was an incapable ILLR. Once again, the United States filled the vacuum.

This time, the Federal Reserve provided nearly $600 billion in credit to a group of 14 advanced and emerging economies starved for dollars. Why did the Fed act in such an unprecedented way? I argue that the international dimensions of the crisis threatened US financial interests in two key ways. First, systemically important US banks and money market funds were directly exposed to foreign financial institutions that were blocked from frozen dollar-funding markets. Thus, without an ILLR, the US financial system was facing an existential threat from a wave of potential foreign defaults. Moreover, the IMF was incapable of providing the amount of liquidity that the global financial system needed as its financial resources were seriously constrained. Second, the seizure of global credit markets severely impaired the transmission of the Fed's interest-rate cuts to the real economy. Only by providing dollars to a global economy desperate for liquidity could the Fed ensure that the US economy got the stimulus it needed by cutting rates to historically low levels. In support of my argument, this chapter presents a variety of evidence including case-study analysis of the financial risks facing the US economy from foreign sources, statistical analysis of the Fed's swap line selection, and chronological process tracing drawing from a review of FOMC transcripts during the crisis. Collectively, the data I present in the chapter support these points.

This book concludes by discussing its contributions to the field of international political economy and to the literature on financial crisis governance. First, it presents a far more complete picture of how international financial crises have been managed following World War II. Until very recently, scholarly interest in the ILLR role has focused almost exclusively on the IMF. Yet, as I show here, the IMF's provision of international liquidity is only part of the story. For decades, ad hoc, unilateral state action has complemented (and sometimes even substituted for) the IMF's multilateral bailouts. Second, the book highlights how the IMF has been consistently dogged by two chronic weaknesses as an ILLR: the problems of resource insufficiency and unresponsiveness. The regularity with which these shortcomings of the Fund have limited its ability to effectively respond to international financial crises provides useful insights into how the institution should be reformed if it is to become a more effective crisis manager. Third, this book reveals how the globalization of finance has resulted in the globalization of national lender of last resort mechanisms. Over a 50-year period, the United States has repeatedly adapted to the changing nature of the international financial system by using existing institutions to meet new, unexpected, and sometimes unprecedented financial needs.

CHAPTER 2

The ILLR in Theory and Practice

The funds available to the IMF are wholly inadequate for it to play the role of an international lender of last resort.

> Mervyn King, Deputy Governor of the Bank of England (2001)

I am sure the IMF would like . . . to become a world bank lender of last resort. That is about the last resort I should think for anything.

> Federal Reserve Chairman Alan Greenspan (FOMC meeting, 1995)

B ecause this project turns on the concept of the international lender of last resort (ILLR), I begin this chapter with a brief intellectual history of the concept. Looking first to the work of Walter Bagehot and others, I consider the nineteenth-century origins of the classic lender of last resort mechanism. Then I quickly turn to the work of the American economist Charles Kindleberger, who in the 1970s applied Bagehot's ideas to the international financial system and attributed the role of global financial stabilizer to the "hegemon"—the world's leading economy and global financial center. By the 1990s, however, the analytical focus of scholars shifted as the IMF took on a more prominent role in international financial crisis management. As researchers became increasingly focused on the IMF as an ILLR, analyses of direct lending between states outside of that institution fell by the wayside. Yet as the Fund took on a more prominent role in stabilizing the international financial system, a handful of scholars raised doubts about the IMF's ILLR capabilities. Building on these critiques, I next explain how the problems of unresponsiveness and resource insufficiency were woven into the IMF's institutional fabric at Bretton Woods followed by a closer look at each of these shortcomings. Finally, I end with an overview of the key US ILLR mechanism at the Federal Reserve and Treasury: emergency loans via reciprocal currency swaps with foreign central banks. Besides discussing how this works in practice, I consider why the *unilateral* provision of liquidity via these channels more closely approximates Bagehot's ideal-type lender of last resort for the global economy. In particular, I point to the independence of the Fed and the Treasury's Exchange Stabilization Fund (ESF) from Congress. This autonomy enables swift action. Additionally, I argue the Fed has the ability to provide virtually unlimited international liquidity by creating dollars, the closest thing the world economy has to truly global tender.

1. AN INTERNATIONAL LLR: A BRIEF HISTORY OF A CONCEPT

The notion that the central bank ought to act as a nation's lender of last resort has British roots. Unsurprisingly, it was an idea born out of crisis. During the nineteenth century and early twentieth century, financial crises were fairly common occurrences. Bank runs led to drains on central bank gold reserves, often prompting monetary authorities to contract credit. And although this response intuitively seemed the proper course of action, it invariably served to worsen the crisis.[1] Sir Francis Baring is recognized as the originator of the term when he referred to the Bank of England as the *dernier ressort* from which all other banks could acquire liquidity during times of crisis.[2] Henry Thornton built on Baring's novel term, noting the central bank's distinctive role as the ultimate source of liquidity during financial panics.[3] Walter Bagehot further refined Thornton's ideas and is often cited as the father of the concept (even though his writing on the subject came decades after Thornton's). Recognizing the self-fulfilling nature of financial crises, Bagehot argued that the central bank should do just the opposite. The only way to end such a mania is to immediately assure the public that there is no shortage of liquidity. Bagehot forcefully articulated his argument as follows: "Theory suggests, and experience proves, that in a panic the holders of the ultimate Bank reserve (whether one bank or many) should lend to all that bring good

---

1. Goodhart and Illing 2002.
2. Baring (1796) 1967.
3. Thornton ([1802] 2008) cited two reasons for this. First, it possessed gold reserves from which distressed institutions could draw from and, second, it could print its own paper currency, which was considered as good as gold. And while Thornton saw the primary role of the central bank as regulating the money supply at a noninflationary pace, he argued that, in times of panic, the central bank should actually increase the money supply so as to provide a stabilizing mechanism and meet public demands for paper.

securities quickly, freely, and readily. By that policy they allay a panic; by every other policy they intensify it."[4] In other words, when faced with panics, the monetary authority ought to provide *unlimited* and *automatic* credit to any party with good collateral.[5]

The lender of last resort was not simply doing the banks a favor, however. Thornton and Bagehot each recognized that allowing a solvent bank to collapse, perhaps because of a rumor or speculation about its health, was just as bad for the public as it was for the bank—especially since panics often quickly spread among institutions, threatening the stability of the broader, national financial system. As Thornton put it, the lender of last resort's responsibility was not to any one bank but rather to "the general interests."[6] The ideas of Thornton and Bagehot have changed little over the last two centuries as the need for central banks to perform the lender of last resort function for the national economy has not changed much over time. Indeed, the emergence of large commercial banks has, if anything, increased the need for central banks to act as guardians of the financial system as a whole.[7] However, neither scholar considered the need for or composition of an *international* lender of last resort. This was left to intellectuals of the late twentieth century.

1.1. The ILLR and the Hegemon

Modern scholarly interest in the ILLR concept owes much to the work of the US economist Charles P. Kindleberger, who made the issue central to his research on the Great Depression and subsequent contributions to the hegemonic stability theory debates of the late 1970s and

---

4. Bagehot 1873.

5. However, he added that this lending should take place at a high rate of interest relative to the precrisis period; Bagehot called this lending at a "penalty rate." Any institution that was unable to present good collateral was to be deemed insolvent and should be allowed to fail.

6. Thornton (1802) 2008.

7. Freixas et al. (2002) conclude that there are two fundamental justifications for why central banks should assume lender of last resort responsibilities. The first is the problem of information asymmetry, which leaves otherwise solvent banks exposed to deposit withdrawals and/or the seizing of interbank lending during a crisis, which can, in turn, cause insolvency and a welfare loss for the bank's stakeholders. The second justification, which is more recent in its origins, is the "too big to fail" concept. If an otherwise solvent major bank fails (or a collection of smaller banks), the entire financial system may be unable to perform its basic functions, including the "smooth operation of the payments system, and the intermediating between savers and borrowers with an efficient pricing of risk" (45). The lender of last resort function is not without its detractors, however. The criticism most commonly levied at the concept is that it introduces moral hazard into a national financial system. Critics argue that it makes risk-taking behavior on the part of financial institutions more likely, which increases the likelihood of future crises (Kaufman 2002).

1980s. Kindleberger recognized that when national financial systems are integrated at the global level, financial crises tend to spill across borders. Thus, in order to maintain stability in the world economy, a Bagehot-style mechanism was needed at the *international* level. Three conclusions are consistently echoed in his body of work on the topic. First, historical evidence from the pre–Bretton Woods era suggested that the ILLR role was something that fell within the purview of the global economic hegemon, or, as he sometimes put it, "the leading financial center of the world."[8] Kindleberger's contention was that crisis-prone financial markets generate a social demand for liquidity provision. However, the provision of this public good is undersupplied by markets and, therefore, the responsibility falls on governments. Yet Kindleberger assumed that cooperation among multiple states to provide the good would be difficult if not impossible; thus, the hegemon was the one actor that should be both willing and able to go it alone and stabilize the system.[9]

Kindleberger's second conclusion was a normative one: ILLR actions are not just good for the dominant economy, they are good for global economic stability. In his master work on the Great Depression, Kindleberger concluded that the severity of the global economic collapse would have been far less severe—perhaps even averted altogether—if Great Britain or the United States had responded with countercyclical lending and the maintenance of open markets for distressed foreign goods.[10] Elsewhere he argued that when the leading economic state is willing to play the role of the ILLR, international crises are far less severe. On the other hand, "when there is no such lender, as in 1973, 1890, and 1931, depression following financial crisis is long and drawn out—this in contrast to episodes when there is one and crisis passes like a summer storm."[11]

Finally, Kindleberger reaches a third conclusion: The world economy cannot count on the hegemon to act as the ILLR forever. Over time, the leading economy's ability and willingness to provide the good declines and eventually vanishes. For example, "after about 1971, the United States, like Britain from about 1890, has shrunk in economic might relative to the world as a whole, and more importantly, has lost the appetite for providing international economic public goods . . . [including] last-resort

---

8. Kindleberger 1996, p. 164.

9. Lake 1993, p. 463.

10. Kindleberger 1973. Eichengreen (1995) disagrees somewhat with Kindleberger on this point, arguing that an ILLR would have only made a difference if the crisis were the result of "a temporary loss of confidence in the stability of fixed parities"; no amount of countercyclical lending would have solved the global economy's problem if the crisis was a result of a general lack of confidence in economic fundamentals.

11. Kindleberger 1996, p. 164.

lending."[12] Kindleberger's assertion was echoed by other scholars writing on the same subject. Barry Eichengreen notes that, in the aftermath of World War II, the United States had such a preponderance of economic power that it maintained the international monetary system's stability by "discounting freely, providing countercyclical lending, and maintaining an open market." However, he also contends that such instances are rare, saying, "For a leading economic power to effectively act as a lender of last resort, not only must its market power exceed that of all rivals, but it must do so by a very substantial margin."[13]

By the 1990s, interest in the hegemonic stability research program had peaked. Meanwhile, beginning with the Latin American debt crisis in 1982, the IMF had taken on a more prominent role in managing international financial crises. The confluence of these two trends resulted in an intellectual shift within the field of international political economy (IPE). Attention moved away from the role that states play in international financial crisis management and toward the role of multilateral institutions, like the Fund, in providing such global economic public goods.

1.2. The ILLR and the IMF

Created in an era of very limited international capital mobility where financial crises emerged slowly within the current account and were more easily contained, the Fund was not designed to function as a Bagehot-style crisis lender for the global economy. Yet, shortly after the collapse of the Bretton Woods monetary regime in the early 1970s, Henry Wallich pointed out that the IMF's role in helping countries facing balance of payments difficulties "has some of the characteristics of a lender-of-last resort operation." He also presciently speculated that "over the course of time, this role of the IMF may expand."[14] Twenty years later, it became normal for scholars to refer to the Fund as the world economy's de facto ILLR. With the benefit of hindsight, James Boughton reviewed the IMF's evolution into its role as a crisis manager and determined that the Fund's

12. Kindleberger 1986, p. 9.
13. Eichengreen 1995, pp. 238–239. This line of argument is a central component of theories of hegemonic stability. The basic line of reasoning says that hegemonic systems are inherently unstable as the burden of maintaining the stability of the system ultimately hastens the decline of the hegemonic power. Eventually, the leading economy grows "weary and frustrated" with free riders as well as the fact that its economic partners gain more from the liberal economic order than it does. Over time, the hegemon is both less willing and less able to provide the public goods it once did (Gilpin 1987, p. 78; Gilpin 1981).
14. Wallich 1977, p. 97.

role changed significantly in 1982.[15] It was at this time that the institution fully matured into its ILLR role by bailing out Mexico and other debt-ridden economies.[16]

Scholarly interest in the ILLR concept grew in the 1990s as an onslaught of currency crises struck developing economies from Latin America to Asia. Many such crises were accompanied by big international financial bailouts where, once again, the IMF appeared to take the lead. The increasingly important role of the IMF in international financial crisis management fueled an impressive research program that sought to explain variation in IMF lending activities. Scholars conducted studies identifying why some countries received larger loan packages than others or why the number of conditions imposed on one government varied from others.[17] Other scholars focused on whether or not crisis lending via the IMF was the appropriate ILLR mechanism for the global economy. Stanley Fischer penned a strong treatise in defense of the Fund's ILLR capabilities, but he also suggested ways that its ability to manage crises could be improved.[18] The US government even jumped into the debate when it commissioned and later released the so-called Meltzer Report. This study suggested how the Fund could be molded into a more effective "quasi-lender of last resort to solvent emerging market economies."[19]

At the same time, others presented critical analyses of the IMF's ILLR capacity, questioning whether or not the Fund could even be considered for the role in the first place.[20] Anna Schwartz (2002) offered the most forceful critique of the IMF as ILLR. She identified three primary attributes that an actor must have in order to function as a "true" ILLR in line with Bagehot's classical conception: (1) the ability to create money, (2) the ability to act quickly and respond to a crisis at a moment's notice, and (3) the ability to act without the consent of any other relevant actor. Schwartz concludes that because the Fund does not meet any of these requirements it is ill equipped to effectively operate as an ILLR. Below,

---

15. Boughton 2000.

16. Sachs (1995) also identifies the Latin American debt crisis as the turning point in the IMF's actions as the ILLR.

17. See Broz and Hawes 2006; Copelovitch 2010; Dreher and Jensen 2007; Dreher, Strum, and Vreeland 2009; Dreher and Vaubel 2004; McDowell 2016; Moser and Sturm 2011; Nelson 2014; Oatley and Yackee 2004; Stone 2004, 2008, 2011; Thacker 1999; Vaubel 1986; Vreeland 2003, 2007; Willett 2002.

18. Fischer 1999. See also Bolton and Skeel 2005, Calomiris 2000, and Mishkin 2000.

19. Meltzer 2000, p. 43. This was the final product of the International Financial Institution Advisory Commission, which was commissioned by the US Congress in November 1998 to consider the current effectiveness and future roles of the major international financial institutions (IFIs).

20. Capie 1998; Goodhart 1999; Schwartz 2002.

I build on these critiques of the Fund's ILLR credentials by more carefully considering the problems of unresponsiveness and resource insufficiency.

2. THE IMF'S LIMITATIONS AS AN ILLR

Born out of the Bretton Woods negotiations in 1944, the IMF reflects the United States' particular vision for how international financial stability would be maintained following World War II. Although the United States could have opted to provide international liquidity on its own, it preferred an institutionalized and decidedly multilateral approach. At the same time, the United States opposed creating a true ILLR. In the classical sense, a lender of last resort should provide automatic and unlimited credit when the financial system is gripped by panic. Britain's John Maynard Keynes, representing his country at Bretton Woods, favored the creation of just such a mechanism for the international economy. Keynes's idea was to create a quasi-global central bank (dubbed the International Clearing Union, or ICU for short), which would hold considerable resources equal to three-fourths of prewar international trade, issue its own currency called the "bancor," and provide automatic, on-demand disbursements to countries facing balance of payments problems.[21] His position was quite clear in one correspondence where he noted, "Our view has been very strongly that if countries are to be given sufficient confidence they must be able to rely in all normal circumstances on *drawing a substantial part of their quota without policing or facing unforeseen obstacles.*"[22]

In contrast to Keynes, the US architect at Bretton Woods—Harry Dexter White—pushed for a far less ambitious international co-insurance scheme, about one-fourth the size of Keynes's initial proposal.[23] This "International Monetary Fund" was to acquire resources from member states, each of which would be assigned a quota. This "fund" would stipulate how much of its own currency (and some gold) it would deposit with the IMF. The Fund could then make these resources "temporarily available to [members] . . . providing them with the opportunity to correct maladjustments in their balance of payments."[24] Unlike Keynes' ICU, White's IMF was not designed to provide automatic financing. Because resources were relatively scarce, loans would only be provided after assessments of policy changes that would address the underlying causes of the balance of

21. Frieden 2006, pp. 256–260; Piffaretti 2009, p. 9.
22. Quoted in Boughton 2002, p. 16. Emphasis added.
23. Bordo and Schwartz 2001; Boughton 2002.
24. See IMF Articles of Agreement, Article I.

payments problem.[25] In other words, the use of conditionality reflected US preferences to place the burden of adjustment on debtor countries. Thus, from the very outset, the IMF's capacity to provide substantial liquidity in times of need was constrained by member contributions. Its capacity to respond swiftly to crises was constrained by institutional rules precluding automaticity.[26] The problems of resource insufficiency and unresponsiveness, discussed more below, were built right into the Fund's DNA.

2.1. The Problem of Unresponsiveness

There is a standard normative argument in favor of an ILLR mechanism. As an international financial crisis is unfolding, such a mechanism can restore market confidence in an afflicted country's financial system (or, as was the case in 2008, the entire international financial system) by keeping lines of credit open when markets have seized on risk fears. In doing so, the ILLR can stop the crisis from spreading and/or intensifying, preventing localized disturbances from going global and serious panics from becoming catastrophic. The ability for an ILLR to act quickly matters because crises themselves typically unfold quickly.[27] Even if an ILLR has announced that a response is coming, if there is too long a delay before releasing funds, the damage may be done before a bailout is provided in the first place. As Eduardo Fernández-Arias and Eduardo Levy-Yeyati argue, it is desirable that an ILLR provide "timely, immediate disbursements to *prevent crises* rather than cure their consequences or, if already underway, mitigate and resolve them at minimum cost."[28] Based on the classic conception, ideally, an ILLR should preempt market panic by stating that it will lend freely to solvent countries at a moment's notice. Then, in the event of a crisis, it should promptly follow through on this promise. The issue of independence is also related to the underlying issue of speed.

25. Boughton 2006, p. 13.

26. Automaticity is the idea that a member country should be able to borrow automatically from the IMF without condition. The use of conditionality was not mentioned in the original Articles of Agreement. However, in the immediate years after World War II, the United States felt that most European countries were not particularly creditworthy. The United States preferred that IMF lending be made contingent on reforms. The Executive Board approved a new tiered system of borrowing known as the "tranche policy" in February 1952. The principle of automaticity still applied, but only to the first 25 percent of a member's quota (what was known as the "gold tranche"). Borrowing above this would kick in an application of conditionality and surveillance; repayment was expected within a period of three to five years.

27. See Bordo and James (2000), who argue that the increased depth of financial markets has made the speed of crisis response increasingly important today.

28. Fernández-Arias and Levy-Yeyati 2010, p. 15. Emphasis added.

Dependence on the consent of additional actors slows down an ILLR's ability to respond to a developing crisis. This is not unlike the role of "veto players" in the literature on political institutions. Veto players, simply put, are actors whose consent is necessary in order to enact a policy.[29] This introduces additional uncertainty from the perspective of markets since it may portend time-consuming negotiations between the financial gate-keepers. If markets know that a lender's decisions depend on the consent of others, they will be more inclined to doubt the timeliness and effectiveness of an eventual response.

The process by which a member country obtains financial assistance from the IMF consists of two main stages. In the first stage, the member country approaches the Fund and expresses its interest in seeking assistance. However, before formally requesting a loan, the country must enter into discussions with IMF staff. In these discussions, the two sides negotiate the proposed loan's terms including its size, maturity, and conditions designed to adjust the borrower country's economic policies to "overcome the problems that led it to seek financial aid from the international community" in the first place.[30] These negotiations—which can span weeks or even months—represent the first hurdle a country must overcome before it receives the financing it needs. Upon the completion of negotiations with IMF staff, an official "Memorandum of Economic and Financial Policies" is written by Fund staff outlining the objectives and macroeconomic and structural adjustments that the borrower government has agreed to implement in exchange for the loan as described in the memo. The memo is then submitted by the staff on behalf of the borrower government, along with a dated "letter of intent" to the executive board of the IMF. The program is placed on the board's schedule. On that date, the board votes whether to approve or reject the request. Exactly how slow is the IMF as a crisis lender in practice? Ashoka Mody and Diego Saravia find that between 1977 and 2004, an average of *17 months* transpired between the onset of a crisis and the initiation of a Fund-supported program.[31] Figure 2.1 displays yearly data that isolate the second stage of the IMF lending process: the number of days that transpires between a formal loan request and approval of that request by the board.[32] The mean

29. Tsebelis 2002.
30. Quote from the "IMF Lending Factsheet," available at http://www.imf.org/external/ np/exr/facts/ howlend.htm (accessed 9 February 2012).
31. Mody and Saravia 2013, p. 192.
32. More specifically, these data depict the number of days that transpired between dates listed on every standby arrangement (SBA) and Extended Fund Facility (EFF) letter of intent and the date on which the executive board approved that loan request. Since the IMF's creation, the SBA has been the institution's "workhorse" emergency lending mechanism for countries facing short-term balance of payments problems. In the mid-1970s, the

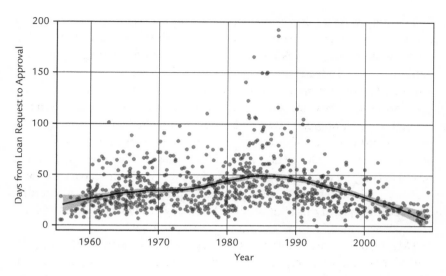

Figure 2.1
IMF Loan Approval Periods, 1955–2009

loan approval period for the sample of requests is slightly more than one month (at about 37 days). As is apparent in the figure, considerable variation exists across time and requests. In some cases, borrowers were forced to wait several months before receiving assistance; in others, the executive board approved requests relatively swiftly (this is especially true in recent years). However, for most of the IMF's history, borrowers waited several months before receiving assistance. In sum, because of the bureaucratic, multistage process through which loan requests must pass, the Fund generally falls far short of Bagehot's ideal of a speedy LLR mechanism.

2.2. The Problem of Resource Insufficiency

Since Bagehot first expressed his ideas, it has been understood that if emergency funding is to be effective, it must be unlimited—at least in principle. Within the national context, central banks have long been identified as the proper locus of the crisis-lending mechanism because they control the

IMF introduced the EFF as a complement to the SBA for countries needing medium-term assistance. SBA request and approval dates were collected by the author at the IMF archives in Washington, DC, and on the IMF's website. SBA request and approval dates as well as all EFF request and approval dates were collected by an assistant via the IMF's digital archives, the IMF's website, and various hard copies of the IMF's annual reports. One outlier is not shown in Figure 2.1 as the y-axis is capped at 200 days in order to improve interpretation.

money supply. As a crisis is unfolding, how much liquidity is necessary in order to calm a financial panic is often unclear. Thus, the central bank's ability to create money makes it especially well suited for managing national liquidity crises. Indeed, the mere presence of a willing crisis lender with unlimited resources may be sufficient to prevent a crisis in the first place. As a former US Treasury secretary, Henry Paulson, once explained in testimony before Congress: "If you have got a squirt gun in your pocket, you may have to take it out. If you have got a bazooka and people know you have got it, you may not have to take it out."[33] A lender of last resort with limited resources may be unable to reassure markets that it has the capacity to provide the credit necessary to meet threatened financial institutions' liquidity needs. Consequently, its efforts will be less likely to have the desired effect.[34] "Partial insurance," it turns out, "is no insurance at all."[35]

IMF resources are limited in two ways. First, in individual cases, the size of IMF loans are constrained by its rules and, in some cases, bureaucratic politics. Each member country's drawing rights are constrained by the amount of money it has paid in. The amount of resources the IMF will lend to each country at one time and in a given year is linked to the size of the member's quota. This cap is called an access limit. Such limits have been gradually increased over time and loans can exceed the cap if the board deems the circumstances to be "exceptional." Yet this added flexibility did not become common until the 1990s when larger rescue packages became necessary to address large capital outflows from emerging markets in crisis. Moreover, the Fund's ability to significantly exceed access limits is constrained in another way: Loans far in excess of these limits can generate political pushback from executive directors who feel a package is too generous. Thus, the possibility always exists that the board may reject a package because it is viewed as being too large. This can constrain the size of loan proposed in the first place.

Such bureaucratic pushback relates to the second way IMF resources are constrained: The institution's total lendable resources are finite. Access limits are necessary in order to ensure that a few borrowers cannot severely deplete Fund resources such that it renders the IMF incapable of assisting other members in times of distress. In aggregate, IMF resources are largely constrained by the amount that all of its members pay into the Fund based on their assigned quota.[36] Of course, the IMF can expand its

---

33. US Senate 2008, p. 19.
34. For more on this subject, see Jeanne and Wyplosz 2001.
35. Cottarelli and Giannini 2002, p. 3.
36. The Fund can, however, temporarily augment its resources by borrowing from members willing to lend additional funds.

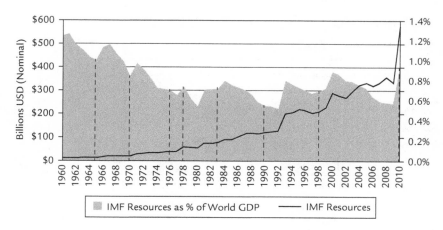

Figure 2.2
IMF Resources in Relation to World GDP, 1960–2010

resource base by increasing member quotas. However, this process takes time as it requires an 85 percent supermajority of voting power within the organization to approve any quota change. In many cases, the time between beginning a general quota review and the actual implementation of quota increases has taken years.[37] Consequently, when unanticipated crises erupt that require financing significantly in excess of its lendable resources, the institution may find its resources are insufficient. In other word, it may find itself holding a squirt gun rather than a bazooka.

To help illustrate these points, Figure 2.2 depicts the IMF's resources over time in relation to world gross domestic product (GDP). Dotted vertical lines identify years in which the Fund adopted a resolution to increase IMF quotas upon review.[38] Thus, they indicate moments when the IMF believed its ability to meet the financing needs of its members was growing inadequate. The figure shows how, over time, the Fund's resources relative to world GDP shrinks before requiring a quota increase. Of course, world GDP is not the best yardstick by which to measure the sufficiency

37. For example, the IMF adopted a resolution in favor of increasing quotas by 50.9 percent in December 1978. However, because of the time needed to round up sufficient member support (in particular, from the United States) for the increase, Fund quotas did not reflect the increase until November 1980.

38. IMF resource data were compiled from relevant IMF annual reports available at http://www.imf.org/external/ns/cs.aspx?id=326 and http://www.imf.org/cgi-shl/create_x.pl?liq. Total resources represent the highest aggregate amount and do not equate to "usable" resources; they include total member quotas as well as monies available under the General Arrangements to Borrow (GAB) and New Arrangements to Borrow (NAB). World GDP was calculated by the author using data from the World Bank's World Development Indicators (WDI) database available at http://databank.worldbank.org/data/home.aspx.

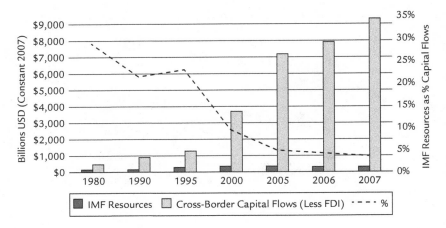

Figure 2.3
IMF Resources in Relation to Global Cross-Border Capital Flows

of IMF resources. The IMF is charged with stabilizing the international financial system, which, relative to world GDP growth over the past fifty years, has expanded at a much faster rate. Thus, Figure 2.3 displays the IMF's resources in relation to global cross-border capital flows (both in constant 2007 dollars) from 1980 to 2007.[39] Total capital flows presented include, at the aggregate level, all cross-border portfolio debt and equity investments, deposits, and all other lending.[40] The Fund's resources (in constant dollars) have not expanded at the same rate as the global financial system. Indeed, the differential growth here is quite staggering. In 1980, the IMF maintained resources equivalent to 28 percent of international capital flows; by 2007 this stood at just 3.6 percent! Consequently, the Fund's ability to effectively manage a systemic international financial crisis has declined over time. In sum, because of its constrained resource base, the Fund falls short of Bagehot's ideal ILLR mechanism that lends freely during panics.

3. THE UNITED STATES' ILLR MECHANISMS

As the remaining chapters of this book will document, when the Fund's unresponsiveness and resource insufficiency have threatened vital US

39. IMF resource data are from relevant IMF annual reports. Global cross-border capital flow data are from Farrell et al. (2008) and Lund et al. (2013).

40. Foreign direct investment (FDI) is excluded because such investments tend to be less subject to volatility and are not typically implicated in international financial crises.

economic interests, the United States has consistently chosen to act as the ILLR by providing credit to afflicted countries unilaterally. Historically, either the US Federal Reserve or the Treasury has been the source of these rescues. In this section, after briefly describing the process through which US bailouts are provided, I explain how these two ILLR mechanisms enable the United States to unilaterally respond more swiftly to crises and bring more resources to bear than the IMF.

3.1. The Mechanics of Currency Swaps

Both Fed and Treasury foreign rescues are orchestrated via what is known as a "currency swap." Charles Coombs, a former vice president of the Federal Reserve Bank of New York, once explained that currency swaps create an increase in the international reserves of both central banks "out of thin air."[41] When a swap is activated, each of the two parties to the agreement (the Fed or Treasury on the one side and a partnering foreign central bank on the other) agrees to exchange its currency for the currency of the other party, based on the market exchange rate at the time of the initial transaction. Typically, the parties agree to a prearranged limit on the amount that will be swapped as well as a specified period of time before the swap is to be reversed. A swap is reversed when the two parties swap back the same quantity of their currencies at the initial transaction's exchange rate.[42] Consequently, both parties are insulated from the effects of exchange-rate volatility: the losses (or gains) that accompany fluctuations in the two currencies' exchange rates.[43] During the swap term, the Fed or Treasury holds the foreign exchange it has acquired in a special account at the foreign central bank while the "borrower" uses its newly acquired dollars to address its financial needs. In short, while the mechanics might be a bit more complex, in practice currency swaps function as collateralized loans.

3.2. Speed and Independence

Pedro-Pablo Kuezynski likened ESF and Fed bailouts to the actions of a financial fire brigade that responds to crises quickly in an effort to prevent

---

41. Coombs 1976, p. 76.

42. Edwards 1985, pp. 137–138.

43. Of course, the transaction is not entirely risk-free. For instance, if the exchange rate changes, one country loses in the sense that it could have acquired the foreign currency at a more favorable rate.

them from spreading elsewhere.[44] Implicit in his analogy is the observation that, relative to IMF credits, US ILLR mechanisms can respond far more swiftly to unfolding crises. Unlike Fund programs, which must pass through numerous veto players involved in a lengthy, two-stage approval process, credits via the Fed or Treasury can be deployed at a moment's notice. Although the IMF cannot make lending decisions independent of its member states, both US ILLR mechanisms have near complete autonomy. For instance, Fed swap lines have, for their entire history, operated free of congressional restraint. When the central bank initiated its first currency swap agreements in the early 1960s (a case I consider in chapter 3), congressional approval was neither sought nor necessary due to the Fed's independence. Indeed, former Federal Reserve chairman William McChesney Martin believed that a major advantage of central bank currency swaps was that the Fed could "undertake the task without new legislation and the inevitable horse-trading that went with it."[45] Moreover, unlike IMF loans, which generally require policy reforms on the part of the borrower, Fed swap lines do not impose conditionality on the borrower. This further speeds up the lending process because negotiating such reforms can be bypassed.

Like the Fed, the Treasury's use of ESF resources has largely been independent of Capitol Hill. Congress created the ESF in 1934 for the purpose of intervention in foreign exchange markets on behalf of the dollar and updated its mandate in 1976, directing the Secretary of the Treasury to use ESF resources "as he may deem necessary to and consistent with the United States' obligations in the International Monetary Fund."[46] Thus, by law the Secretary of the Treasury is the lone authority controlling ESF resources, contingent only on the consent of the president. In effect, the ESF is a tool that enables the president to autonomously bail out a foreign economy in crisis without having to undertake the time-consuming and potentially contentious process of seeking congressional appropriation of funds. Unlike Fed swaps, ESF credits typically come with one condition attached: The borrower must seek long-term financial assistance from the IMF. However, the lengthy process of negotiating a reform program is outsourced to the Fund so that ESF assistance can be provided up front. In chapters 4 and 6, I explain how the United States regularly tapped the

44. Kuezynski 1984. Similarly, the ESF's contribution to the financial rescue of Mexico in 1982 is referred to as a "classic example of a 'fire brigade' exercise" by Robert Pringle in the preface to Joseph Kraft's book, *The Mexican Rescue* (1984).

45. Bremner 2004, p. 167.

46. US Senate 1976, p. 18. For a detailed historical account of the ESF's origins, see Henning 1999.

ESF to provide "bridge loans" to heavily indebted countries in the 1980s, in effect providing speedy loans while the IMF worked to hammer out long-term policy reforms to complement the financing.

Of course, both mechanisms have limits to their independence. Both the Fed and the Treasury's ESF operate with legal mandates granted to them by Congress. Occasionally, some members of Congress have opposed the use of these mechanisms. For instance, various Fed chairmen have been called before Congress to explain and justify their foreign activities.[47] However, at no time has Congress imposed limits on the central bank's ability to open currency swap agreements. With respect to the ESF, its role in bailing out foreign economies has raised the eyebrows of some members of Congress as well. The first such action came in 1978 when Congress passed legislation that required the Treasury to provide monthly statements on ESF activities to the House and Senate. However, this only served to increase the transparency of its use. Treasury maintained full control over the use of ESF resources.[48] The most ambitious effort to restrict Treasury's autonomy over the ESF came in 1995 after its resources were used to provide a $20 billion bailout to Mexico. A bill introduced by Senator Alfonse D'Amato (R-NY) in 1995 passed both houses of Congress, which, for the first time, temporarily imposed constraints on the president's ability to use ESF resources for foreign credits. The new law required congressional approval for loans greater than $1 billion and with maturities beyond 60 days unless the president assured "in writing to the Congress that a financial crisis in that foreign country poses a threat to vital United States economic interests or to the stability of the international financial system."[49] The amendment remained in place for the fiscal years 1996 and 1997. With the exception of this brief interlude, however, the institutional independence of the ESF has been otherwise unchallenged.

3.3. Lending Capacity

If an ILLR does not have sufficient resources to put out a financial conflagration, markets will view any proposed response as inadequate and the crisis will continue unabated. Partial insurance is the same as no insurance.

---

47. For instance, as recently as 2010, Federal Reserve Chairman Ben Bernanke was called to testify before Congress to justify the use of central bank swaps. Representative Mike Pence (R-IN) expressed his displeasure with the Fed saying, "From Johnstown, Pennsylvania, to Muncie, Indiana, the American people have had it with bailouts" (Hilsenrath 2010).
48. Osterberg and Thompson 1999.
49. US Congress 1996, p. 109.

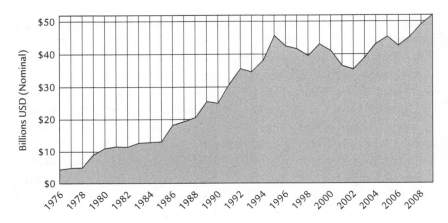

Figure 2.4
ESF Total Assets, 1976–2009

This is why central banks—with their capacity to create liquidity—are the ideal locus of the lender of last resort role within the national context. Like the IMF, the ESF's resources are finite. Figure 2.4 displays the total assets of the ESF from 1976 until 2009 based on year-end totals.[50] To date, the largest foreign credit provided by the ESF was the $20 billion rescue package for Mexico in 1995. Yet, as I will discuss in chapter 6, even this action required assistance from the Federal Reserve. Because it cannot create liquidity, the ESF has limited capacity to fight global financial crises. Indeed, although the ESF's ability to respond swiftly to crises gives it a leg up on the IMF, its lending capacity has always been considerably more limited than even the Fund's. Thus, the typical ESF rescue has capitalized on its comparative advantage as a speedy crisis responder. Much of its foreign lending has been designed to address the problem of IMF unresponsiveness.

Some ESF credits have been used to address IMF resource insufficiency. However, the Treasury has typically pledged such credits *alongside* an IMF loan with the intent of augmenting the overall financing package. Conversely, the Federal Reserve's lending capacity is virtually unlimited due to its ability to create money. Of course, not just any kind of money can address international financial crises. In the domestic context, institutions in need of emergency financing require that credit be denominated in their respective national currency. However, in the context

50. Data were collected by a research assistant from relevant US Treasury bulletins. ESF assets have historically been denominated in a select few hard currencies, including the US dollar, the German deutschemark (later the euro), the Japanese yen, and also Special Drawing Rights (SDRs).

of international financial crises, institutions and governments in need
of assistance generally need liquidity in *foreign* currencies. Discussing
the need for an ILLR in a globally integrated financial system, Charles
Goodhart explains,

> Just as commercial banks will turn to their [central bank] when they cannot bor-
> row . . . on acceptable terms in money markets . . . national governments and [cen-
> tral banks] will want to turn to an international LLR when they, or their private
> sector, *cannot borrow foreign currency* on acceptable terms in the international
> money market.[51]

Of course, Goodhart is not just talking about any foreign currency here.
In the international financial system, not all currencies are created equal.
Most national currencies are used sparingly, if at all, in international
financial markets. Only a small number of currencies can be considered
truly global currencies that are not bound by geography. At the top of the
currency hierarchy lies the US dollar.[52] The dollar is widely used outside
of the United States. It lies at the heart of the global financial system.[53]
It is the most used currency in international trade settlement and in foreign exchange transactions. It is the dominant global reserve currency
and competes with the euro for the world's most widely used investment
currency in banking and securities markets.[54] Understanding the dollar's
dominance in the international currency hierarchy is central to the discussion of the ILLR function in the global economy. Because there is no
global central bank that prints one world currency, the degree to which a
currency is "internationalized" has serious bearing on the extent to which
it could actually be useful to a foreign country or financial institution facing a credit crunch.

Take, for example, a government facing a balance of payments (or currency) crisis. In such an event, sovereigns face market pressure on their
official fixed exchange rate from capital outflows and speculation.[55] In
order to defend the exchange rate, the government must intervene in
international currency markets by buying its own currency and selling foreign exchange. For the purpose of intervention, the country will

---

51. Goodhart 1999, p. 349. Emphasis added.
52. Cohen 1998.
53. For more on the concept of international currencies, see Cohen 1971, 1998, 2006.
54. Cohen and Benney 2014; Goldberg and Tille 2008.
55. The literature modeling currency crises is typically divided into three generations. For
a first-generation model, see Krugman 1979; for the second generation, see Obstfeld 1986;
for the third generation, see Dooley 2000 and Kaminsky and Reinhart 1999.

want to use a foreign currency that will most swiftly generalize the impact on its currency's exchange rate. This is a matter of economies of scale—or what economists refer to as "network externalities"—and suggests a preference for the dominant currency, the dollar, in official foreign exchange intervention.[56] However, if the government spends down all of the dollars in its reserves, it may need the assistance of an ILLR to provide liquidity in dollars so that it can continue to support its currency and avoid devaluation.

Alternatively, consider the needs of a government on the verge of a default on its external debts. In this case, a country experiences excessive growth in terms of public budget deficits, rendering the government incapable of servicing its current international liabilities. Acquiring new loans from private debt markets also becomes more difficult. In many cases, governments may be forced to seek external financing from an ILLR in order to avoid a disorderly default. The need for external financing is related to the fact that most governments (and many private companies) borrow in foreign currencies—a problem referred to as "original sin."[57] Thus, a government cannot simply print more of its own currency to pay off its debts because what it needs is *foreign* exchange. It needs assistance denominated in one of a few select currencies that dominate global debt markets. Prior to the introduction of the euro in 1999, the dollar was the dominant currency in international debt markets. The euro has emerged since its introduction as the second key currency in debt markets, though the dollar has recently been expanding its role again.[58] In sum, an effective ILLR must be capable of providing liquidity in the proper currency. In most cases, the proper currency is the dollar.[59]

---

56. Countries are also more likely to rely on the currency that is most commonly used to settle their foreign trade transactions. Therefore, one would expect that peripheral European countries—which trade predominantly with the European Union—would lean toward using the euro; Latin American economies and oil exporters, on the contrary, would favor the dollar. On a global scale, we know that, based on the available data, about half of global exports are invoiced and settled in US dollars. This is followed by the euro, which accounts for 15 to 20 percent of exports (though this is concentrated around Europe). The remaining 30 percent or so is composed of a mix of monies, though in comparison they are marginal compared to the dollar and euro (Cohen 2013; Goldberg and Tille 2008). From this angle, then, the dollar and the euro are the most obvious choices for intervention purposes.

57. Eichengreen and Hausmann 1999, 2005.

58. Hiroyuki and Rodriguez 2015.

59. Others have made similar points. Keleher (1999, 4) once noted that the world's top currency is "for all practical purposes analogous to monopoly issuance" at the global level. He added, "In global financial crises (liquidity shortage) situations, managers of dominant international currencies should accept responsibility to supply needed world liquidity: to act as international LLR." Similarly, Kindleberger once implicitly acknowledged that the ILLR responsibility falls to managers of dominant reserve currencies (1983, 84–87).

When it comes to lending capacity in dollars, no entity can compete with the Federal Reserve. Because of its ability to create liquidity denominated in the tender that most closely approximates global money, its capacity to fight international financial crises is virtually unlimited. Consequently, unlike the ESF, the Fed is ideally positioned to address the problem of IMF resource insufficiency, especially during "five alarm" global financial crises like what occurred in 2008.

3.4. Division of Labor

ESF and Federal Reserve swaps are analogous to two separate fire crews working under the direction of the same fire department. Although each crew has the same broad goal—that of putting out fires within the jurisdiction—each has an area of expertise and a traditional clientele. Residential fires get one crew, commercial fires the other. Similarly, the Federal Reserve and the Treasury's ESF each have their own specialties that they bring to bear when confronting an international financial conflagration. In a statement before Congress at hearings on the ESF in 1976, Federal Reserve Chairman Paul Volcker summed up the division of labor between the two American ILLR mechanisms as follows:

> The Federal Reserve, in time of need, can bring very substantial resources to bear . . . . The ability to marshall [sic] large amounts of resources in one currency or another through these Federal Reserve swap arrangements at a time of need remains important in dealing with specific problems as they arise . . . . The ESF, although its resources are much smaller, can respond in a greater variety of ways to contingencies not envisaged in guidelines for Federal Reserve operations. The ESF can, for instance, engage in transactions with countries that may not be included in the [Federal Reserve] System's overall swap network . . . . The ESF can respond more flexibly to unusual or special circumstances attaching such conditions and specifications to these financings as may be appropriate with each operation . . . . Because of some of these differences, the flexibility with which the U.S. could approach a particular situation has sometimes been enhanced by having both the System and the ESF participate in its own way.[60]

The Federal Reserve's most important asset is its theoretically unlimited pool of financial resources. The Fed's ability to create liquidity in US dollars renders its capacity to respond to systemic global financial crises

---

60. US House of Representatives 1976, p. 82.

unparalleled by any other actor in the world. In circumstances when the IMF faces the problem of resource insufficiency, the Federal Reserve is generally best equipped to step in and fill the ILLR role on its own. Historically, its lending has *substituted* for IMF credits. However, a downside of the Fed's swap lines is that the US monetary authority has typically been very reluctant to extend swap lines to nonindustrialized countries. The Fed is quite circumspect with respect to the countries with which it is willing to transact. This is at least in part due to the institution's informal "red line," whereby it will only extend credit to countries that are signatories to Article VIII of the IMF's Articles of Agreement.[61] Article VIII, in short, requires that countries make their currencies convertible for current account transactions.[62] Since it was not until after 1993 that even a majority of IMF members had signed Article VIII, this red line precluded most countries from receiving a bailout via the Federal Reserve for the majority of years considered here.[63] As such, advanced industrial countries have been the typical Fed swap line recipient.[64]

By comparison, what the ESF lacks in resources, it makes up for in flexibility and agility. Unlike the Federal Reserve, the ESF has no informal restrictions regarding which countries it will lend to. In practice, this has meant that the ESF tends to serve a different population of borrowers than the Fed does. Historically, ESF credits have been extended almost exclusively to developing or emerging market economies. Moreover, because the ESF's resources are limited, its financial rescues have almost always *complemented* IMF lending. On many occasions, it has aided Fund lending by quickly providing bridge loans while IMF programs are negotiated. On other occasions, it has aided Fund actions by providing supplemental credits aimed at increasing the overall size of the financing package.

Figure 2.5 presents a spatial map of ILLR capability based on Bagehot's classical conception of a mechanism that can automatically provide

---

61. Federal Reserve Chairman Paul Volcker mentions this during a 1982 Federal Open Market Committee (FOMC) meeting where the group discusses the possibility of extending a swap line to either Argentina or Brazil. At one point in the conversation, Volcker notes, "Argentina is an Article VIII country, which is one place where we draw the ring around swap agreements. Brazil is not" (FOMC 1982c, 62).

62. Or, to put it differently, Article VIII prohibits countries from imposing restrictions on payments and transfers for current international transactions.

63. IMF 2006, 7. By 2005, this percentage had jumped to nearly 90 percent.

64. There are a few exceptions to this rule, however. Most notably is Mexico, which has been the beneficiary of Fed swaps in 1982, 1990, 1995, and 2007–2008. Furthermore, Mexico has enjoyed a permanent swap line with the Fed since 1967; since 1994 a $3 billion swap line has been maintained as part of the North American Framework Agreement (NAFA), a financial agreement between Canada, Mexico, and the United States that preceded the more famous trade agreement by a similar name.

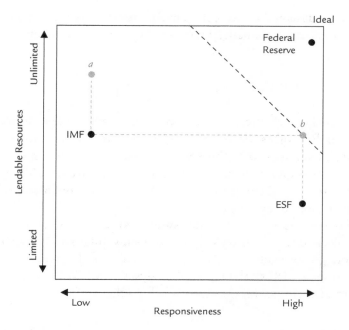

Figure 2.5
Spatial Map of ILLR Capability

unlimited liquidity. Both axes are theoretically conceived of as continua. Moving up the y-axis signifies that the mechanism's aggregate lendable resources are closer to the "unlimited" liquidity ideal. Moving to the right on the x-axis signifies that the mechanism's responsiveness to borrower needs is more proximate to the "automaticity" ideal. Thus, the closer the mechanism is to the upper right corner of the figure, the closer it is to the ideal-type ILLR. Although the specific points depicted do not correspond to a precise measure on either scale, the figure is meant to depict the various strengths and weaknesses of the IMF, ESF, and Federal Reserve as potential ILLR mechanisms. By virtue of its ability to independently open swap arrangements with foreign central banks and its capacity to create liquidity in US dollars, the Federal Reserve most closely approximates an ideal-type ILLR mechanism. Although the ESF's lendable resources are quite limited, its ability to complement IMF lending through (1) providing supplemental resources (point *a*) or (2) swiftly providing bridge loans while longer-term credits are being worked out (point *b*) has the effect of moving the *combined response* closer to the ILLR ideal point. Thus, although the United States prefers that the IMF assume the ILLR role, its shortcomings may under some circumstances threaten vital US interests. When faced with such situations, the United States' unilateral ILLR actions are designed to protect its economy from harmful spillovers by making international financial crisis management more effective.

4. CONCLUSIONS

Using Bagehot's classical conception of the lender of last resort, upon which Kindleberger's concept of an ILLR was based, I have explained why the IMF's effectiveness in this role has been consistently limited by the problems of resource insufficiency and unresponsiveness. These shortcomings are embedded in the Fund's DNA. The United States relies on two institutions to execute unilateral ILLR actions: the Federal Reserve's ability to open reciprocal currency swap arrangements with partner central banks and the Treasury's ability to open similar swap arrangements with foreign governments by using ESF resources. The remainder of the book presents historical, empirical analyses of US ILLR actions in an effort to further uncover the motives behind these efforts.

CHAPTER 3

The United States Invents Its Own ILLR, 1961–1962

We are accustomed to thinking of ourselves as a nation with almost limitless productive resources—a nation capable of turning out goods and services sufficient for our own needs and for a sizeable foreign demand, without undue monetary strain . . . . This is true. But time moves swiftly.

Robert B. Anderson (*Foreign Affairs*, 1960, p. 419)

In the preceding chapter, I explained how at its creation the International Monetary Fund (IMF) reflected a distinctly US vision for how the international financial system following World War II would be stabilized in times of stress. Rather than follow John Maynard Keynes's plan to create an entity resembling a global central bank, Harry Dexter White and the US delegates advocated for a multilateral institution without the capacity to create its own money, with relatively limited resources, and that would not provide credit automatically. In short, the problems of resource insufficiency and unresponsiveness—which reflected US preferences at the time—were part and parcel to the Fund's anatomy at its birth. Yet, fewer than 20 years after the negotiations at Bretton Woods concluded, the US Federal Reserve was lending hundreds of millions of dollars to a handful of countries in need of short-term balance of payments assistance. However, unlike the Fund, the Fed provided these credits automatically and without conditionality. In effect, the Fed was acting as the global central bank that it resisted creating just a few years before.

Why did the United States change course so dramatically in such a short period of time? What motivated the United States to begin providing short-term liquidity to foreign countries when the IMF had been created for that very purpose not two decades earlier? Broadly speaking, two factors explain the shift. First, the IMF's shortcomings as an international lender of last resort (ILLR) took 15 years to fully reveal themselves to US policymakers. The problems of resource insufficiency and unresponsiveness were not really problems at all during the initial postwar years. In that era, international capital mobility was severely restricted and crises were small and developed slowly. However, by the early 1960s, things were changing. Restrictions on capital flows were eased and cracks in the IMF's ILLR credentials were made manifest. Second, for the first time since World War II had ended, the US found *itself* in need of an ILLR. The United States had designed the Fund to place the burden of adjustment on debtor countries at a time when US policymakers did not anticipate that the United States would soon become a debtor country itself. The changing nature of global finance and the Fund's weaknesses as ILLR directly threatened two vital US economic interests that were intimately related to one another: the stability of the dollar's exchange rate and the country's gold stock.

Top US policymakers wanted a more effective ILLR mechanism that would give the United States access to substantial, on-demand financing. It was the Federal Reserve that ultimately delivered the goods. Between 1962 and 1963, the Fed negotiated an ad hoc system of swap agreements with 11 foreign central banks that gave the US monetary authority access to foreign exchange at a moment's notice, outside of the auspices of the Fund. In exchange, the Fed had to make dollars available to its partner central banks under the same rules. In a matter of two years, the United States ended up as the primary liquidity provider in the system. Indeed, the Fed largely assumed the ILLR mantle from the IMF on behalf of those countries involved in the swap system. Yet the United States did not create the system because it wanted to provide easy credit to its partners. Reciprocity was just the price of admission. The United States pushed for the system of credit lines because it wanted a more effective ILLR mechanism for *itself*: one that could protect its own interests better than the IMF.

1. MORE DOLLARS, MORE PROBLEMS

The dollar was the cornerstone of the international monetary order following World War II. Fixed to gold at $35 per ounce, it was the reference point to which all other currencies were pegged. Because the currencies of Europe were not fully convertible for current account transactions until the late 1950s, most international transactions were settled in dollars.[1] The

1. Britain's pound sterling still had an important role, albeit a declining one and restricted mainly to the so-called sterling area.

growth of world trade and the reliance on the dollar meant that the dollar was in high demand—but for years it was also in short supply. Following World War II, Europe was in the midst of a consumption and investment frenzy. Still recovering from the destruction of the war, these countries were in desperate need of dollars to import food and capital equipment.[2] The IMF played a modest part in filling the dollar gap through its lending. The United States also responded by providing funds directly to Europe via foreign aid. The Anglo-American Loan Program and Marshall Plan were developed as a means to address the shortage by providing dollars to a recovering Europe.[3] However, by the late 1950s, the global dollar short-age transitioned into a global *oversupply* of dollars that threatened the sta-bility of the dollar and the US gold stock.

1.1. From Dollar Gap to Dollar Glut

This shift from dollar scarcity to dollar glut was the consequence of sev-eral factors, but at its base it was a consequence of official and private capi-tal flows out of the United States. In 1958, the major European economies returned their currencies to external convertibility for current-account transactions, meaning that for trade purposes the currencies were now freely tradable with other foreign exchange. This was soon followed by the relaxation of exchange controls and the explosion of the offshore "euro-dollar" market in London.[4] Together, these changes created conditions where short-term international capital transfers increased in size and fre-quency. In the words of Susan Strange, "Between 1958 and 1961 it is no exaggeration to say that there had taken place *a major renascence of inter-national financial and money markets* . . . . [This] united Western Europe and North America for the first time since the war into a single interna-tional market for foreign exchange."[5] Capital movements were driven by interest-rate differentials as well as expected changes in par values.[6]

2. De Vries 1987, p. 13.
3. Helleiner 1994, pp. 58–62.
4. For an excellent historical account of the development of the euro-dollar market and the role that states played in its creation, see chapter 4 in Helleiner 1994.
5. Strange 1976, p. 58. Emphasis added. The integration Strange speaks of was primarily through the offshore deposit or "euro-dollar" market, which started in London around 1958 and took off in the 1960s. Direct integration of national financial markets only came later (see Cohen 1986).
6. The economic boom taking place in Europe caused those countries to raise interest rates. On the contrary, with the United States in recession, the Federal Reserve preferred lower rates to stimulate the US economy. This led to the interest-rate differentials that were, in part, driving liquid capital flows. For example, the spread between UK and US Treasury

Bretton Woods was getting its first taste of speculative capital flows. Private capital outflows rose throughout the 1950s, reaching nearly $4 billion in 1960. Meanwhile, even after the Marshall Plan ended, US overseas military spending and foreign aid continued to increase by almost $2 billion annually over 1952 levels.

All the while, Europe's economy had recovered. By 1954, industrial production in most European countries reached levels 50 percent *above* those prior to World War II. World trade had also recovered. The total volume of international trade was about 65 percent larger than it had been before the war. As European countries exported more, they sought to increase their own foreign exchange reserve stock as insurance against trade shocks. Due to the inconvertibility of their own currencies, an increase in reserves meant an increase in *dollar* holdings. By the latter half of the 1950s, a number of onetime trade deficit countries—including Belgium, France, the Federal Republic of Germany, Italy, and Japan—were all running trade surpluses and rapidly stockpiling dollars.[7] The combination of overseas US government spending, a transformed international financial system increasingly characterized by private, liquid capital flows from the United States to Europe, and growth in European governments' foreign exchange reserves resulted in a growing supply of dollars pooling outside of US borders. The rapidly changing international financial system generated two new threats to the US economy.

1.2. Two Threats: The "Gold Drain" and Speculation

The growing international supply of dollars led to a feeling that the dollar was overvalued. As Barry Eichengreen explains,

> The problem was less that the dollar was fundamentally overvalued relative to the yen and the European currencies; it was more that the dollar was increasingly overvalued relative to gold, reflecting the inelasticity of monetary gold supplies and the growing overhang of foreign dollar balances.[8]

bill rates, which in the summer of 1960 was 3.1 percent with the United Kingdom offering a rate of 5.5 percent while the United States sat at 2.4 percent, see *Financial Times* 1960.

7. De Vries 1987, p. 25. This reserve accumulation was, in part, due to US overseas military spending and foreign aid transfers. But it was also a consequence of the dollar's role as the world's top currency. Since most trade was settled in dollars, countries running current account surpluses naturally found their dollar reserves increasing as a result of their involvement in international trade.

8. Eichengreen 2000, p. 5.

This was especially problematic because the currency was convertible into gold at 1/35th an ounce per $1. By the end of 1957, foreign countries had invested their excess dollars into $13.6 billion of liquid assets in the United States. Of that sum, $7.9 billion were "official" assets: predominantly short-term US treasury securities that could be converted into gold on demand. The remaining $5.7 billion was privately held in the form of US bank deposits. At that time, the United States maintained a total of $22.9 billion in gold holdings compared to the rest of the "free world," which possessed only $14.8 billion in gold.[9] It became apparent that if the countries of Western Europe continued to grow and increase their dollar reserves and subsequently their dollar-denominated assets, they might begin to convert some of these assets into gold. A modest redistribution of gold from the United States to its allies abroad was not viewed as a serious threat to the US economy or the international financial system. However, what was unfolding was not a modest redistribution. The rate at which gold was flowing to Europe was alarming to US officials. As a result of foreign dollar-gold conversions, from 1957 through 1960, US gold holdings fell to $17.8 billion. In just five years, the United States had lost nearly a quarter of its bullion.[10]

The United States had a vicious cycle on its hands as it related to gold conversions. As foreign economies amassed billions of dollars in US treasury bonds, they began to worry that the United States might one day not have sufficient gold reserves to back its growing obligations to foreign creditors. Suspicion was building that the United States might have to devalue the dollar by increasing the dollar price of gold in order to stop the drain.[11] This suspicion, in turn, increased the incentive of foreign governments to convert at least a portion of their dollar-denominated assets into gold as a way of protecting themselves from experiencing losses if the dollar were devalued. As one scholar writing on the subject has put it, "Around 1960 it became clear that the [gold] reserves in Fort Knox were not adequate to cover foreign liabilities.[12]

The dollar also faced a second threat from private capital holders. The development of European financial markets in the early 1960s meant that

9. For added perspective, in 1945, US gold holdings totaled $29 billion. Distribution of gold holdings among major economies was as follows: Germany, $2.5 billion; United Kingdom, $2.3 billion; France, $0.6 billion; Italy, $0.5 billion. See Knipe 1965, p. 158.

10. Ibid., pp. 159–61.

11. Bremner 2004, p. 166. See also Naftali 2001, p. 385. These concerns were not limited to foreign finance ministries, either. For instance, in an interview with the *New York Times* in the spring of 1959, an economist and former research director of the IMF, Edward Bernstein, stressed the need for the United States to deal with the international dollar glut before the dollar became a "weak" currency; see *NYT* 1959a.

12. Zimmermann 2002, p. 111.

US and foreign investors alike had many new investment opportunities in currencies other than the dollar. Fears about dollar devaluation generated concerns among private market participants as well. A devalued dollar would mean investments in the currency would lose value when converted into foreign currency. If investors believed a devaluation was inevitable, they had incentives to move their money into foreign currency–denominated assets. However, such a move meant that these foreign investors would be effectively selling dollars to foreign central banks (in exchange for foreign currency) already flush with dollar reserves. Such a move would just increase the pressure on European monetary authorities to continue converting dollars into gold. The mere anticipation that the United States might be forced to devalue the dollar could create a self-fulfilling speculative flight from the dollar. Hence, the United States was vulnerable to the threat of a "bank-run-like crisis. If private investors converted their claims on the [United States] into foreign currencies *en masse*, the dollar would come tumbling down."[13] The United States needed the help of an ILLR to protect its gold stock and increase global confidence in the dollar-gold peg.

2. IN SEARCH OF AN ILLR

Although the Bretton Woods monetary order had already weathered several crises, this was the first that threatened the stability of its linchpin currency.[14] If a speculative attack on the dollar were to unfold, the United States would need access to an external source of credit in foreign currencies other than the dollar. For instance, borrowing French francs would enable the United States to slow a speculative flight from the dollar by entering into foreign exchange markets and selling francs to buy excess dollars that were being moved out of the country. Or, alternatively, it could exchange francs for dollars being held by the French central bank in order to preempt a conversion of those dollars into gold. At the time, the IMF was the closest thing the world economy had to an ILLR. However, the majority of the IMF's resources were in US dollars.[15] In November 1961, for example, the United States had rights to borrow $5.8 billion from the IMF. However, the Fund's holdings of the major industrial country

---

13. Eichengreen 2000, p. 33. For more on these two threats to the dollar, see Gavin 2004, pp. 33–88.

14. Previous crises include the wave of devaluations (led by sterling) in 1949 and the sterling crises in 1951, 1953, and 1957.

15. Indeed, the vast majority of its lending at this time was in dollars. Until 1960, 87 percent of all drawings were in that currency (Strange 1976, p. 104).

currencies, other than British pound sterling, only amounted to $1.6 billion.[16] Thus, the Fund was really only equipped to provide to the United States a loan in its own currency. Such a loan would do nothing to defend the dollar from the risks it was facing.

The IMF had insufficient resources to cover a potential drawing from the United States.[17] In light of this, both US economic policymakers and executives at the IMF began to consider ways they could bolster the institution's access to currencies other than the dollar. What ultimately developed was a proposal for a new lending agreement, known as the General Arrangements to Borrow (GAB), among the major industrial powers. Yet, even as the new arrangement increased US access to foreign exchange, it also increased the number of hoops that the country would have to jump through in order to access this financing. In other words, the GAB addressed the IMF's problem of resource insufficiency and replaced it with the problem of unresponsiveness.

2.1. The General Arrangements to Borrow

The purpose of the GAB was to replenish the IMF's resources with currencies other than the dollar. These additional resources would be available to help the United States address the concerns about a speculative flight from the dollar on the part of private-market actors and the threat of gold conversions en masse on the part of official dollar holders. The basic functionality of this new lending arrangement, as explained by then Chairman of the Federal Reserve William McChesney Martin Jr., was as follows:

> The IMF would sell to the United States for dollars the major foreign convertible currencies that the IMF would borrow from the other participating countries. The United States could then use these currencies to buy up dollars offered in the market by private holders, and to redeem dollars acquired by foreign central banks in excess

---

16. Solomon 1982.

17. Even more so than a potential US drawing, what really kept the IMF executives up at night was the potential for a simultaneous drawing by the United States and the United Kingdom. There was a very real fear that in such an event there would not be sufficient resources to go around. This concern became especially acute in light of a drawing by the United Kingdom in the summer of 1961. The British withdrew $1.5 billion; however, only one-third of this was in dollars due to US insistence that the majority of the loan be in the nine other convertible currencies held at the Fund. This single drawing nearly exhausted the IMF's lendable resources—in fact, it was forced to sell $500 million of its own gold to rebuild its currency stock (Strange 1976, p. 108).

of the amounts they are willing to hold. This would tend to prevent dollar holdings of foreign central banks from becoming a drain on our monetary gold stock.[18]

Although the mechanics of how a new IMF lending arrangement would work were quite straightforward, the process of creating such an arrangement was not. The negotiation of the GAB signified a major shift in the postwar international political economy. During the Bretton Woods negotiations in 1944, the US delegation led by White so dominated the proceedings that Britain's Keynes complained that "a cooperative international agreement was being undone as Americans reworked the Bretton Woods institutions to guarantee American preponderance."[19] By 1961, the pendulum had swung the other way. It was now the United States, not the Europeans or Japanese, that needed liquidity.[20] This asymmetry in need determined the negotiating positions of the parties from the outset. The United States, as the country most likely to borrow and directly benefit from the new lending arrangement, had little leverage. The continental European countries, as the likely lenders, held nearly all the cards.[21] GAB negotiations involved many months of "tough bargaining and, often, bitter disagreement."[22]

Two fault lines defined the difference between US and European preferences over the new arrangement: (1) the extent to which a new arrangement would be tied to the IMF and (2) the size of the arrangement. The original plan for the GAB, proposed by the United States and supported by IMF's managing director, Per Jacobsson, was to put in place "firm commitments by the creditor nations to reinforce the IMF as a whole."[23] That is, the rules that already governed IMF lending would remain in place for any new resources provided to the Fund. The United States supported this approach because it retained the largest percentage of votes within the Fund. Thus, tying any new arrangement directly to IMF governance would give the United States substantial influence over how quickly any new funds would be released and what conditions would be attached. The French delegation led the European Economic Community (EEC) members in opposing this approach. France had long resented what it believed to be a UK-US alliance that dominated global monetary relations since Bretton Woods. France worried that if the GAB was completely subsumed

18. US House 1962, p. 91.

19. Frieden 2006, p. 259.

20. The exception here was the United Kingdom, which was also facing significant balance of payments issues of its own.

21. A press report at the time summed the likely positions up this way: "As things look now, the United States is more likely to become a borrower than a lender" (*Washington Post* 1961).

22. Strange 1976, p. 105.

23. Ainley 1984, p. 7.

by the IMF, where the United States maintained unrivaled power, it would be difficult to impose the tough but necessary conditions on the United States in the event of a drawing.[24] France favored an approach that would only give the IMF limited influence over the use of the newly committed funds. In terms of a new arrangement's size, as the likely borrowers, the United States naturally preferred that more resources be made available. President Kennedy wanted $4 billion in drawing rights for the United States.[25] On the other side, the EEC—which would be putting up the bulk of the money—preferred to have a smaller arrangement and proposed making only $2 billion available to the United States.

In November 1961, GAB negotiations officially began in Paris. In total, 10 industrial countries agreed to participate in the negotiations. This elite group earned two monikers: the Group of Ten (G-10) or, alternatively, "the Paris Club."[26] The EEC countries entered with a strong bargaining position. They were the key surplus countries being courted and, at that time, had no foreseeable need of drawing on the arrangement. On the other hand, the United States' negotiating position was weakened by the obvious self-interested motives behind the proposal. From the outset, the prospective creditors controlled the negotiations. The French, Belgians, and Dutch had three demands they insisted be met, or otherwise talks would not proceed. The first was that they would have much greater say over the use of funds than they did in the IMF itself. This included the possibility that there could be a separate review of the prospective borrower's domestic policies. The second demand was that the creditor countries themselves would decide whether or not the Fund could borrow from them and loan the offering to a deficit country. Finally, they wanted concessions that the use of the new lines of credit would be limited to fighting a speculative attack against a major economy or to finance a

24. As evidence of this, the French pointed to recent history. The United Kingdom was just behind the United States in terms of voting power within the IMF. In August 1961, Great Britain drew on Fund resources. Yet the French felt that the IMF had not imposed as strict an array of conditions on Great Britain as it had on the French when they borrowed from the IMF in 1958. France believed that Britain received easier terms due to its more powerful role within the institution and its close alliance with the United States on monetary issues (Strange 1979, p. 109). This occurred despite the fact that Jacobsson had told UK contacts that they had to willingly accept a stringent adjustment program in exchange for a loan because smaller countries would only submit to the Fund's demands if countries like the United Kingdom did as well (Jacobsson 1979, p. 368).

25. According to Per Jacobsson's account, when US Treasury's representatives met with him during the negotiation process, they proposed a plan that would allow any one country to borrow up to 125 percent of its quota. Jacobsson concluded that this was "obviously thought to be to the benefit of the USA" (Jacobsson 1979, pp. 378, 381).

26. Participating countries include Belgium, Canada, France, Germany, Italy, Japan, the Netherlands, Sweden, the United Kingdom, and the United States.

Table 3.1 GAB: INDIVIDUAL CREDIT ARRANGEMENTS

Participant	Units of Participant's Currency	US Dollar Equivalent (*in Millions*)	Percentage Share
United States	US$ 2,000,000,000	2,000	33.33
United Kingdom	£ 357,142,857	1,000	16.66
Deutsche Bundesbank	DM 4,000,000,000	1,000	16.66
France	NF 2,715,381,428	550	9.16
Italy	Lit 343,750,000,000	550	9.16
Japan	¥ 90,000,000,000	250	4.16
Canada	Can$ 216,216,000	200	3.36
Netherlands	f. 724,000,000	200	3.36
Belgium	BF 7,500,000,000	150	2.50
Sveriges Riksbank	SKr 517,320,000	100	1.66
Total		6,000	100.00

normal drawing by the United States.[27] In short, the ECC countries made it known that they did not want to create an institution that would rubber-stamp a bailout of the United States without imposing tough economic reforms. The United States had little choice but to accept these terms.

The US Treasury representative in Paris, Donald J. McGrew, visited with Jacobsson to describe the compromise that had been struck regarding the GAB. Jacobsson strongly opposed this approach, even calling the ECC demands "strange and silly!"[28] He felt that by ceding most of the control over to the industrial creditor economies, the IMF would be marginalized. He made the case that any arrangement must meet three standards: (1) respect the Articles of Agreement, (2) not impair the authority of the IMF, and (2) give the IMF the authority to decide whether to borrow (participating countries could, however, decide whether to lend). In the end, the EEC countries conceded these points to Jacobsson and pacified at least one important US demand by agreeing to make a total of $4 billion in resources available to the United States. Table 3.1 lists the agreed-upon contributions of each country to the GAB.[29]

Regardless of these concessions, which were by no means trivial, the final design of the GAB was a victory for the EEC countries. When the G-10 agreed on terms in December 1961, French Finance Minister M. Wilfrid

27. Strange 1979, p. 111.
28. Jacobsson 1979, pp. 376–377.
29. Table adapted from Ainley 1984, p. 13.

Baumgartner triumphantly explained that the new resources would not be available to the IMF without restraint. Rather, they would "be submitted to scrutiny and discussed by the finance ministers of the [G-10]."[30] Any loan under the new agreement had to be agreed upon based on a cumbersome, if cleverly designed, procedure. A letter from Baumgartner to the other GAB participants sums up the agreed-upon system:

1. To start with, the country in need of a loan is to first consult with the Managing Director of the IMF and then with the remaining participants in the arrangements.
2. The Managing Director decides whether to formally ask for resources, in which case the participants (excluding the borrower) will enter into discussion. The aim is to reach a unanimous decision in favor or against the loan.
3. If a unanimous agreement cannot be reached, the question will go to a vote (again, excluding the borrower). Requests must:
   a. be approved by two thirds of the remaining nine participating countries and,
   b. garner a three-fifths majority of votes, which were distributed in accordance with the resources each country put into the arrangement.
4. If the loan is approved, then the creditors then enter into additional consultations with the Managing Director regarding the amount of each currency that will be loaned to the Fund. In these consultations, participants have the ability to object to the proposal made by the Managing Director.[31]

The GAB was not designed to function as a well-oiled ILLR. Moreover, the final design of the GAB shifted power away from the IMF and toward the EEC countries. The United States had far less power within the GAB relative to normal operations of the IMF. This was best embodied by the voting structure, the specific formula of which the EEC had developed with the explicit aim of giving veto power to their countries. As Baumgartner's letter states, any loan had to garner a three-fifths majority of votes, which were determined by each country's contribution. Susan Strange ably summarized how the veto was designed to function in practice:

> The arithmetic would work as follows: a U.S. drawing would be the full amount
> less its own commitment, i.e. [$4 billion]. Three-fifths of this amount would be

---

30. Strange 1979, p. 112.
31. EBS 1961, p. 13.

[$2.4 billion]. But non-ECC participants (Britain, Canada, Japan, and Sweden) could only muster [$1.55 billion] "votes" between them.[32]

Thus, if all ECC members collectively opposed the terms of a US loan request, they could effectively block it.

During an IMF executive board meeting one month after the Paris negotiations, the United States' top representative at the Fund, the executive director Frank Southard, voiced his country's disapproval of the arrangement's ultimate design. Although he begrudgingly admitted "the scheme was, of course, a compromise," Southard pointed out the GAB's "limitations" highlighting two issues. First, the GAB did not provide the Fund with "supplementary resources for its ordinary operations"— alluding to the fact that the control of the new funds were outside of the IMF's control, where the United States maintained significant influence. Second, Southard explained that the United States would have preferred a system that did not require the Fund to consult with the prospective lending countries. In other words, here Southard was objecting to the rule that allowed the creditor ECC countries to deny a loan if they had sufficient votes to block it. It would have been better had the agreement empowered the managing director, after consulting the other executive directors, to decide "whether a particular exchange transaction or stand-by arrangement was necessary to forestall or cope with an impairment of the international monetary system."[33]

In sum, the US officials felt that borrowing from the GAB was unnecessarily cumbersome and gave too much power to the EEC. This posed another problem from the United States' perspective. If the United States were to borrow from the GAB, it would be subject to a list of policy conditions and austerity measures that the ECC would insist be a part of any loan. The ECC countries felt that the United States needed to adjust its domestic economic policies in order to reverse the private capital flowing out of the US economy; flows that were contributing to the global dollar glut. In the years leading up to the GAB negotiations, European policymakers signaled that they felt that threats to the dollar were partly a consequence of domestic inflationary pressures. The Fed needed to raise interest rates. According to an entry in Jacobsson's diary, the Europeans also "expected that the Americans would have to do more or less the same things as they had done themselves—including the holding back of wage increases."[34]

---

32. Strange 1976, p. 118, footnote 44.

33. EBM 1961, pp. 10–11.

34. Jacobsson's diary quoted in James 1996, p. 157. Jacobsson himself was prone to feeling this way. In the spring of 1959, he was quoted in the *New York Times* as saying the US gold

This prospect made drawing on the new arrangement all the more unpalatable to the Kennedy administration, which was focused on implementing a domestic economic program designed to stimulate the US economy—the exact opposite of what the ECC wanted.

Despite myriad US objections, the Kennedy administration and the Federal Reserve strongly lobbied Congress to ratify the arrangement. Their dissatisfaction with its design notwithstanding, they understood that the GAB remained an important signal to markets (even if they had no intention of using it). In the event of an attack on the dollar either by speculative capital flows or demands at the gold window, the United States now had access to an additional $4 billion in foreign currencies. Combine this with the resources available via traditional IMF sources and the United States now had rights to some $5.2 billion in foreign currencies. It was a start. But US officials were still not content.

3. AN ALTERNATIVE ILLR: CENTRAL BANK CURRENCY SWAPS

The creation of the GAB helped address the IMF's problem of resource insufficiency by increasing its access to foreign currencies. Yet, even as the new arrangement alleviated one problem, it intensified another: the problem of unresponsiveness. For the United States, acquiring the resources it might need was now more difficult and more costly than ever. A prospective drawing from the GAB was a relatively risky proposition, both economically and politically. First, in the event of a speculative move against the dollar, the IMF could not disburse GAB funds on demand. Accessing credit via the new mechanism had considerable red tape. Deliberation among the creditor economies that controlled access to the funds could take weeks or months. In the meantime, the very threat that a drawing was aimed at mitigating may have already done its damage. Second, there was the issue of conditionality. Early in the IMF's existence when it was thought the United States would not need to borrow from the Fund, the United States pushed for the adoption of conditionality. Now, the European countries—which had initially opposed the IMF's use of conditionality—flexed their newfound muscle by making GAB drawings

---

drain "represents a warning about the trend of costs and prices in that country" (1959b). US policymakers were aware of the European's position as well. In a 1960 Federal Reserve meeting, one board member noted that US allies were fearful that the United States would not take "adequate measures" to correct the balance of payments crisis and would "succumb to excessive monetary ease and fiscal laxity" (FOMC 1960, p. 15).

dependent on a domestic adjustment program they would design. What the US policymakers really needed and wanted was an ILLR that could act quickly and independently in the event of a crisis: a system that would give the United States access to countercyclical, on-demand financing free of conditions. As it happened, just such a system was being developed, even as the GAB negotiations were under way. The solution to US concerns about the IMF's inadequacies as an ILLR was a new kind of liquidity arrangement.

3.1. The Fed's Novel Idea

As chairman of the Fed, William McChesney Martin believed that his institution was the ideal candidate to act in international currency markets to address the threats to the dollar. As he put it, it was the only actor that could "undertake the task without new legislation and the inevitable horse-trading that went with it."[35] Due to its political independence, the Fed was more nimble, more flexible in this realm than any other US institution. Martin proposed a novel solution to the threats posed by the gold drain and a potential speculative attack: the central bank currency swap. These deals would enable the Fed to "swap" dollars for the currency of a foreign partner for a prearranged period of time. Thus, they would give the United States access to foreign exchange much more swiftly than the IMF, and without conditionality. They could be used to "counter speculative attacks on the dollar" and "to avoid unnecessary U.S. Treasury gold losses resulting from rapid accumulation of excess dollar balances by foreign monetary authorities."[36] In other words, the foreign exchange the United States would acquire via swap activation could be used in two ways. First, it could intervene in foreign exchange markets by buying dollars being sold by private holders, thereby warding off a speculative attack on the currency. Second, and most important, it could sop up dollars being held by foreign central banks in excess of what they were willing to hold, thereby preventing conversions at the gold window.

The United States negotiated the first swap with the French central bank on March 1, 1962—a full eight months before Congress approved the GAB. The first agreement was essentially a pilot program. It was quite small at only $50 million, and the agreement expired in a short three months. Nonetheless, the sheer monetary magic of the agreement was not lost on Charles Coombs, then the vice president of the Federal

35. Bremner 2004, p. 167.
36. Rainoni 1973, pp. 551–552.

Reserve Bank of New York, who negotiated the swap line with the Bank of France. As he put it, "As central banks endowed with the privilege of creating money, the Federal Reserve and the Bank of France thus produced out of thin air . . . an increase of $100 million of international reserves."[37] The ease with which the United States and France reached a deal encouraged Martin that the agreement with France could be duplicated with any number of partner central banks, thereby knitting together an informal lending network that would give the United States access to short-term financing denominated in the important currencies of Europe as well as Canada and Japan. Although Martin did not have to seek the approval of Congress to implement the swap deals, he did have to convince his fellow members of the Federal Reserve Board of Governors that the program should be expanded.[38] Some members were skeptical that the swap lines would be effective at protecting the dollar and advocated for a more classical approach to adjustment. Governor Robertson, speaking on behalf of a number of other governors and Fed staff, argued, "There are no gimmicks by which the position of the dollar can be maintained in the world. It would be unwise to resort to devices designed to hide the real problems. The United States must practice what it has long preached about the need for monetary and fiscal discipline."[39] Moreover, many skeptical members of the board felt that the Treasury, not the central bank, should manage the swap program.

At this time, Treasury was using its own special cache of foreign currencies that it held in the Exchange Stabilization Fund (ESF) to make forward purchases of dollars in exchange markets. These transactions had a similar structure to the Fed's swap arrangements. However, the limited resources of the ESF constrained the Treasury. The Fed had the ability to quickly increase the size and number of its swap arrangements almost at will—a distinct institutional advantage that the central bank had over the Treasury. Consequently, the Treasury's Undersecretary for Monetary Affairs Robert Roosa wrote to the Federal Reserve Board informing the governors that, in the face of a crisis, "only the central bank can make the prompt, smooth

---

37. Coombs 1976, p. 76. Coombs cites an increase of $100 million in reserves because both parties in the swap gain an increase in their reserves of $50 million.

38. That is not to say the Fed did not face criticism from Congress. Indeed, some members felt the central bank had overreached with this move. For instance, one representative expressed his dissatisfaction with Martin, saying, "To me this is a tremendous power you have taken upon yourself, and I must serve notice on you right now that I consider this an usurpation of the power of Congress. I don't think you are authorized to do this at all, and you give us only the vaguest generalities about what kind of arrangements you are going to make with foreign Central Banks" (US House 1962, p. 91).

39. FOMC 1961a, p. 71.

Table 3.2 FEDERAL RESERVE RECIPROCAL CURRENCY SWAP
ARRANGEMENTS, 1962–1969 (US DOLLARS, MILLIONS)

Partner	1962	1963	1964	1965	1966	1967	1968	1969
Austria	**50**	50	50	50	*100*	100	100	*200*
Belgium	**50**	50	*100*	100	*150*	225	225	*500*
Canada	**250**	250	250	250	*500*	750	*1,000*	1,000
UK	**50**	*500*	*750*	750	*1,350*	*1,500*	*2,000*	2,000
France	**50**	*100*	100	100	100	100	*1,000*	1,000
Germany	**50**	*250*	250	250	*400*	*750*	*1,000*	1,000
Italy	**50**	*250*	250	*450*	*600*	*750*	*1,000*	1,000
Netherlands	**50**	*100*	100	100	*150*	225	*400*	300
Switzerland	**100**	100	*50*	50	*150*	*350*	*550*	550
BIS	**100**	*150*	*300*	300	*400*	*1,000*	*1,600*	1,600
Japan	—	**150**	150	*250*	*450*	*750*	*1,000*	1,000
Sweden	—	**50**	50	50	*100*	200	*250*	250
Denmark	—	—	—	—	—	**100**	100	*200*
Mexico	—	—	—	—	—	**130**	130	130
Norway	—	—	—	—	—	**100**	100	*200*
Total	900	2,050	2,350	2,800	4,500	7,080	10,505	10,980

adjustments that are called for."[40] In light of Roosa's letter, the board quickly reversed its position and unanimously supported the program. Martin did not waste any time expanding the program. By the end of 1962, the Fed had negotiated a total of ten swap lines totaling $900 million—and that was just the beginning. Over the course of the decade, the Fed's swap program grew to include 13 partner central banks as well as the Bank for International Settlements (BIS) and had expanded to a sizable total of $11 billion. Table 3.2 presents the growth of the swap program from its inception through 1969.[41] The totals represent the size of each swap agreement at the end of each year. Totals in **bold** represent new arrangements; totals in *italics* represent a change in the size of the swap from the previous year.

3.2. Who Needs the IMF?

Within a very short period of time, the Federal Reserve had crafted an ad hoc system of financing that provided all of the benefits of an IMF

40. FOMC 1961b, p. 85.
41. Data are from relevant historic Federal Reserve *Monthly Review* publications, available at http://www.ny.frb.org/research/ monthly_review/1963.html.

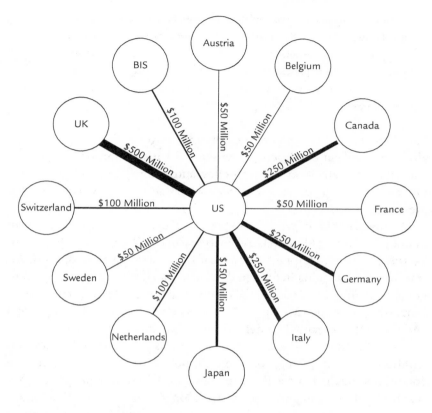

Figure 3.1
Federal Reserve Swap Network, 1963

loan without the drawbacks. As Figure 3.1 depicts, by the end of 1963 Chairman Martin had in place a system that gave the Fed access to $2.3 billion in foreign exchange. More importantly, these swap lines had a number of advantages over alternative means of external financing. Central bank swaps were incredibly flexible and could be expanded at a moment's notice over the phone. This contrasted greatly with the months of difficult negotiation that were necessary to implement the GAB. Additionally, swap credits were available on demand *without* negotiation. Thus, swap resources could be deployed far more swiftly during a quickly unfolding crisis. Charles Coombs summed up just how fast and flexible the swap lines were:

It is quite true . . . that many of these defenses were quickly improvised, sometimes within a matter of hours, to deal with sudden emergencies. In most cases, they were negotiated on a bilateral basis and may give the impression of being no more than an unrelated patchwork. But these bilateral defenses have the most important advantage of being solidly based on market and institutional realities in each country and are capable of being flexibly adapted to new and unforeseeable needs. One cannot overemphasize the importance of being able to move quickly—on the basis of telephone consultations if necessary—against speculative pressures before they gain momentum.[42]

Speed and flexibility were not the only advantages either. Swap drawings also came *without* conditions, meaning the United States could borrow and still maintain its domestic policy autonomy.[43] Finally, swaps also met an occasional "desire for secrecy which an IMF drawing could not provide."[44]

One need not look further than the actual use of the central bank swap lines by the United States relative to its use of the GAB to see which facility was preferred. Despite the fact that the central purpose of the GAB was to make financing in foreign currency available to the United States, not once during the 1960s did the United States activate the arrangement. Borrowing from the IMF and GAB was a cumbersome and slow process and was not well suited to defend the dollar in the face of speculative pressure. Furthermore, as one scholar explains, "Successive U.S. administrations were unwilling, for domestic political reasons, to accept the conditions attached by the Fund to drawings."[45] The swap network meant that the United States and its partners no longer needed the IMF for assistance. They had "managed to develop sources of liquidity [they] deemed preferable."[46] Or, in Richard Cooper's words,

> The apparent need of the United States for swap facilities suggest certain deficiencies in the International Monetary Fund as a source of and supplement to international liquidity. IMF lending was evidently felt to be *too costly, too clumsy to arrange, too small in amount, or too visible to the public to satisfy the requirements of the countries in need.*[47]

42. Coombs 1976, p. 91. A great example of this flexibility came in the immediate aftermath of the assassination of President Kennedy when, within minutes, the Fed had increased its swap lines with the Swiss National Bank and the BIS by 50 percent each "in a move to head off any panic or speculative sale of dollars for other currencies" (Cowan 1963).

43. Creditors did retain the discretion to activate the swap, and so they could ask for certain assurances during the period of consultation. At times, such assurances included a promise to turn to the IMF, if needed, rather than request a swap renewal (Henning 1999, pp. 51–52). In practice, however, this was uncommon.

44. Cooper 1968, p. 214.

45. Ainley 1984, p. 26.

46. Bird and Rajan 2001, p. 10.

47. Cooper 1968, p. 213. Emphasis added.

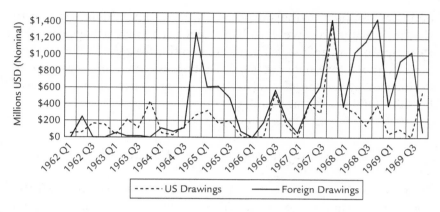

Figure 3.2
Aggregate Swap Credits by Quarter, 1962–1969

In contrast, the United States consistently drew on its swap arrangements throughout the decade and beyond. They emerged as a clear alternative to the IMF that was far closer to Walter Bagehot's ideal ILLR. Figure 3.2 plots aggregate quarterly swap drawings from 1962 through the end of 1969.[48] Foreign central bank drawings from the Fed are indicated by the solid line. Fed drawings from foreign central banks are indicated by the dotted line.

Perhaps the only downside to the swap arrangements, as compared with borrowing from the IMF, was the fact that the former were quite short-term in nature. Typically, a swap drawing formally expired in three months and therefore in principle had to be reversed in that same time frame. This meant that while they were great at addressing short-term dollar outflows and pressures at the gold window, they were not designed well for financing medium- to long-term imbalances. However, in practice, it turned out that the swap lines effectively provided longer-term assistance as well. Robert Roosa made this point to President Kennedy in a meeting with his economic advisors in 1962. Roosa explained to the president that, practically speaking, swaps are not short term: "They are, in general, renewable. The usual practice in these is you simply roll them over until they are reversed. They can go on for years if they have to." In practice, Roosa was correct. All the swap lines opened in 1962 were consistently renewed, without exception, for decades to come. In addition, Roosa pointed out that the "technically" short-term nature of the swaps was desirable for domestic political reasons: "It keeps us in control . . . . We

48. Data were collected by the author from relevant historic Federal Reserve *Monthly Review* publications.

don't want the lights to [be] put out, you see. We've had our problems with the Congress on this. We don't like to put out a swap arrangement that they say, well, you're just really getting into this for good."[49] These seemingly contradictory statements highlight another reason swaps were so desirable: they had the effect of looking temporary but, in practice, could be quite durable and long-standing.

3.3. How the Swap Lines Protected US Interests

Swaps were also quite effective. As indicated above, the United States considered swap lines to be an added line of defense against the joint threats of a speculative attack on the dollar and the gold drain. In the event of a speculative flight from the dollar, the Fed could draw on the swap lines and use the currency it acquired to intervene in the foreign exchange market to support the dollar.[50] By buying and selling foreign currencies, the central bank could subdue and even deter speculative movements that were harmful to the dollar by making such movements less profitable and hence riskier. As Roosa put it, "The central bank can . . . by varying the extent of its own intervention in the forward market, allow the cost of [a] speculative hedge to go as high or as low as it wishes." Roosa added, regarding the purposes of the swaps, "While these swaps have, to be sure, been drawn upon to meet various kinds of short-run swings in reserve needs, their usefulness as a backstop to forward transactions has been crucial for the fulfillment of operations that successfully thwarted the cumulative development of speculative pressures against the dollar."[51]

Regarding the gold drain threat, the United States could tap a swap line when a foreign central bank had accumulated more dollars than it wanted to hold. If, for example, the German central bank was flush with dollar reserves, the United States could activate its swap with the Deutsche Bundesbank and use the borrowed marks to buy the superfluous dollars. This would effectively give the German central bank "cover against the risk of a dollar devaluation for the duration of the credit."[52] On its face, this may seem contradictory since the swap activation has the effect of *increasing* Bundesbank's dollar holdings. Even if the United States were to use its acquired marks to buy $250 million in dollars back from the Germans, Bundesbank would still have an additional $250 million dollars

49. Naftali 2001, pp. 499, 509.
50. Rainoni 1973.
51. Roosa 1965, pp. 30–32.
52. Odell 1982, p. 103.

it acquired in the swap. This is true. However, what made the deal work was the fact that the dollars acquired in the swap were *guaranteed* to be exchanged at the *initial exchange rate* when the swap is reversed. So in this example, Bundesbank is swapping dollars that are at risk to a potential devaluation for dollars that are protected. And, once protected against devaluation, much of the motivation behind converting those dollars into gold is eliminated.[53]

3.4. Why Did Europe Cooperate?

An important question remains. Many of the European economies had been keen to flex their newfound monetary muscle during the GAB negotiations to ensure they would have significant control over the new arrangement and, potentially, over US economic policy if a drawing were made. So why were they so quick to agree to US requests for swap arrangements? In essence, in agreeing to the swaps, they gave back everything they had gained in the GAB negotiations. Although it is true the arrangements eventually made the GAB redundant and diluted its power, they were not initially seen this way—at least from the European perspective. A key reason why the Europeans supported the swap arrangements has to do with the fact that they were viewed as only a "first line of defense" for the United States. If longer-term financing were needed, the Europeans expected the United States to convert any outstanding swap into a standby arrangement with the IMF or GAB.[54] Therefore, the Europeans did not initially think of the swaps as a mechanism that would almost entirely displace the need for the United States to seek IMF assistance, but only as the first of several steps the United States would progress through in correcting its own imbalances.[55]

Besides this, countries that partnered with the Fed stood to benefit from the swap lines in the future if their own economic fortunes changed.

53. However, there was no provision in the swap agreements that would prevent a partner central bank from taking the dollars acquired in the swap and demanding gold. C. Douglass Dillion and Roosa explained to a concerned President Kennedy that this would not happen as "we don't make a swap with anybody if we don't already know what their practice is with respect to the holding of dollars" (Naftali 2001, p. 501).

54. Roosa felt that the only likely circumstance where the United States would have to convert a swap line into an IMF standby arrangement is in the event of an "emergency situation," that is, if the United States became involved in hostilities in Vietnam, and European countries, in protest, attempted to convert dollar reserves into gold en masse (Naftali 2001, p. 502).

55. Fed Chairman Martin described the use of the swaps in the same way before Congress: "The Federal Reserve would help to deal with minor pressures before they reach

As was the case with the GAB, it was clear from the outset that the United States was going to be a borrower in these arrangements—at least in the near term. However, there was no guarantee that those countries with balance of payments surpluses in 1962 would not find themselves in deficit within a few short years. Therefore, because the swap lines were reciprocal, opening up such an arrangement made dollars available to these countries as well (the value of this was not to be discounted for the European partners: after all, the dollar remained the key international currency despite its struggles). As one journalist at the time put it, "It is possible that the swaps will prove useful to some other country suffering a payments deficit and pressure on its currency. Indeed, American officials look forward to the day when they can come to the aid of some other central bank."[56] Swaps, then, naturally appealed to the European countries because they were a source of on-demand, flexible, unconditional credit. In one of several meetings with President Kennedy where the swap lines were discussed, Roosa makes this point, saying of the Europeans, "They are perfectly free to use these dollars if their balance of payments requires it."[57] In the end, this is exactly what happened. As Figure 3.2 indicates, the Fed became the *primary provider of liquidity* in the system not long after its creation.

A third reason the countries of Europe chose to cooperate with the Fed in the swap arrangement was the very real fact that there was a collective interest in maintaining a stable monetary system and the dollar-gold peg was the foundation of that system.[58] In a sense, Europe faced a classic prisoner's dilemma scenario where individual incentives push actors to consider actions that are collectively suboptimal. Individually, official dollar holders had incentives to defect and convert their dollars into gold given the constant fear that the United States would increase the dollar price of gold. However, if they all defected and rushed for the exits at the same time, they understood this would force dollar devaluation and bring about the unraveling of Bretton Woods. This would have been the worst outcome for everyone. What was needed was a system that would assure everyone the dollar could be defended against any serious onslaught, either by an

a scale commensurate with IMF action. And it could take prompt action in more serious circumstances while IMF arrangements are being worked out. . . . [T]he System would not enter into long-term foreign exchange commitments . . . it would not make arrangements under which the United States would acquire foreign exchange for a period of 3 to 5 years, as under IMF procedures. Federal Reserve foreign-exchange transactions and the proposed IMF arrangement would, therefore, complement each other. Both would play important roles in maintaining an efficient international payments system" (US House 1962, p. 91).

56. *New York Times* 1964, p. 118.
57. Naftali 2001, pp. 501–502.
58. Eichengreen 2000, p. 7.

official source or private-market actors, thus reducing the incentive to defect. The swap arrangements helped to provide this assurance. In this case, the surplus countries had a very real incentive to provide easy credit to the United States. That is, "the potential lenders discovered that it was really in their interest to lend."[59]

4. CONCLUSIONS

At the beginning of this chapter, I posed the following question: What motivated the United States to begin providing short-term liquidity to foreign countries when the IMF had been created for that very purpose less than two decades earlier? As I have argued in this chapter, the answer has to do with (1) the recognition of the IMF's limitations as an ILLR and (2) the fact that the United States *itself* wanted on-demand access to credit without delays or conditions. The Fed's system of swap deals gave the United States what it wanted. However, the price of admission was that the United States, too, had to be willing to provide credits to its swap partners. It did not take long for the Federal Reserve's swap net-work, originally designed to protect the US dollar, from evolving into what became a truly multilateral system of short- to medium-term credit operations between countries. Within a few years, the United Kingdom, Italy, Canada, and others had all tapped their own swap lines with the Fed as borrowers. In the end, it was the Fed that was the primary provider of short-term liquidity to its partners. Not surprisingly, given the speed, flex-ibility, and lack of conditionality that accompanied financial swaps, the other G-10 countries increasingly turned to the United States for help via swap credits instead of the IMF. Thus, this episode marks the entrance of the United States onto the world scene as an ILLR. Ultimately, the swap network was one of a number of arrangements that helped to sustain the Bretton Woods monetary order until its dénouement in 1971 when under-lying economic realities made ad hoc stop-gap measures no longer viable defenses for the fixed dollar price of gold. In the following chapters, I show how the United States applied the lessons of the 1960s and adapted this once novel technique to the post–Bretton Woods global financial system.

---

59. Stein 1965, p. 204.

CHAPTER 4

The Exchange Stabilization Fund and the IMF in the 1980s and 1990s

In order to support and give meaning to a nation's international economic and financial policy, its monetary authorities require a mechanism to undertake foreign exchange operations. For the US Government that instrument is the [ESF] . . . . Globalization of the world economy and financial markets has changed the nature and scope of strains on the balance of payments adjustment . . . indebtedness problems have arisen with serious implications for world financial markets.

> David C. Mulford, Undersecretary of the Treasury for International Affairs (*Hearings before the Subcommittee on International Trade, Investment and Monetary Policy*, 1984)

International financial markets have changed from where they were under the Bretton Woods structure, the emergence of private global finance has to a very substantial extent made much of the purposes of the Bretton Woods structure of dubious merit in the current environment.

> Federal Reserve Chairman Alan Greenspan (FOMC meeting, 1995)

President Richard Nixon's decision in 1971 to take the dollar off of gold eliminated the gold drain and speculative attack threats. It also ended the Bretton Woods system of fixed exchange rates. This meant that neither the United States nor its European counterparts needed to defend their exchange rates in the same manner they did under the par value system. Consequently, use of the system of swaps that had been so carefully crafted in the 1960s began to decline. However, this was not the case for the governments of developing economies, most of whom maintained pegged exchange rates for many years after the end of the Bretton Woods monetary order. At the same time, many developing countries also began borrowing from private international credit markets. The combination of increased international capital mobility, growing external sovereign debt held by private financial institutions, increasing foreign portfolio investment in emerging market economies, and the maintenance of pegged exchange rates contributed to two decades of financial instability in the developing world.

While the International Monetary Fund (IMF) took center stage in managing international financial crises in the 1980s and 1990s, the United States stepped in to complement the Fund's efforts by providing credits to economies in crisis on more than 50 different occasions via the Treasury's Exchange Stabilization Fund (ESF). Why did US economic policymakers feel acting as an international lender of last resort (ILLR) alongside the Fund was necessary rather than letting the IMF manage crises on its own? In this chapter, I explain how changes in the nature of the international financial system following the dénouement of the Bretton Woods order revealed IMF shortcomings as a de facto ILLR. It was precisely these shortcomings that provide the backdrop for US involvement in foreign bailouts. In the 1970s and early 1980s, the rise of global bank lending was the key driver of change. The onset of sovereign debt crises in the 1980s led to an expansion of the Fund's role as an international financial crisis manager. Yet the strategy it adopted—known as "concerted lending," which I discuss in more detail below—made the institution's crisis response agonizingly slow. On a number of occasions, the United States stepped in to provide "bridge" loans via the ESF to borrowers that were waiting on a plodding IMF to disburse much-needed financial support. Change again came in the 1990s with the rise of footloose global portfolio investment. Volatile short-term capital flows sent a number of emerging market economies into crisis and caused their currencies to crash. These new capital account crises required an ILLR to respond with both great speed *and* great force. If loan packages were not sufficiently large, the heterogeneous pool of global investors would not view the package as a credible backstop and the stampede out would continue. In this context, the ESF provided credits designed to *supplement* IMF loans by increasing the size of the overall financing package. Together, the joint credits were intended to calm market jitters with an overwhelming use of financial force. Taken together, this chapter highlights how the United States' unilateral bailout actions were designed to complement IMF credits in a way that would move the crisis-management effort closer to Walter Bagehot's ideal.

1. THE EXCHANGE STABILIZATION FUND

In 1978, IMF member nations passed the Second Amendment to the IMF Articles of Agreement to reflect the new realities of the international monetary system. In short, the amendment "established a new code of conduct for exchange arrangements" after the Bretton Woods par value system collapsed earlier that decade.[1] Under the Bretton Woods regime, member countries' ability to adjust their exchange rates was severely restricted. Member countries had to express par values in gold, either directly or by way of their peg to the US dollar. Any member that opted to adjust the value of their currency outside of preset limits set by the Fund would lose their drawing rights at the institution. Beginning in 1973, most major currencies began floating. However, member nations had not amended the IMF Articles of Agreement to reflect this; thus, most of the major industrial economies were in technical violation of the IMF's original Articles of Agreement. The Second Amendment gave member countries total freedom to decide what type of exchange arrangement they wanted. It was no less than "a complete departure from the par value system."[2] Prior to the adoption of the Second Amendment, the US law that authorized US participation in the IMF, known as the Bretton Woods Agreements Act of 1945, required Congress to pass its own amendment to the aforementioned Act, formally acknowledging the shift in the rules of the global monetary system. Congress considered the amendment in 1976. Besides authorizing these reforms at the Fund, Congress also reconsidered the mandate of the Treasury's ESF, as it had also become outdated.

In 1933, President Franklin D. Roosevelt had taken the dollar off of the gold standard, resulting in a substantial decline in the dollar's value. The following year Congress created the ESF when it passed the Gold Reserve Act of 1934. In that law, Congress gave the Secretary of the Treasury full authority over the fund (subject only to the consent of the president) and authorized the secretary to use the resources of the ESF "for the purpose of stabilizing the exchange value of the dollar."[3] Over the intervening years, ESF resources were typically used for this purpose.[4] This mechanism was especially valuable under the par value system of Bretton Woods until the early 1960s when the central bank swap network somewhat marginalized its role. When the dollar was allowed to float in the

---

1. IMF 2006, p. 1.
2. Ibid., p. 1.
3. US Senate 1934, p. 1.
4. However, there were also a considerable number of cases where, prior to 1977, the ESF was used to provide credits to foreign governments.

early 1970s, stability gave way to flexibility. The ESF's relevance declined further. Add to this the emergence of private balance of payments financing and the continued maintenance of the central bank swap network and the ESF had become a relic of a bygone era. That was until the passage of amendments to the Bretton Woods Agreements Act and its enactment on October 19, 1976, which marked an important new beginning for the ESF. The congressional amendments, which paved the way for the Second Amendment's implementation at the IMF, gave the ESF a new mandate that adapted it to the monumental changes taking place in the international financial and monetary systems. Moving away from the specific language regarding the stability of the dollar, Congress now directed the Secretary of the Treasury to use ESF resources "as he may deem necessary to and consistent with the United States obligations in the International Monetary Fund."[5]

In practice, the new role that Congress and (more importantly) the Department of the Treasury envisioned for the ESF was essentially that of a financial "first responder." The basic idea was that Treasury could tap the ESF to provide short-term assistance to countries that had already entered into negotiations with the IMF. However, the borrower might need funds immediately that could bridge the gap between a request for IMF financing and the actual approval and disbursement of funds. Such credits were appropriately referred to as bridge loans. To be clear, Congress had not authorized the ESF to compete with the Fund; rather, it had instructed Treasury to *assist* it. At the same time, however, Treasury was not interested in building bridges to all IMF loans. ESF lending was to be far more selective. While serving as Under Secretary of the Treasury for Monetary Affairs for the Carter administration, Anthony Solomon explained to Congress that from now on ESF credits were to be used

> primarily [as] bridging operations to countries that are entering stabilization programs with the Fund and will therefore be drawing from the Fund's, and our credit operations, which are very few as you know, very selective, and designed to help the country get into a condition to . . . qualify for [the] . . . kinds of international standby conditions that the Fund would require and to meet the Fund's conditions vis-à-vis that country.[6]

To ensure that the ESF would assist, but not replace, the Fund, the US Senate added an amendment to the 1976 bill that emphasized that "the goal for the [United States] is to place primary reliance on the IMF

5. US Senate 1976, p. 18.
6. US Senate 1977, p. 24.

and to confine foreign exchange lending operations outside the IMF to *short-term operations*."[7] However, a 1977 amendment made allowances for longer-term financing when "unique or exigent" circumstances made this necessary. Yet once again it was noted that "in none of these cases should the ESF compete with the IMF, however, and every effort should be made to bring all medium- and longer-term financing within the framework of the IMF or other appropriate multi-lateral facilities."[8]

Table 4.1 lists ESF credits to foreign governments by country and year from 1977 (the first full year after the ESF's congressional mandate was revised) to 2002 (the last year Treasury made an ESF credit to a foreign government). Table 4.1 also reports the total net resources committed to each recipient for that calendar year in constant 2010 dollars. By *net* resources I mean the sum total of all credits provided within a particular calendar year. This is relevant because, in certain cases, countries received multiple credits over the course of a year. Sometimes this means Treasury renewed an expired credit at the same amount; in other cases, it means Treasury provided an additional credit on top of a preexisting swap line. Thus, the total number of credits provided is also listed in Table 4.1 along with whether or not the loan was bilateral (involving only the United States and the borrowing country) or multilateral (involving additional creditors). Multilateral loans involved US cooperation with additional central banks, which was typically coordinated via the Bank for International Settlements (BIS).[9] Totals listed represent the US portion of such multilateral packages. On a few rare occasions, the ESF acted to guarantee portions of loans to sovereigns made by the BIS.[10] These are denoted in the table as well.

Collectively, Treasury provided a total of 54 credits on behalf of 24 foreign countries, totaling almost exactly $100 billion in 2010 dollars during these years. Of course, unlike the IMF, whose raison d'être as a multilateral international institution is to provide emergency financial assistance to its members, the United States is not bound by any such mandate. Hence, in contrast to IMF lending, a decision by the United States to extend a bailout to a financially distressed government is entirely discretionary and

7. US Senate 1995, p. 447. Emphasis added.

8. US House 1995a, p. 380.

9. Unfortunately, I was unable to acquire the names of the other lenders in each of these multilateral cases. The BIS will not release this information, nor will the central banks or finance ministries of the likely suspects: France, Germany, Japan, and the United Kingdom. Each were contacted and declined to reveal which multilateral BIS rescues they participated in. For more information on the BIS's role as a crisis lender, see Howell 1995 and Siegman 1994.

10. Under the ESF statute, a guarantee is treated the same as a credit (US House 1995a, 357).

Table 4.1 ESF CREDITS, 1977–2002

Country	Year	Net Size, 2010 USD (Billions)	Number of Credits	Bilateral or Multilateral
Argentina	1984	1.679	2	B
Argentina	1985	0.304	1	M
Argentina	1987	0.816	2	B/M
Argentina	1989	1.502	2	M
Argentina[+*]	1995	0.358	1	M
Bolivia	1986	0.199	1	B
Bolivia	1989	0.484	3	B
Brazil	1982	4.474	5	B/M
Brazil	1983	0.875	1	B
Brazil	1988	0.461	1	M
Brazil[+]	1999	6.689	1	M
Costa Rica	1990	0.047	1	B
Ecuador	1986	0.298	1	B
Ecuador	1987	0.060	1	B
Guyana	1990	0.053	1	M
Honduras	1990	0.137	1	M
Hungary	1990	0.033	1	M
Indonesia	1998	4.013	1	M
Jamaica	1983	0.109	1	B
Korea	1998	9.102	2	M
Macedonia[+]	1994	0.007	1	M
Mexico	1982	3.614	2	B/M
Mexico	1986	0.543	1	M
Mexico	1989	7.253	1	M
Mexico	1990	1.001	1	B
Mexico	1994	17.769	3	B/M
Mexico	1995	30.762	2	B/M
Netherlands	1981	1.199	1	B
Nigeria	1986	0.074	1	M
Panama	1992	0.225	1	B
Peru	1993	0.709	1	B
Philippines	1984	0.094	1	B
Poland	1989	0.352	1	M
Portugal	1977	1.079	1	B
Romania	1990	0.064	1	M
Uruguay	2002	1.805	1	B
Venezuela	1989	0.791	1	B
Venezuela	1990	0.174	1	M
Yugoslavia	1983	0.164	1	M
Yugoslavia	1988	0.092	1	M

[+] Denotes these were ESF guarantees of BIS credits to the borrowing country.
[*] Denotes long-term financing was provided by the World Bank, not by the IMF.

highly selective. What explains Treasury's decision to use these resources for these purposes? As I have argued, the United States will act as an ILLR when either the IMF is too slow or its resources are too constrained to protect vital US economic interests. In the following sections, I consider how the global financial system changed in the 1980s and then again in the 1990s in ways that called into question the IMF's crisis-management capabilities. In response, US policymakers used the ESF as a means to correct for the Fund's flaws and protect the US economy.

2. GLOBAL BANKING AND THE DEBT CRISIS: 1980S

After the dissolution of the postwar monetary order, the global financial system changed dramatically. The most notable changes were that industrialized countries widely adopted floating exchange rates and their further relaxation of restrictions on international capital flows. The balance sheets of commercial banks in the advanced economies—once confined within their national borders—began to absorb more and more international assets. Leading the charge in this new era of global banking were US banks. Seeking out new opportunities for profit around the globe, they capitalized on growing worldwide demand for the almighty US dollar. Meanwhile, the US government supported, even encouraged, the trend. Finance was becoming an increasingly important sector of the national economy. Beginning in earnest under the Reagan administration, the central aim of US international financial policy was to create a truly global financial system with the United States at the core.[11] Figure 4.1 plots the impressive growth in US banks' cross-border claims from 1977 to 1982.[12] In under five years, total foreign claims more than doubled from $164 billion to $353 billion. Almost half of this lending went to developing countries. US bank claims grew in these countries from around $79 billion to $180 billion in the same time span. A significant source of demand for US bank loans came from Latin American sovereigns. Indeed, by year-end 1982, more than 10 percent of US banks' total foreign claims ($38.6 billion) were against Latin American governments.[13]

---

11. Helleiner 1994.
12. Data reported are consolidated unadjusted claims; data collected by the author from relevant Country Exposure Lending Surveys (CELS) via the Federal Reserve archive available at http://fraser.stlouisfed.org/ publication/?pid=333.
13. Totals from December 1982 CELS report.

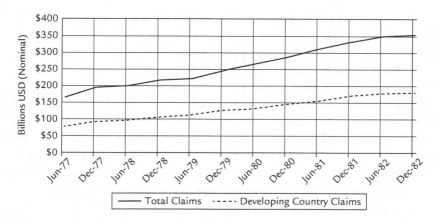

Figure 4.1
US Banks' Claims on Foreign Residents, 1977–1982

A necessary consequence of the internationalization of US banks' balance sheets, however, was that a major foreign financial crisis could now directly threaten the stability of the US financial system. In August 1982, that is exactly what happened when Mexico announced that it was suspending payments on its external debt obligations. The crisis quickly spread. One year later, 27 developing countries were in negotiations to restructure their loans.

Major global banks, many of them in the United States, were facing losses larger than their entire capital stock, and the global financial system was facing its most serious financial crisis since the Great Depression. It was in this context that the IMF asserted itself as the world's de facto ILLR.[14]

2.1. The IMF's "Concerted Lending" Strategy and the Problem of Unresponsiveness

As described in chapter 1, the IMF typically makes loans available after a two-stage process. First, countries must approach the Fund and express their interest in borrowing and then enter into negotiations to determine the size, maturity, and conditions of the loan. This process itself can be quite lengthy. After reaching an agreement with Fund staff, the prospective borrower submits a letter of intent to the IMF executive board along with a memorandum outlining the reforms that will be made in order

14. Boughton 2000; Sachs 1995.

to ensure timely repayment. At this point, with a simple majority vote, the board will make the determination whether to approve the loan. Prior to 1982, when a country approached the IMF for a loan, the standard practice for Fund staff was to first determine how much financing the borrower could expect to acquire from private as well as other official creditors before calculating the amount of financing the borrower needed from the institution. The Fund staff, in conjunction with the borrowing government, would spell all of this out in the letter of intent and memorandum of understanding. As Boughton explains, "That strategy collapsed, at least for the most heavily indebted countries, with the Mexican crisis of August 1982."[15] After the Mexican default, commercial banks actively sought ways to reduce their exposure to the most heavily indebted countries. This came as a shock to the Fund as well as US authorities. In the recent past, when the Fund got involved, the banks did not look to cut and run. Indeed, just a few years earlier Anthony Solomon helped convince Congress that the ESF's new mandate would not lead to its increased use for international bailouts, explaining,

> Usually when a country undertakes [an IMF] stabilization program, then the private capital markets typically increase their lending to that country. They do not bail out. On the contrary, the record shows quite clearly that they increase their lending after they get the so-called Good Housekeeping Seal from the IMF.[16]

In other words, prior to 1982, IMF loans had the effect of "catalyzing" private lending.[17] But this crisis was different from anything policymakers had ever experienced. As the Fund was increasing its lending to the economies in crisis, many commercial banks were preparing to do just the opposite. The result would have been little to no net increase in financing for the borrower country. Although it was in the banks' *collective* interest to keep lending as a group, thereby keeping the indebted government liquid so it could continue servicing its debts, it was in their *individual* interests to pull out and let the IMF and other banks pick up the slack. Of course, as each bank pulled out, the risks facing the other banks that stayed in only grew. The banks faced a classic collective action problem: a counterproductive, pro-cyclical lending dynamic was unfolding that threatened to undermine the Fund's efforts to stop the bleeding. In response, the IMF decided to alter its traditional approach and adopt a new strategy that became known as "concerted lending." In short, the concerted lending

---

15. Boughton 2001, p. 406.
16. US Senate 1977, p. 32.
17. For more on this see Guitian 1992.

strategy adopted by the Fund during the debt crisis relied on issuing an ultimatum: The IMF would not approve loan requests until the group of commercial banks (referred to as a "syndicate") agreed to *increase their exposures* to the indebted economies.[18] If the banks could not collectively act on their own, the Fund would make them.

In practice, concerted lending worked as follows. First, IMF staff and government officials would negotiate program details. Once agreement was reached, the prospective borrower would formally submit a letter of intent to the IMF. This was business as usual. However, things changed with the next step. Rather than immediately scheduling a board vote, the Fund would take the program as proposed in the letter to the banking syndicate. The board informed the syndicate that a vote would not be scheduled until it agreed to provide additional loans to the borrower in question. Only when a deal was reached would the managing director put the program to a vote before the board. Thus, concerted lending injected an additional round of negotiations between the Fund and the syndicate into the loan approval process. Unsurprisingly, this tended to slow down the IMF's response speed. The process behind Argentina's 1984 standby arrangement (SBA) request, a case I discuss more in chapter 6, is illustrative of this. On September 25, Argentina signed and filed a letter with the Fund requesting $1.2 billion in assistance. Despite the large size of the request, the Fund calculated that Argentina needed an additional $8 billion in financing to repay arrears to banks and official creditors, and to replenish its dwindling foreign exchange reserves. Managing Director Jacques de Larosière set up a series of bilateral meetings with official creditor countries and bank syndicates in order to round up additional money. These negotiations took months to complete. Once all parties had signed on, the Board approved the loan on December 28—a full 94 days after Argentina first filed its request for assistance.[19] This is substantially higher than the 37-day mean for all loan requests between 1955 and 2009 (see Figure 2.1).

In effect, concerted lending allowed the Fund to secure larger overall financing packages by getting new money from banks. However, concerted lending also made the Fund an even less responsive ILLR. A review of executive board minutes early on in the crisis reveals that executive

18. Boughton (2001) describes the moment this became the Fund's new approach: "The turning point came at the November 1982 meeting in New York . . . at which the Managing Director informed the banks that the Fund would not approve Mexico's requests for an extended arrangement until the banks provided him with written assurances that they would increase their exposure by enough to cover a substantial fraction ($5 billion) of Mexico's scheduled interest payments for 1983" (p. 406).

19. Boughton 2001, pp. 393–394.

directors were aware that the strategy impacted the Fund's responsiveness. One director remarked that the "ultimatum" approach resulted in "undue and costly delays," while another noted that such delays were particularly worrisome in cases "where speed was essential to maintain confidence and momentum of adjustment."[20] Board members also cited a number of other drawbacks to the strategy, including fears that its overuse would render it ineffective and that it jeopardized the Fund's impartiality in debt negotiations.[21] In light of these concerns, a few directors suggested that concerted lending should only be used in "exceptional cases"—specifically, situations where the stability of the international financial system was threatened.[22]

Despite these drawbacks, de Larosière remained a staunch advocate of concerted lending. In one meeting he forcefully argued that the strategy remained necessary in many cases. Without it, the managing director argued, the institution faced "uncertainties" about whether new loans from banks would reach satisfactory levels to fully address borrowers' financing needs. Insufficient commercial bank participation would jeopardize the success of Fund programs and put the institution's resources at risk.[23] One executive director echoed the managing director's sentiments noting that when it came to deciding in which cases the strategy was appropriate, his preference was "to err on the side of caution and lengthen the list." In the end, the executive board decided against formally limiting the use of the strategy and instead opted for a "case-by-case" approach. Concerted lending would remain the "prevailing strategy" for managing the debt crisis through at least 1987.[24]

In a sense, the Fund's decision to employ the concerted lending strategy is best viewed as a trade-off. Because of its finite resources and quota system that limited the overall size of individual loan packages, the institution was incapable of providing sufficient financing to fill the entire financing gap of some heavily indebted countries. However, by issuing

20. EBM 1983a, pp. 17, 37.
21. At one meeting, an executive director suggested that the IMF find a new crisis-management strategy that would not "jeopardize [our] neutrality as an intermediary between debtors and creditors" (EBM 1983b, 29). Others worried that banks were becoming dependent on the strategy and that the actions were being interpreted as a "guarantee by the Fund for the security of bank loans" (EBM 1983b, 32). Lastly, others suggested that overuse of the strategy would weaken the Fund's leverage vis-à-vis the banks and render it ineffective (EBM 1983b, 28).
22. EBM 1983a, p. 21; EBM 1983b, pp. 22–23; Erb 1983.
23. EBM 1983b, pp. 29, 35–36.
24. Boughton 2001, p. 481. Bird and Rowlands (2004) date the strategy from 1982 through 1986, while Caskey (1989) notes that the strategy was adopted during the Mexican debt adjustment program through 1987. For a discussion on the end of the concerted lending strategy, see Volcker and Gyohten (1992, p. 215).

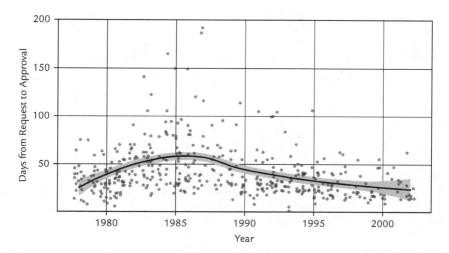

Figure 4.2
Days between IMF Loan Request to Approval, 1977–2002

banks an ultimatum, the Fund believed it could forcibly catalyze private lending to these countries, which would increase the size of the over- all financing package. Thus, while the Fund could not "lend freely" like Bagehot's ideal crisis manager, it could—through negotiations with com- mercial banks—indirectly increase its financial firepower. However, this strategy came with a price tag: The IMF gave up the ability to respond to the crisis swiftly. In essence, the Fund could not have both. Ultimately, it chose *large* lending packages over *fast* loans.

The effect of the concerted lending strategy on IMF responsiveness during the 1980s was substantial. Figure 4.2 plots the number of days that transpired between the date that borrower country governments filed letters of intent with the executive board and the date on which the board approved these loan requests. A total of 439 SBAs and Extended Fund Facility (EFF) requests between 1977 and 2002 are represented.[25] On average, the mean approval period for IMF loan requests was 42 days with a standard deviation of 29 days. Notably, the lowess curve is elevated throughout the 1980s when the IMF managed the international debt

25. Data were compiled by the author and assistants by recording the date on all SBA and EFF letters of intent between 1977 and 2002 via the IMF digital archives and counting the number of days until executive board approval of the request. The IMF's digital archives can be accessed at http://www.imf.org/external/adlib_is4/default.aspx; dates of Fund loan-request approvals after 1983 are available at http://www.imf.org/external/np/fin/ tad/ extarrl.aspx. Additionally, to improve the figure's readability, the following outlier is excluded: Belarus (1994) at 277 days. A lowess smooth curve with a 95 percent confidence interval is included.

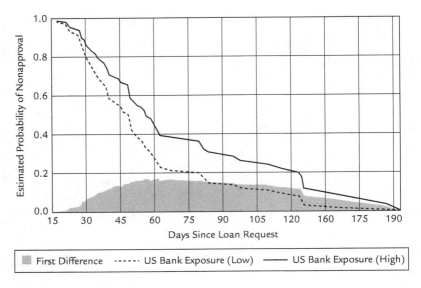

Figure 4.3
US Bank Exposure and IMF Responsiveness, 1983–1987

crisis. Between 1982 and 1989—the conventional dates assigned to the crisis—the board's approval period lengthened, averaging 55 days with a standard deviation of 32. Moreover, on average, waits for approval were longer for borrowers where US banks were heavily exposed. Figure 4.3 plots survival curve estimates that model the probability a loan request will still be waiting for approval after a given number of days. As the figure indicates, a request by a borrower where US banks were highly exposed (about 3.4 percent of their foreign claims) was about 17 percent *more likely* to still be waiting on board approval after 60 days compared to a request by a country where US banks were less exposed (about 0.7 percent of their foreign claims).[26] Thus, during the 1980s, the concerted lending strategy not only hurt the IMF's responsiveness broadly speaking but also led to disproportionately longer waits for borrowers where US financial interests were elevated.

2.2. The ESF and "Bridge Loans": Correcting for the Problem of IMF Unresponsiveness

The newly minted role that Congress created for the ESF in 1977 came just in time for the debt crisis. The Federal Reserve had essentially ruled

---

26. The Cox proportional hazards model is discussed in more detail in the appendix.

out the prospects of opening up swap agreements with the indebted countries as they tended not to be Article VIII signatories—a red line that the central bank has historically drawn when considering opening these credit lines.[27] However, the newly resuscitated ESF was free of the central bank's inhibitions. Consequently, it became the mechanism of choice for US ILLR actions beginning in the 1980s. Russell Munk explains that the Treasury employed the ESF when the Fund or another international financial institution (IFI) "had been called upon to help, and its management had indicated that it was coming, but it was coming at a rather deliberate speed. The house was likely to burn before the IFI arrived."[28] Although the Fund's responsiveness was hamstrung by its standard, two-stage approval procedure—and further constrained by concerted lending—ESF credits were not bound by such a cumbersome process.

First, unlike the IMF, ESF emergency loans came with only one string attached: that the borrower seek assistance from the IMF for its medium- to long-term financing needs.[29] This is because the Treasury has traditionally required that in cases where it makes ESF credits to foreign governments there is an "assured source of repayment."[30] Second, unlike the IMF, there is no executive board at Treasury where multiple governments debate and vote on a request. Rather, Treasury disburses resources immediately upon the consent of the Secretary of the Treasury and the president. Consequently, emergency loans via the ESF could be deployed rapidly and bridge the time between the date a government initially approached the IMF for help and when it actually received its first dollars.[31] Thus, when the ESF was used during the debt crisis, it was essentially the financial "first responder." It arrived quickly to the scene of

27. The exception to this is Mexico, which has maintained a standing bilateral swap line with the Federal Reserve since 1967. Because of the Fed's historic relationship with the Bank of Mexico, on some occasions during the 1980s and 1990s, the Fed participated alongside the Treasury in providing emergency financing to Mexico.

28. Munk 2010, p. 222. There are cases where US funds were released prior to IMF financing being agreed upon. For example, in 1982, outgoing Mexican President José López Portillo acted contrary to IMF orthodoxy by nationalizing the banking system and introducing capital controls—acts that put IMF financing in jeopardy. Disaster was averted only because ESF resources were released in concert with a larger BIS bailout package, buying time until an IMF loan was eventually worked out (Helleiner 1994, pp. 177–178).

29. On rare occasions, borrowers were allowed to seek assistance from another IFI like the World Bank or Inter-American Development Bank. In almost all cases, however, the IMF was involved.

30. US Senate 1984, p. 12.

31. Because IMF credits are paid out in "tranches" rather than up-front all at once, in some cases Treasury used ESF credits to bridge the gap until the next tranche of money was released by the Fund if conditions facing the country had deteriorated since initial IMF approval.

the crisis to prevent the fire from spreading or getting worse. Meanwhile, the IMF now had time to hammer out a long-term loan program with the government, enter into negotiations with private creditors, and take care of any other bureaucratic business that was necessary. Throughout the 1980s, Treasury used the ESF repeatedly for such bridging operations. However, into the 1990s, the ESF's role in supporting IMF bailouts would shift from providing loans in advance of Fund disbursements to providing loans alongside Fund credits designed to augment the size of the overall financing package.

3. PORTFOLIO FLOWS AND CAPITAL ACCOUNT CRISES: 1990S

The global financial system of the 1990s was dramatically different from the one that existed at the start of the debt crisis in 1982. Although big commercial banks had been the primary driver behind the expansion of global finance in the 1970s and early 1980s, it was global portfolio investment that exploded in the 1990s. Between 1990 and 1994, roughly $670 billion of foreign capital flowed into countries in Asia and Latin America as investors around the world began putting their money into emerging market economies' stock and bond markets.[32] Governments in these capital receiving countries, once dependent on commercial banks, began to rely more on the issuance of debt securities (bonds) in international credit markets. To illustrate this trend, Figure 4.4 presents net portfolio investment in three emerging market economies from 1982 until 1999.[33]

This is not to say that foreign lending by US commercial banks was insignificant during the 1990s. However, it was now only a fraction of global financial flows. Figure 4.5 presents total cross-border lending by US banks from 1982 to 1998 and points to two trends.[34] First, there was considerable retrenchment in US banks' foreign lending throughout the 1980s as the debt crisis unfolded. Second, this trend began to reverse itself in the early 1990s as US banks once again began to expand their foreign portfolios. For added clarity, Figure 4.6 presents the volume of a variety

32. Calvo, Leiderman, and Reinhart 1996, p. 123; Prasad et al. 2003; Truman 1996, p. 201.
33. Data were collected by the author from the IMF balance of payments statistics via Data-Planet. Unfortunately, time-series data on US-only flows to these countries are unavailable for these years.
34. Adjusted foreign claims data were collected by the author from relevant CELS reports via the Federal Reserve archive, available at http://fraser.stlouisfed.org/publication/?pid=333.

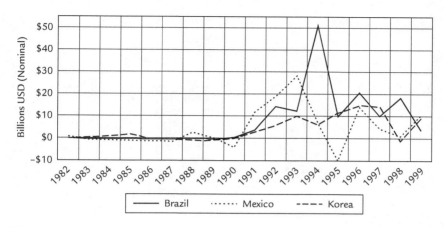

Figure 4.4
Net Portfolio Investment in Three Emerging Markets, 1982–1999

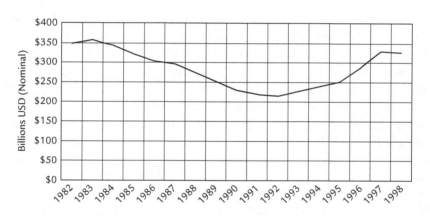

Figure 4.5
Total Cross-Border Claims of US Banks, 1982–1998

of financial flows from the United States to foreign markets in 1994 and 1997.[35] In 1994, US residents' foreign portfolio investments were nearly four times the size of US banks' cross-border lending; by 1997, US foreign portfolio flows were more than six times foreign bank lending!

Just as the complexity of the global financial system was changing, the nature of financial crises also changed in the 1990s. In the previous

35. Securities and equities data were collected by the author from the US Treasury's Annual Cross-US Border Portfolio Holdings data, available at http://www.treasury.gov/resource-center/data-chart-center/tic/Pages/fpis.aspx. Unfortunately, the US Treasury did not begin the annual collection and reporting of data on US residents' holdings of foreign debt securities and equities until 2000. Consequently, data for years prior to 1994, as well as 1995 and 1996, are unavailable. Banking data are from CELS reports.

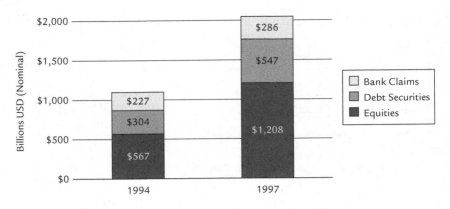

Figure 4.6
Total US Foreign Claims by Type, 1994 and 1997

decade, sovereign debt crises were the predominant variety. They centered on the reluctance of a relatively small group of large commercial banks to continue rolling over the debts of heavily indebted developing country governments. When sovereigns partially or wholly default on their debt obligations to their creditors, they directly impose losses on financial firms with large foreign balance sheets. Although the threat of sovereign default did not disappear in the 1990s, financial crises in that decade tended to be of a different breed. They developed in a country's capital account as a result of short-term capital flows.[36] The prevalence of these "capital account crises" was exacerbated by the entrance of investment funds and individual investors participating alongside the big banks. These new entrants in financial markets were far more prone to what some observers dubbed "herd" behavior. A few pieces of bad information about a national economy could spark a group of investors to pull their money out. Other investors witness this and assume that things must be bad and the race is on for the exit. Moreover, improvements in technology now meant that these investments could be pulled out of a country "with little more than the flick of a computer key."[37]

In these situations, spooked investors looking to get off of a sinking ship before it is too late exchange the local currency for dollars, or other hard currencies. This, in turn, forces the emerging market central bank to spend down its foreign exchange reserves. Meanwhile, speculators

36. Calvo (1998) referred to the crises that developed in the 1990s as "capital account crises" to distinguish them from current account crises, which were the dominant variety in previous decades.
37. Calvo, Leiderman, and Reinhart 1996, p. 127.

looking to make a quick profit added to the mounting pressure by placing bets against the monetary authority's ability to maintain the fixed
exchange rate. If the herd is large enough, it can force a significant and
painful devaluation of the currency. Such "currency crashes" increase
the likelihood that governments and firms will default on foreign debts.
A major devaluation in a currency's exchange rate can inhibit a borrower's ability to pay back external debts if they are denominated in a foreign
currency, as is typically the case with developing and emerging market
economies.[38]

3.1. Capital Account Crises and IMF Resource Insufficiency

The IMF was designed by its founders to address misalignments in member countries' current accounts that tended to develop slowly. It was not
designed to manage fast developing capital account crises. In this new era,
effective crisis management required swift action from an ILLR. Although
speed has never been the IMF's strong suit, the problem of unresponsiveness that had dogged the IMF in the 1980s faded somewhat the following
decade. The Fund's newfound speed was a result of two key developments.
First, the move away from concerted lending in the late-1980s meant that
IMF loan approvals were no longer contingent on up-front bank financing. Thus, the Board could approve requests without having to wait on
the conclusion of negotiations with banking syndicates. Second, as I will
discuss more below, the Fund implemented reforms after the Mexican
peso crisis in 1995 that enabled the institution to accelerate loan approval
in a matter of days when faced with exceptional circumstances. Yet, even
though the Fund proved to be a speedier emergency responder during the
1990s, the problem of resource insufficiency reemerged to challenge the
institution's ILLR credentials.

The number of actors active in global financial markets had grown
exponentially from the early 1980s to the mid-1990s. In the midst of a
panic, reversing capital outflows became more difficult as the number of
creditors grew. No longer could Fund management simply haul a handful

---

38. Economists call this "original sin": If a country is forced to devalue its currency and
its liabilities are predominantly denominated in a foreign currency, debts become more
difficult to service, which can lead to a crisis, see Eichengreen and Hausmann 1999, 2005.
Existing empirical research supports the original sin argument as a recent study found that
as the ratio of foreign currency debt to total debt increases, the likelihood that a country will
experience a debt crisis also increases: see Bordo et al. 20010.

of banks to New York, press them to roll over existing debts, and fill in the financing gap as they had during the 1980s debt crisis. To complicate matters, the 1990s also witnessed a rapid increase in the accumulation of short-term debt in emerging market economies. This trend has been linked to the occurrence of more severe financial crises and capital flight.[39] Concerted lending was no longer an effective way to catalyze private capital flows on behalf of borrowers in trouble. Financial crisis management had to adapt to these new realities.

The approach that emerged has been compared to the so-called Powell Doctrine in military affairs: Once policymakers decide to intervene in a financial panic, it must be implemented with overwhelming force in terms of the size and speed of the rescue package.[40] The best way to prevent a disparate, disorganized herd of foreign investors from stampeding out and crashing an economy is to act quickly and shock markets with a massive bailout package. For instance, Manuel Guitian noted that "capital account problems typically require a rapidly agreed and relatively large financial support package."[41] If creditors do not believe a rescue package is sufficient to backstop the entire market, it will have no impact on their behavior. As Bagehot argued, partial insurance during a panic is essentially no insurance at all.[42] Thus, during the 1990s, the Fund sought to provide much larger loans that sent stronger signals to financial markets in the face of developing capital account crises. This was necessary "in order to generate 'catalytic financing' from a disaggregated, heterogeneous group of private international lenders."[43]

The Fund's new crisis-management strategy was embodied in reforms borne out of the G7 Halifax Summit in mid-June 1995. There, the IMF examined the "adequacy of the Fund's current mechanisms" and proposed "the establishment within the IMF of a new standing procedure—'Emergency Financing Mechanism' [EFM]—involving a fund arrangement with strong conditionality but with *high up-front access and faster procedures* to access Fund resources in crisis situations under the 'exceptional circumstances' clause."[44] In effect, the Fund was pledging that, when necessary, it could move itself closer to an ideal-type ILLR that could provide sizable loans much more swiftly than it had in the past.

Despite these reforms, the new model of crisis management posed a challenge for the IMF. In theory, providing much larger credits to borrowers facing capital account crises was the right strategy. However, making

39. Rodrik and Velasco 1999, p. 3.
40. Jeanne and Wyplosz 2001; Zettelmeyer 2000.
41. Guitan 1995, p. 817.
42. Cottarelli and Giannini 2002, p. 3.
43. Copelovitch 2010, p. 9.
44. Halifax 1995. Emphasis added.

good on this promise would prove difficult because of the Fund's inability to create liquidity like a central bank. As discussed in chapter 2, the institution's lending capacity was limited in two key ways. Together, these limitations brought the institution's problem of resource insufficiency to the fore once again. First, vis-à-vis individual borrowers, member quotas effectively cap the amount of resources a government can borrow from the Fund. Specifically, IMF "access limits" constrained member country borrowing. In 1994, annual access limits were set at 68 percent of a member country's quota, although this was temporarily increased to 100 percent at the end of that year. Cumulative access limits were left at 300 percent.[45] Of course, the IMF did have some flexibility since it could exceed these limits under the "exceptional circumstances" clause as determined by the executive board. However, the board directors could push back on a decision to lend an amount significantly above a borrower's access limits if they felt a package was too generous. Thus, even under such cases, the proposed size of any given loan may be constrained by the potential threat of opposition by some on the board.

One reason for such opposition relates to the second way in which Fund resources are constrained: the possibility that IMF's total resources become strained as too many loans significantly exceed member countries' access limits. Because the Fund's lendable resources are finite, its ability to fight several significant financial fires at once can quickly run up against its financing capacity. The institution ran into this problem in the late 1990s after it provided large loans to several members during the Asian financial crisis. The IMF's 1998 annual report noted that because of "very high demand for the use of IMF resources . . . its liquidity position weakened considerably" and the board "considered the IMF's liquidity position vulnerable and expected it to remain under considerable strain in the period immediately ahead."[46] Ultimately, the IMF raised new funds by increasing quotas. However, as I discussed in chapter 2, such reviews generally take many months to be fully realized—time that often cannot be spared if a crisis is to be adequately addressed.

3.2. The ESF and Supplemental Loans: Correcting for the Problem of IMF Resource Insufficiency

The Fund's improved responsiveness in the 1990s meant that the ESF became less important as a bridging financing mechanism. On the other

45. EBM 1994, p. 31.
46. IMF 1998, p. 82.

hand, ESF credits were valuable in that Treasury could provide them alongside an IMF loan, offering additional resources in an effort to "shock" financial markets with a large rescue package. Thus, in the 1990s, policymakers tended to use ESF credits to *supplement* IMF loans. Even though the Fund could provide loans in excess of borrowers' access limits in extreme cases by using the exceptional circumstances clause, the question often remained: Will it be enough? This kind of uncertainty surrounding financial rescues in the 1990s had a lot to do with how the United States used the ESF during that decade. Indeed, in several cases where Treasury provided supplemental bailouts alongside IMF credits in the 1990s, it is clear that US economic policymakers did not feel that—on its own—the IMF package was sufficient to calm market jitters. This was especially true in the case of credits to Mexico in 1995 and Korea in 1997. In both cases, which I survey in detail in chapter 6, the United States provided ESF credits in an effort to augment the packages being provided by the Fund. Policymakers believed that larger bailouts would stand a better chance of calming markets by convincing them that a sufficient backstop had been provided. In short, by providing supplemental bailouts during the 1990s, the ESF sought to complement and improve the effectiveness of the IMF by pushing its rescue efforts closer to Bagehot's ideal of an ILLR that lends "freely and readily."

4. CONCLUSIONS

This chapter illustrated how structural change in the global financial system during the 1980s and 1990s altered the ways in which the IMF worked to manage international financial crises. Additionally, it explains how the IMF's effectiveness as an ILLR was called into question in different ways during each of these decades. In the 1980s, the Fund was dogged by the problem of unresponsiveness; in the 1990s, the problem of resource insufficiency reemerged. It was precisely these shortcomings that necessitated the involvement of another entity that was both willing and able to act as an ILLR alongside the Fund. On more than 50 occasions, the US Treasury played this role. Although this chapter explains why US economic policymakers did not believe the Fund was equipped to manage a number of financial crises on its own, it left another important question unanswered. What motivated US economic policymakers to act as an ILLR on behalf of some countries during these years but not for others? Although many countries were the beneficiaries of ESF credits, the United States did not provide supplemental credits to every country that approached the IMF during this period. In fact, most countries that sought assistance during these turbulent years did not receive a US bailout. Why did Treasury intervene on behalf of some countries but not others? In the following chapter, I begin to answer this question by developing an empirical model of US ESF credit selection between 1983 and 1999.

CHAPTER 5

Who's In, Who's Out, and Why?
Selecting Whom to Bail Out,
1983–1999

Why should the US taxpayer be involved in bailing out the bad loan decisions of the money center banks?

> Rep. Denny Smith (R-OR) (*Hearings before the Subcommittee on*
> *International Trade, Investment and Monetary Policy,* 1984)

When the Exchange Stabilization Fund is used, it is used to try to stabilize the world economy, not to help another country but to defend our own country, to defend our own prosperity, to defend our own jobs.

> Rep. David Obey (D-WI) (House floor debate on HR 2490, *Treasury*
> *and General Government Appropriations Act, 2000,* 1999)

U S actions as an international lender of last resort (ILLR) during the 1980s and 1990s were intended to complement the International Monetary Fund (IMF)'s effectiveness as an international financial crisis manager. At times, Exchange Stabilization Fund (ESF) credits were designed to provide a quick liquidity injection until IMF funds could be disbursed; in other cases, the United States provided supplemental resources designed to increase the overall size of the international financing package being provided. Either way, the United States opted to provide liquidity outside of the Fund in order to correct for that institution's shortcomings as an ILLR. However, although the IMF's problems of unresponsiveness and resource insufficiency generated the *need* for US actions, they do not fully explain why some countries received US assistance and others did not. What interests were US economic policymakers acting to protect? What "selection process" did Treasury use in determining

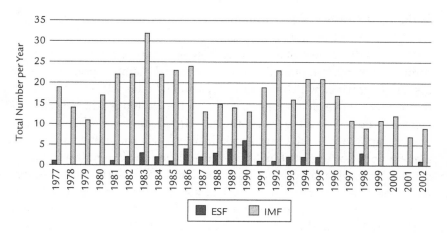

Figure 5.1
IMF Loan Requests and ESF Credits, 1977–2002

whom to bailout? In his testimony before the Senate in 1977, Anthony Solomon—who served at Treasury under President Carter and then later as president of the Federal Reserve Bank of New York (FRBNY) from 1980 to 1984—summarized the process by which ESF credits are made:

> It may be that some country that will be approaching the IMF which we feel is subject to very difficult circumstances, and yet is making a major effort to undertake a stabilization program with the IMF. If such a country approaches us, we would consult with the chairman of the committees and the subcommittees . . . before we would consider this ESF financing. *We believe that [it] should be used very selectively, and in relatively few cases is it justified.* It is such a short-term bridging operation that it can be of use only in limited circumstances.[1]

Solomon was making assurances to Congress that US dollars would not be put at risk willy-nilly. Treasury would use utmost discretion in making decisions about which countries to rescue and which countries to pass over. In practice, Solomon's statement was quite accurate. Although a select group of countries benefited from US bailouts (see Table 4.1 in chapter 4), most countries facing financial hardship that approached the IMF during the 1980s and 1990s did not find themselves on the receiving end of US assistance. To illustrate this, Figure 5.1 reports the total number of requests for IMF assistance by year from 1977 through 2002.[2] Next

---

1. US Senate 1977, p. 28. Emphasis added.
2. These include only standby arrangement (SBA) and EFF requests, the two primary lending mechanisms for addressing short- to medium-term balance of payments imbalances. Concessional IMF loan requests are excluded.

to the total number of Fund requests are the number of countries that received an ESF loan the same year.

Why did the United States decide to act as an ILLR on behalf of some countries but not others facing similar problems? Put more precisely, what criteria determined which countries the United States selected for rescue? In the quote above, Solomon indicates that the United States was likely to consider countries facing "very difficult circumstances." Of course, any country approaching the Fund for a loan is likely to be in that boat, so alone it does not really tell us much. In addition to economic and financial hardship, what factors increased the likelihood that the United States would provide an emergency credit to countries in need? It is my contention here that the primary driver behind Treasury's bailout selection during the 1980s and 1990s was policymakers' desire to protect vital US financial interests from threatening foreign spillovers. In the first section below, I further develop this argument. Next, I present an empirical model of ESF bailout selection and then test my argument. The results support my assertion that increased US bank exposure is associated with a higher likelihood of an ESF bailout; however, this relationship only holds when systemic risk facing the broader financial system is elevated.

1. US FINANCIAL INTERESTS AND ESF BAILOUT SELECTION

The international expansion of US bank lending that began in the late 1970s and launched the modern era of financial globalization meant that financial disturbances in foreign economies were no longer isolated to the country of origin. They now had direct channels through which they could spill over into and threaten US financial markets. While hundreds of financial institutions in the United States make loans outside of the United States, the majority of this foreign lending was concentrated in the hands of a few banks known today as systemically important financial institutions (SIFIs).[3] As Lawrence Broz and Michael Brewster Hawes explain, SIFIs "specialize in wholesale and international banking and are located in financial centers such as New York, Chicago, and San Francisco. Their clients include governments, corporations, and other banks."[4] Institutions like Bank of America Corp., Citigroup Inc., JPMorgan Chase & Co., and

---

3. In the past, these were referred to as "money center" banks. They are also sometimes called "large financial institutions" (LFIs).
4. Broz and Hawes 2006, p. 376.

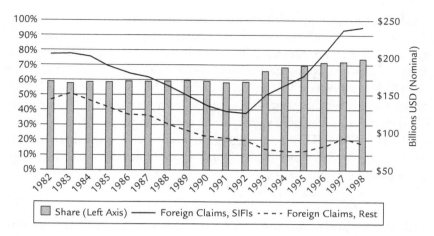

Figure 5.2
SIFI's Share of US Banks' Foreign Claims, 1982–1998

Wells Fargo & Co. fall into this category.[5] SIFIs lie at the core of domestic banking systems and are viewed as having more "systemic importance"—defined as "the damage a bank's failure inflicts upon the rest of the system"—than smaller banks.[6] For instance, for the entire period under investigation, SIFI's foreign claims have comprised more than 55 percent of total US foreign bank claims. Figure 5.2 visually displays this by plotting the total aggregate (nominal) foreign claims of these supersized banks alongside all other reporting US banks from 1982 until 1998. The figure also reports SIFI claims as a share of all US bank claims.

I argue that US economic policymakers were most likely to deploy ESF resources on behalf of foreign economies in crisis where these systemically important US banks were most at risk. The IMF's unresponsiveness, due to the concerted lending strategy, during the 1980s debt crisis increased the likelihood that a sovereign would be forced to default on its debt obligations to US banks. In the 1990s, the IMF's inability to provide sufficiently large credits meant that Fund programs alone may have left the crisis unresolved, leaving US banks and other financial institutions active in those economies at great risk. Thus, I expect that elevated exposure of SIFIs should be associated with an increase in the likelihood of a US financial rescue. Major commercial banks are a well-organized, well-financed political lobby. Banks are also keenly aware that financial crises in foreign jurisdictions threaten their profits—and even their health—if

5. The total number of banks classified as SIFIs has varied from as many as nine in 1982 to as few as six in 1998.
6. Craig and von Peter 2010, p. 22.

a sufficient percentage of their claims are concentrated in that location. They also know that Treasury has the capacity to provide rescue packages to these countries in crisis. Additionally, banks clearly benefit from these kinds of bailouts. Research has shown that bank stock prices rise when the IMF announces it will be bailing out countries to which the banks are exposed.[7] Another study found that when a country facing a financial crisis receives an emergency loan, it uses the money to pay back its private creditors.[8] When SIFIs' interests are threatened by foreign financial crises, I anticipate that they will press top US economic policymakers to take steps that ensure the health and profitability of their institutions—steps like providing foreign ESF credits.[9]

Yet this claim implies that decision making at Treasury was captive to Wall Street, that Treasury made foreign bailouts simply to protect the private interests of big banks and policymakers have no agency. Moreover, this is inconsistent with the broader argument of this book, which asserts that US ILLR actions are designed to protect vital US economic interests— not private financial interests. The likely role of the banking lobby in this story is undeniable. However, it is far too simplistic to depict top US policymakers as marionettes and big banks as holding all the strings. They are also individuals, operating inside state institutions, with their own interests in policy. I expect that policymakers prefer policy choices that increase the likelihood their institution will live up to its mandate. With respect to these cases, the key institutions are the US Treasury and, to a lesser extent, the Federal Reserve. Although these institutions have missions encompassing a number of roles, each is charged with providing a key public good for the US economy: protecting and providing for the stability of the US financial system, broadly construed.[10] In other words, policymakers within these institutions are ordained as the guardians of

---

7. Demirgüç-Kunt and Huizinga 1993; Kho, Lee, and Stulz 2000; Lau and McInish 2003; Zhang 2001.

8. Bird 1996.

9. Because of the substantial resources at their disposal and their small numbers, SIFIs should be more likely to overcome collective action problems and successfully lobby financial authorities for protection in the form of ESF bailouts (Olson 1965). Two existing studies have found convincing evidence that this type of lobbying influences congressional voting behavior (Broz 2005; Broz and Hawes 2006).

10. Treasury is the "steward of US economic and financial systems" with a mission to "[protect] the integrity of the financial system." Additionally, Treasury "works with other federal agencies, foreign governments, and international financial institutions . . . to the extent possible, predict and prevent economic and financial crises." Similarly, one of the Fed's primary purposes is "maintaining the stability of the financial system and containing systemic risk that may arise in financial markets." For more information on the Treasury's mission, see http://www.treasury.gov/about/role-of-treasury/Pages/default.aspx. For details regarding the Fed's mission, see http://www.federalreserve.gov/faqs/about_12594.htm.

US financial stability. I expect their decisions reflect a desire to fulfill their mission.

If exposures to a potential default on the part of multiple foreign borrowers are substantial enough, policymakers may feel that a crisis poses systemic risk to the US financial system. To put it differently, policymakers have an interest in intervening when they believe the probability of a "worst-case scenario"—where the broader financial system faces the prospect of great instability as a result of foreign spillovers—is high enough to justify intervention. Thus, I expect that the effect of SIFI exposure on the likelihood of US foreign bailouts to be conditional on the level of systemic risk facing the US financial system at a given moment. Policymakers should be most concerned about commercial bank losses when the risks facing the entire financial system are elevated. The basic point is this: Individual financial crises do not happen in a vacuum. They occur in a broader international context. Some crises are relatively isolated, occurring in an otherwise stable environment. In such cases, so long as they have sufficient capital in reserve, financial institutions should be capable of weathering losses from the crisis without seriously jeopardizing the health of the US economy. However, there are also moments when individual crises occur within a far more dangerous context. Contagion can cause multiple financial fires to burn at once. Under these circumstances, systemic risk is higher as banks face the possibility of foreign losses on multiple fronts. Threats from individual crises are intensified in this environment. Concerns about the capital adequacy of banks generate fears that banks might fail, threatening the stability of the entire domestic financial system. In such cases, more than just Wall Street profits are at risk. The broader *public* interest is also in danger. When the health of the system is in peril, policymakers should be most likely to act defensively by providing bailouts to those countries where the risks to SIFIs are the greatest. Thus, at the domestic level, US foreign rescues reflect a joint product model where two outputs are produced by the same process: protecting the private financial interests of major banks while also protecting the stability of the national financial system.

The argument is presented visually in Figure 5.3. I expect that the United States will most likely provide ESF credits to countries where SIFIs are highly exposed when the systemic risk facing the broader US financial system from foreign crises is high. This corresponds to quadrant *B* in Figure 5.3. In such cases, the pleas of the bank lobby should be very intense because their survival may be in question. Additionally, US economic policymakers should be most sensitive to the pleas of the bank lobby in such times. Here, the private interests of the banks coincide with

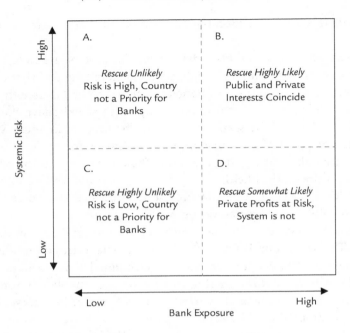

Figure 5.3
Systemic Risk and Bank Exposure Interaction

the broader public interests that policymakers are ordained to serve and protect.[11]

Yet, because the ESF's resources are finite, policymakers' actions are constrained. Consequently, under such circumstances, Treasury should prefer to deploy ESF resources where they will have the greatest effect on stabilizing US markets. Here, the banking lobby acts as an important source of information by relaying to policymakers where they face the greatest risks. All else equal, both Treasury and the big banks should prefer to deploy resources on behalf of countries where SIFIs are most exposed. Conversely, bailouts should be less likely on behalf of countries where SIFIs have little exposure and when international financial waters are calm. This corresponds to quadrant C. Here, banks will have little incentive to ask for protection and policymakers should be reluctant to offer it.

Turning to quadrant A, Treasury is unlikely to provide ESF credits to countries where SIFIs are not highly exposed—even when systemic risk is high. Because ESF resources are finite, when multiple financial fires

11. Gilpin (1975, p. 142) makes a similar argument explaining the spread of US multinationals around the world, noting that "corporate interests and the 'national interest'. . . coincided."

break out at once, I expect Treasury to respond to those that pose the greatest risk to the system. Moreover, in such circumstances, I anticipate that the banking lobby will press policymakers to rescue those economies where they are most exposed. Finally, I expect that policymakers are somewhat likely to provide bailouts to countries where SIFIs are highly exposed, even when systemic risk is low. This corresponds to quadrant D. In these cases, I expect the banking lobby to press Treasury to assist those countries where their claims are the greatest. Yet, in this context, policymakers should be reluctant to act, given that the system does not appear to be under threat. Bailouts in this context would essentially represent an indirect means of protecting profits of big banks. At the same time, in this context, ESF resources are less likely to be under strain from fighting multiple fires at once. Thus, policymakers may be somewhat more amenable to requests by the banks. Additionally, Treasury officials may be persuaded that such a rescue is *preemptive*. Inaction could result in contagion. As other economies become similarly afflicted, systemic risk will elevate, requiring additional bailouts in the future. Thus, while cases in quadrant D should be much less likely to correspond with ESF bailouts than those in quadrant B, they should be more likely to result in rescues than those in quadrants A and C. The remainder of this chapter presents an empirical model of ESF bailout selection where I test my argument.

2. AN EMPIRICAL MODEL OF ESF BAILOUT SELECTION

The first step in constructing an empirical model of ESF bailout selection is identifying an appropriate population for statistical analysis. Ideally, I would have a list of all countries that approached the Treasury for assistance—both those that received rescues and those that were denied—during the period under investigation. Unfortunately, the US Treasury will not release any information regarding foreign requests for US emergency financial assistance that were denied; nor will it say whether the United States has ever extended a bailout only to be rebuffed by the targeted borrower.[12] In other words, the only data available on ESF bailouts are instances where the United States is known to have extended

---

12. I filed a Freedom of Information Act (FOIA) request with the US Treasury asking for (1) a complete list of all ESF loan requests by country/date between 1972 and 2012 and (2) information regarding whether or not ESF loans were ever offered to countries without a request. Treasury's response in a letter to the author was as follows: "A search has been conducted by this office and no records responsive to your request have been located."

a loan to a country in distress. This makes the selection of "negative" cases necessary to build an appropriate population for statistical analysis more complicated than one would like. Without the true population of negative cases, I developed a second-best approach to sample selection. Treasury insists that if a country is to receive assistance from the ESF, it should have filed a letter of intent with the IMF.[13] Again, this is the point at which the borrower government and Fund staff have agreed to the terms of the loan and any required reforms. Based on this information, my sample comprises all countries that requested IMF assistance during the years under investigation. Although nearly all of these loan requests were approved by the executive board, a few were not. However, constructing a sample of requests is more suitable than basing it on actual loan approvals since, as discussed in the previous chapter, in most cases ESF credits were made *prior to* executive board approval. In other words, filing a letter of intent— not board approval—is the proper prerequisite for a developing country to receive an ESF bailout. Finally, the sample is restricted to requests from 1983 to 1999 because of data limitations.[14]

The presence (or absence) of an ESF bailout in a given year is the primary outcome of interest in this analysis. I confirm the presence of a US bailout through documentation of the ESF's use for foreign credits (which I obtained directly from US Treasury by request) as well as additional secondary sources.[15] During the period under investigation, the United States intervened on 34 (yearly) occasions on behalf of 20 different countries via the ESF. However, due to missing data, these numbers drop to 28 and 17, respectively, in my sample.[16]

I rely on two key measures of US financial interests to test my argument. First, to capture the private interests of big US banks, I construct a measure of SIFI bank exposure. This simple measure accounts for the concentration of their foreign loans by country in percentage terms. Precisely, I divide the foreign claims of SIFIs on a given country by total foreign claims of those banks in that same year and then multiply this by 100. Thus, a value of 1 would indicate that 1 percent of SIFIs' foreign claims are concentrated in that country at that time. A higher value indicates increased exposure. The second measure I construct is designed to account for systemic risk. The measure captures changes in the risks facing the US banking system from all foreign financial crises in a given year.

---

13. In rare cases, Treasury provided assistance prior to a letter being completed (i.e., Mexico in 1982); however, in such rare cases the borrower had been in negotiations with the IMF staff working toward agreement.

14. Full details of the statistical sample are available in the appendix.

15. Osterberg and Thompson 1999; Wilson 1999.

16. Coding method of the dependent variable is discussed at length in the appendix.

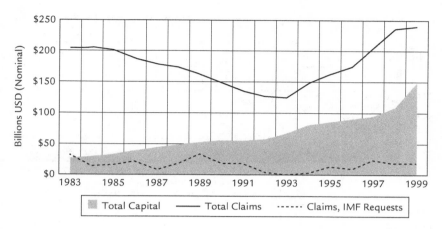

Figure 5.4
SIFI's Foreign Claims and Capital Stock, 1982–1998

I base my construction of this measure on several assumptions. First, I assume that foreign claims of SIFIs are more at risk in countries that seek IMF assistance than in countries that do not. Second, by adding up the total claims of these big banks to all countries that sought an IMF rescue in a given year, we can capture the global risk climate facing major US banks at that moment in time. I assume that, all else equal, in a year when three or four countries to which SIFIs are highly exposed seek IMF assistance, the risks to the broader US banking system are higher than a year when only one of those countries approaches IMF. In such a case, there are multiple financial fires burning in the world and, thus, the risk climate is more threatening. Third, I assume that the vulnerability of the US banking system is not just based on the sum total of bank claims to economies facing financial crises. It is also based on the capital stock that banks hold in reserve. If the capital held by SIFIs rises relative to their total foreign claims, all else being equal, the system should be less vulnerable to foreign shocks. Banks should be more capable of weathering the storm by drawing down their own reserves. Figure 5.4 plots total foreign claims, total foreign claims on countries requesting IMF assistance each year, and total reported capital of SIFIs.

Building on these assumptions, we can estimate systemic risk facing the US banking system from foreign sources by taking the sum total of SIFI claims on countries seeking IMF assistance in a given year (the dotted line in Figure 5.4) divided by total capital held by SIFIs (the shaded area in Figure 5.4). The result is an index that reveals how US banks' capital stacks up in relation to their outstanding loans to economies in crisis over time. Figure 5.5 displays this systemic risk index for US banks,

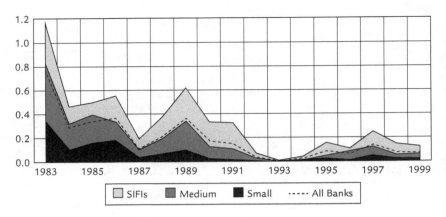

Figure 5.5
Systemic Risk Index, 1983–1999

disaggregated across groups as well as in the aggregate. A point higher up the y-axis represents a higher level of risk, whereas moving down represents decreasing risk. For instance, the measure of 0.62 for SIFIs in 1989 means that the sum total of bank loans to countries requesting IMF assistance that year were equal to 62 percent of their total capital. Unsurprisingly, systemic risk was the highest in 1983 as the IMF was flooded with requests from developing countries during the first full year of the international debt crisis and US banks held a relatively small amount of capital in reserve. Systemic risk remained elevated throughout most of the 1980s before dropping in the 1990s. Risk was most elevated in that decade in 1997 as the Asian financial crisis erupted. To test my argument, I interact both measures of US financial interests: SIFI bank exposure and the systemic risk index. I anticipate that when both of these measures are elevated, the probability of ESF rescues will be the highest (corresponding to quadrant *B* in Figure 5.3). Both of these variables are discussed in more detail in the appendix.

I also include a number of additional covariates in the model to control for potentially confounding factors. Other considerations outside of financial interests may also motivate policymakers to bailout economies in crisis. For example, scholarly accounts of the decision by policymakers to provide ESF credits to South Korea in 1997 point to that country's strategic value as an ally in Asia as influencing the decision.[17] To account

---

17. While defending his department's decision to use ESF resources in defense of Korea and Indonesia in the midst of the Asian financial crisis, then Treasury Secretary Robert Rubin explained, "Our nation's economic *and national security* are vitally at stake in the situation in Asia" (Stevenson 1998a; emphasis added).

for US geostrategic interests in a foreign country, I account for its United Nations General Assembly (UNGA) ideal point distance with the United States.[18] Smaller (larger) ideal point distance indicates that countries' foreign policy preferences are closer to (farther from) US preferences. Although UNGA votes may not carry much actual weight in international relations, they may be useful symbols of support, solidarity, and common interests between countries. As has been argued elsewhere, "Even though UN votes may not be very important, they may still be an accurate signal of alliances and common interest . . . . They may be correlated very strongly with important strategic interests."[19] To control for the possibility that nonfinancial economic ties influenced US bailout selection, I control for countries' share of trade with the United States.[20] Another factor that may influence US bailout decisions is a country's domestic political institutions. For example, Treasury defended its 1984 Argentine bailout, in part, by pointing to Argentina's transition to democracy. Consequently, I include Polity country scores to account for the regime type of each country in question.[21] I also account for Latin American countries in the model with a dummy variable because the vast majority of ESF credits were provided to countries in that region.[22] It may be the case that policymakers felt a greater responsibility to take care of countries in the United States' "backyard" and less responsibilities for countries in other regions.[23]

It may also be the case that Treasury's decisions to act as an ILLR were influenced by borrower-country need. Policymakers may have weighed

18. Specifically, I employ data from Bailey, Strezhnev, and Voeten 2015. The authors show that ideal point estimates improve upon conventional dyadic similarity indicators such as Affinity or S-scores (Gartzke 1998; Signorino and Ritter 1999) by allowing for more valid intertemporal comparisons: distinguishing UN agenda changes from changes in state preferences.

19. Dollar 2000, p. 38. A related body of research on the determinants of IMF lending has consistently found evidence that Fund loan selection (Thacker 1999), loan size, and loan terms are influenced by the borrower countries' voting record in the UNGA (Dreher and Jensen 2007; Dreher, Strum and Vreeland 2009; Oatley and Yackee 2004; Stone 2004, 2008; Thacker 1999; Vreeland 2003, 2005).

20. Specifically, I calculate each country's total trade (imports + exports) with the United States divided by total US trade with the world. I then multiply this by 100. Thus, the variable accounts for each country's annual share of US trade.

21. Marshall, Jaggers, and Gurr 2012. Polity consists of a 21-point scale and range from -10 (least democratic) to 10 (most democratic).

22. Specifically, this is a dummy variable equal to 1 if a country is classified as being part of Latin America (including the Caribbean) by the UN, 0 if otherwise.

23. A conversation during a 1982 Federal Open Market Committee (FOMC) suggests there may have been a perceived geographical division of labor between the United States and Europe when it came to financial crises. At one point during the meeting, Chairman Volcker noted, "It certainly is in [Europe's] mind as are some of these other things: Latin American is your area" (FOMC 1982c, p. 65).

the severity of the economic conditions facing a country in crisis when making financial rescue decisions.[24] Although all countries that approach the IMF for financial assistance are facing financial difficulty (otherwise they would not be asking for help), within this group considerable variation exists. Therefore, I control for a variety of macroeconomic conditions, including total national debt service costs over export earnings, the current account balance, total foreign exchange reserves (minus gold), and the annual GDP growth rate. I also include a dummy variable that accounts for whether a borrower country's currency faced a speculative attack the same year, or the year before, they sought IMF assistance.[25] Variation in such factors may exacerbate or attenuate the severity of the crisis and, therefore, affect the extent to which countries are willing to ask for additional assistance. Such factors may also impact the willingness of the United States to help. In this sense, the Treasury or the Fed may act as international financial physicians that are more likely to treat patients suffering from especially severe forms of economic sickness. In addition to these need-based factors, I include standard macroeconomic control variables such as GDP and GDP per capita in all specifications.

I also include three domestic-level variables to account for the possibility that US political or economic conditions impact the ESF bailout selection process. As noted in the previous chapter, the Secretary of the Treasury decides when ESF resources ought to be marshaled in defense of a foreign economy, conditional on the consent of the president. Because variation in the political party affiliation of the president might affect bailout selection, I account for whether the executive is a Republican or Democrat.[26] It may also be the case that US economic performance has an effect on the likelihood that policymakers will decide to act as an ILLR. When the US economy is in the doldrums, administrations may be more reluctant to send resources abroad to rescue foreign sovereigns. Thus, I also account for the annual US GDP growth rate and the annual unemployment rate (in percentage terms), respectively.[27]

24. For example, former Undersecretary of the Treasury for International Affairs David Mulford once explained to Congress that ESF credits are "considered on a case-by-case basis, *based on a demonstrated need for liquidity* and evidence of adjustment efforts in cooperation with the IMF" (US Senate 1984, p. 13; emphasis added).

25. This variable, equal to 1 in the event of a speculative attack, 0 otherwise, is based on the exchange market pressure (EMP) index developed by Eichengreen et al. (1995) and Kaminsky and Reinhart (1999) as described in Leblang (2003). I discuss how I code this variable, as well as the source of the data, in the appendix.

26. Specifically, I employ a dummy variable equal to 1 if the president at the time of an ESF credit was a Republican, 0 if otherwise.

27. I rely on the World Bank's World Development Indicators (WDIs) for each of the aforementioned economic need-based and domestic-level variables.

To address issues related to temporal dependence in models with binary dependent variables, I include a cubic polynomial.[28] Finally, in keeping with previous studies on international financial rescues, all the aforementioned covariates are lagged one year. This reflects the fact that the process of ESF bailout selection, like IMF loan selection, is based on information that lags behind the date of the actual decision.[29] Given the dichotomous outcome of interests (ESF rescue), I fit four logistic regression models: a first model with only the bank (SIFI) exposure measure and macroeconomic controls, a second that interacts bank exposure with the systemic risk measure as well as the macroeconomic controls, a third that adds in regime type and UN voting measures, and a fourth that adds in US economic controls.[30]

3. RESULTS

Table 5.1 reports the results for all four models. First, I will focus my discussion on the measures of US financial interests. On its own, bank exposure does not appear to impact the likelihood of a financially distressed country being selected for an ESF bailout (see Model 1 results). Although the coefficient is positive as expected, it is not statistically significant at conventional levels. However, when bank exposure interacts with systemic risk, the effect is both substantive and statistically significant across all remaining models. To illuminate the effects of systemic risk and bank exposure on ESF bailout selection, Figures 5.6 and 5.7 present the simulated predicted probabilities of a US rescue as SIFI bank exposure increases from its sample minimum (0 percent) to its maximum (10 percent).[31] The solid lines represent the mean expected probability of a bailout while the shaded gray areas represent 90 percent confidence intervals. Figure 5.6 shows the predicted probability of an ESF credit when systemic risk is low, held at one standard deviation below its sample mean (0.05). As the figure indicates, when systemic risk is low, there is almost no discernible effect of SIFI bank exposure on the probability of an ESF credit line. This suggests that when the risks facing the broader

28. Carter and Signorino 2010.
29. Knight and Santaella 1997, p. 413. The only exception is the covariate accounting for the president's party, since this would have obviously been known at the time the decision was being made.
30. To address potential problems due to clustering in countries and years, I compute Heteroskedastic and Autocorrelation Consistent (HAC) standard errors. All models are fitted using the R package Zelig (Imai, King, and Lau 2007, 2008).
31. This also allows me to avoid the problem of directly interpreting interaction coefficients in nonlinear models. For more on this, see Ali and Norton 2003; Gelman and Pardoe 2007.

Table 5.1 ESF BAILOUT SELECTION REGRESSION RESULTS

	Model 1		Model 2		Model 3		Model 4	
Intercept	-11.820	(8.806)	-6.144	(8.723)	-4.629	(8.945)	-25.952	(19.513)
GDP (log)	0.295	(0.421)	0.106	(0.403)	0.124	(0.405)	0.074	(0.403)
GDP per capita (log)	-0.284	(0.672)	-0.466	(0.658)	-0.623	(0.634)	-0.526	(0.609)
External debt service/exports	0.032	(0.025)	0.029	(0.028)	0.034	(0.030)	0.031	(0.029)
Current account balance	-0.033**	(0.012)	-0.034**	(0.013)	-0.031*	(0.013)	-0.031*	(0.013)
Reserves/GDP	0.0382	(6.952)	-4.110	(7.039)	-2.871	(7.722)	-3.500	(8.499)
GDP growth	-0.033	(0.083)	-0.017	(0.090)	-0.014	(0.090)	-0.023	(0.091)
Speculative attack	1.142*	(0.569)	1.041*	(0.580)	1.093†	(0.632)	1.203*	(0.591)
Share of US trade	0.010	(0.244)	-0.094	(0.210)	-0.003	(0.305)	-0.046	(0.299)
Latin America	2.382**	(0.901)	2.4194*	(0.967)	1.935	(1.242)	2.017†	(1.197)
Democracy (PolityIV)					0.055	(0.067)	0.042	(0.067)
UN ideal point distance					-0.325	(0.864)	-0.262	(0.854)
US unemployment							1.387	(1.281)
US GDP growth							0.335	(0.250)
Republican president							1.586	(2.248)
Year	0.942	(0.747)	1.391†	(0.833)	1.367†	(0.806)	3.914	(2.786)
Year²	-0.089	(0.091)	-0.153	(0.097)	-0.149	(0.091)	-0.366	(0.283)
Year³	0.001	(0.003)	0.004	(0.003)	0.004	(0.003)	0.010	(0.009)
SIFI bank exposure	-0.023	(0.269)	-0.168	(0.229)	-0.187	(0.223)	-0.056	(0.277)
Systemic risk	-1.285	(1.792)	-3.305	(2.398)	-3.132	(2.433)	0.060	(3.528)
SIFI exposure * systemic risk			1.660*	(0.723)	1.886**	(0.685)	1.991*	(0.815)
N	179		179		178		178	
Number of countries	46		46		46		46	
AIC	118.02		116.84		119.83		124.13	

Heteroskedastic and Autocorrelation Consistent (HAC) standard errors in parentheses † $p < 0.10$, * $p < 0.05$, ** $p < 0.01$

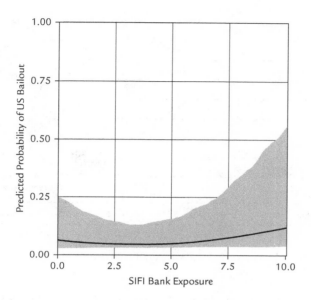

Figure 5.6
Predicted Probability of US Bailout (Low Systemic Risk)

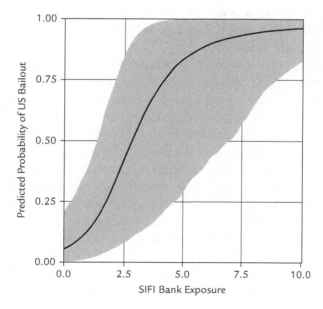

Figure 5.7
Predicted Probability of US Bailout (High Systemic Risk)

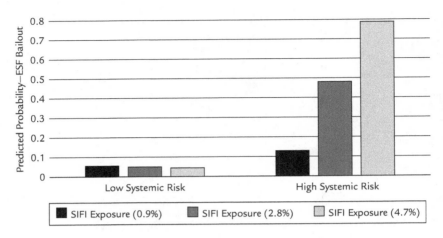

Figure 5.8
Mean Predicted Probabilities of ESF Bailout (Model 4)

US financial system were low, SIFI exposure had little to no impact on US policymakers' decisions to intervene on a distressed country's behalf. For the sake of comparison, Figure 5.7 presents variation in SIFI exposure when systemic risk is elevated one standard deviation above its mean (0.65). The relationship is quite different in this case. When systemic risk is elevated, the effect of SIFI exposure on the probability of a US rescue is positive and quite substantial.

To further clarify this effect, Figure 5.8 presents the mean simulated predicted probabilities of a US rescue when systemic risk is low and elevated as SIFI exposure increases from its mean (0.9 percent of total foreign claims, slightly above the level of Turkey in 1999) to one standard deviation above the mean (2.8 percent, about the level of Argentina in 1984) to two standard deviations above the mean (4.7 percent, between the level of Korea in 1997 and Brazil in 1998). When systemic risk is low, increasing bank exposure from its mean to one and then two standard deviations above the mean has essentially no effect. Conversely, when systemic risk is high, increasing SIFI exposure from 0.9 percent to 4.7 percent of total foreign claims, the probability that Treasury will intervene as an ILLR and provide a bailout increases by a substantial 66 percent.[32] In short, the results indicate that US financial interests do correlate with ESF bailout selection. However, the results suggest that financial interests only impact US decisions to act as an ILLR when the private interests of major banks and the public interests that policymakers are mandated to protect are

32. At the elevated levels of SIFI exposure, the difference is statistically significant at the p<0.1 level.

aligned. When risks facing the broader US financial system from international financial turmoil are high, policymakers are more sensitive to the exposures of major US banks and more inclined to respond to requests by the financial sector for protection. In such cases, policymakers may justify such actions as necessary to protect the broader national interests even though the banks reap a private benefit from the rescue operation. On the other hand, when the risks facing the system are low, ESF bailout selection does not appear to be substantially impacted by SIFI bank exposure. In such cases, policymakers appear to be far less sensitive to the banks' private interests. The empirical results suggest that US policymakers' sensitivity to the exposure of big Wall Street banks depends on the systemic context.[33]

Outside of the key financial covariates, the results indicate that countries with larger current account deficits and countries facing speculative attacks against their currencies were more likely to receive a US rescue. Thus, the results suggest that economic need played a role in the ESF bailout selection process. In all but Model 3, Latin American countries appear somewhat more likely to have been selected for an ESF rescue than countries in other regions. This implies that US policymakers may have been more sensitive to the needs of countries in their own geographic backyard. Neither the geopolitical variables nor the domestic economic controls are statistically significant at conventional levels.[34]

4. CONCLUSIONS

The broad thesis of this book is that the United States will choose to act unilaterally as an ILLR when the IMF's shortcomings threaten vital US economic interests. Chapter 4 explained that, as a result of seismic changes in the global financial system, the Fund's effectiveness as a financial crisis manager suffered from the problem of unresponsiveness during the 1980s and the problem of resource insufficiency in the 1990s. These weaknesses forced the United States to step in and provide unilateral bailouts throughout these decades. Yet not all countries in crisis received US

---

33. This is consistent with Oatley (2011), who cautions and demonstrates that within IPE, studies that focus on domestic politics "in isolation from international or macro processes" can generate inaccurate knowledge (p. 311).

34. In separate specifications (not shown), I included a country's share of US foreign aid as an additional control. The coefficient for US aid was negative and it was not statistically significant. Additionally, its inclusion did not alter the statistical significance of the financial interaction term. I omitted its inclusion here only because it resulted in the loss of 12 observations, including several cases where ESF bailouts were made. Given the small sample size and the scarce number of ESF credits in the model, I opted to exclude this from the analysis.

rescues. Here, I presented an empirical model of ESF bailout selection. The results support my argument that variation in the Treasury's provision of international ESF bailouts is best explained by variation in US financial interests. In a globalized world economy where the US financial system is not confined within the United States' borders, circumstances sometimes require policymakers to extend the lender of last resort mechanism internationally in order to protect the US economy. International rescues are most likely when major banks at the heart of the US financial system are highly exposed to an afflicted economy. In such cases, the banks should press economic policymakers to intervene by providing a bailout, thereby protecting their institutions from threatening spillovers. However, the story is somewhat more complicated than this. As I argued, it is overly simplistic to think of policymakers at Treasury as puppets of the financial industry. They are also stewards of the public interest that have a desire to fulfill their institution's mandate, which includes stabilizing the US financial system. Thus, they should be most sensitive to the needs of the banks when the broader national financial system is facing grave risks. The results support this, as the effect of SIFI exposure on the likelihood of a US bailout is strongly conditioned on the level of systemic risk facing the US economy at a given point in time. Policymakers are most likely to spring into action when the private interests of the financial industry are aligned with the broader public interest. Thus, ESF bailouts reflect a joint-product model where two outputs are produced by the same process. In this case, the joint outputs are (1) the protection of the private financial interests of major banks and (2) the stabilization of the national financial system.

CHAPTER 6

US International Bailouts in the 1980s and 1990s

Nobody likes big banks, especially big New York banks.

Peter Wallison, Former US Treasury General Counsel

(*Miller Center of Public Affairs Interview*, 2003)

A byproduct of programs designed to restore stability and growth may be that some creditors will be protected from the full consequences of their actions.

Robert Rubin, Former US Treasury Secretary (1998)

The statistical results in the previous chapter strongly suggest that policymakers' desire to protect the US financial system was the primary motivation behind Exchange Stabilization Fund (ESF) rescues in the 1980s and 1990s. The interactive effects of bank exposure and systemic risk on the likelihood of US bailouts are both significant and sizable. When big US commercial banks were highly exposed to an economy in crisis at a time when systemic risk facing the US financial system was elevated, policymakers were most likely to deploy ESF resources. However, when the stability of the domestic financial system was not at risk, the exposure of systemically important financial institutions (SIFIs) to an economy in duress did not affect the likelihood of a US rescue. Thus, the empirical model supports the argument that US economic policymakers were most likely to act as an international lender of last resort (ILLR) during this period when the private interests of SIFIs were aligned with the broader *public* interest.

Although the statistical analysis shows that US financial interests explain a significant amount of variation in foreign ESF credits, it presents only a partial picture of the political economy of US ILLR actions during these years. Quantitative analysis is good at identifying the average relationship between variables—in this case, financial interests and US foreign rescues—across a broad sample of cases. However, it does not truly link the causal chain that begins with policymakers' concerns about the health of the US financial system and ends with the decision to bail out a foreign economy. Nor can it tell us that policymakers were truly motivated by such considerations in individual cases. Additionally, quantitative analysis is not very effective at explaining cases that do not fit the proposed model. Not all ESF bailouts fit my argument, yet the statistical results do not tell us much about why these rescues were made. Lastly, the statistical analysis does not directly tie concerns about the International Monetary Fund's (IMF's) ineffectiveness as an ILLR to the bailout decisions. Case studies offer a way to correct for these weaknesses. They enable us to trace the process through which these events actually unfolded and identify the factors that had the greatest influence on the decision-making process. In an effort to address these issues, this chapter explores seven cases where the United States rescued foreign economies in duress as well as two cases where troubled economies were passed over for help.

1. CASE SELECTION

Case selection in case-study research should have two main objectives: (1) obtain a representative sample with (2) useful variation on the dimensions of theoretical interest.[1] In order to satisfy these objectives, I employ what John Gerring refers to as the "diverse case method."[2] This technique aims to select a set of cases that represent the full range of values that characterize a specific relationship between an explanatory variable (in this case, the interaction between two measures of US financial interests) and an outcome of interest (ESF credits).[3] Figure 6.1 presents a modified version of Figure 5.3 from the previous chapter. Each of the cases is placed into one of the four quadrants, based on whether their values on the two key explanatory variables—SIFI bank exposure and the systemic risk index—are above or below their respective sample means.[4]

---

1. Seawright and Gerring 2008, p. 296.
2. Gerring 2007.
3. For more on this, see Gerring 2008 (p. 300) and Seawright and Gerring 2007 (pp. 97–101).
4. Admittedly, using the sample mean as the cutoff point is somewhat arbitrary. Seawright and Gerring (2008) note that when dealing with continuous variables, as is the case here, it is difficult to identify where these lines should be drawn. The primary goal, however, is to ensure that there is meaningful variation across these variables of interest. The approach I use here accomplishes this.

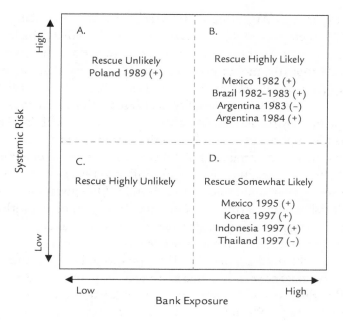

Figure 6.1
Case Distribution across Theoretical Dimensions of Interest

Thus, those in quadrant *B* represent cases where both bank exposure and systemic risk are above average for the sample. Those in quadrant *D* represent cases where SIFIs were exposed at above-average levels but systemic risk was below average. The case in quadrant *A* exhibits below-average bank exposure but above-average systemic risk. Thus, these cases present a range of variation across the two explanatory variables. Additionally, Figure 6.1 also indicates the value of the outcome of interest: whether or not an ESF credit was provided in each case. A plus symbol (+) indicates that a bailout was provided, while a minus symbol (–) indicates the absence of a credit. Thus, these cases also present both possible outcomes of the dependent variable. This case-selection strategy has an additional benefit: It makes it easy to identify "typical" cases that fit the argument's expectations and "deviant" cases that do not.[5]

The Polish (1989) and Argentine (1983) cases are deviant cases in that they disconfirm a deterministic relationship between the explanatory variables and the outcome of interest. My argument appears to poorly explain Treasury's decision to bail out Poland in 1989 given that SIFIs had little exposure to that economy. Similarly, given that big banks were

5. For more on typical and deviant cases, see Gerring 2007.

highly exposed to Argentina in 1983 and systemic risk facing the US financial system was high, my argument would predict a bailout—yet one did not occur in this case. Exploring these cases allows us to move beyond a simplistic, monocausal story by identifying alternative explanations of US ILLR actions. Mexico (1982), Brazil (1982, 1983), and Argentina (1984) are examples of typical cases—those that appear to be well explained by the model. Close within-case analysis of these rescues presents the opportunity to probe whether or not the historical evidence actually validates the argument. All three observations in quadrant *D*— Mexico (1995), Korea, Indonesia, and Thailand (1997)—fall somewhere in between deviant and typical cases. Here, SIFI exposure was high yet systemic risk was below the sample average. Thus, conducting within-case analysis of these particular events represents an important opportunity to assess the extent to which the *private interests* of the banks may have independently influenced US bailouts. If so, this would suggest that at least some US bailouts are not designed to protect the public interest.

Finally, these cases also present significant variation over time. Five cases are from the 1980s; four are from the 1990s. This variation across time is important given the argument I made in chapter 4 about changes in the structure of the global financial system and how this affected the IMF's adequacy as an ILLR. In the 1980s, IMF unresponsiveness should be linked to the need for US intervention. In the 1990s, IMF resource insufficiency should be a key concern of policymakers. Thus, due to the variation over time, the case studies will also help identify whether the supposed weaknesses of the Fund were in fact linked to US bailout decisions.

2. THE CASES

The nine cases are presented here in chronological order. This is helpful as some of these rescues occurred within months of each other. Thus, the conditions surrounding cases sometimes coincide. Individual cases are sometimes discussed in conjunction with other rescues that occurred proximate to one another.

2.1. Mexico, Brazil, and Argentina, 1982–1983

The notion of the Reagan administration bailing out a foreign country in crisis would have seemed far-fetched to an educated observer in 1980. As one *Washington Post* reporter at the time put it, the Reagan administration came into office "dedicated to the 'magic of the marketplace' as a cure for troubled economies and deeply suspicious of international financial institutions and the aid they dispense."[6] Miles Khaler noted that Reagan was initially quite skeptical of intergovernmental cooperation in international financial and monetary affairs.[7] In fact, this skepticism was sufficient to make the administration oppose an IMF quota increase in its first year in office. The administration's position would soon change, however. In August 1982, the Mexican government learned that its foreign lenders were no longer willing to roll over its debts. On August 12, Mexican Finance Minister Silva Herzog called Fed Chairman Paul Volcker and Treasury Secretary Donald Regan. He informed them he was immediately putting in place a moratorium on servicing Mexico's external sovereign debts, effectively defaulting on those obligations. The majority of Mexican debt was held by Western banks, which had been rapidly expanding their foreign lending operations over the previous decade. The Mexican announcement immediately generated fears in financial markets that other countries, especially the debt-ridden economies of Latin America, might soon follow suit. The worst-case scenario facing exposed banks was the possibility that the major debtor economies might form a cartel and collectively repudiate their debts. Such a move would have been cataclysmic. Multiple systemically important US banks would have faced the real prospect of bankruptcy.

In the words of one administration official, the Mexican default had "a major effect" on the Reagan White House's view of the IMF as well as the role of Treasury in managing international financial crises. Mexico's external debt stood at more than $80 billion, $25 billion of which was owed to US financial institutions—a sum that made up more than 7 percent of all US banks' foreign claims and, even more staggering, represented *more than one-third* of their total capital stock. Mexican officials, who had been in close contact with Treasury since April, explained that they needed roughly $3 billion immediately simply to restart making the minimum payments on their debts.[8] As Jeffrey Sachs put it, "Even the ostensibly laissez-fair Reagan administration went swiftly into action" when faced with the Mexican default.[9] On August 15, Treasury Secretary Don Regan authorized a $1 billion ESF loan to the Mexican government, which, at that time, was only just beginning its negotiations with IMF officials about a loan package. With an IMF loan still up in the air, the

6. Oberdorfer 1983.
7. Khaler 1992, p. 69.
8. Oberdorfer 1983, p. A1.
9. Sachs 1988, p. 233.

United States agreed to record the loan as prepayments for Mexican oil purchases. Treasury then drummed up a $1.85 billion multilateral bridge loan package via the Bank for International Settlements (BIS). This included an additional $600 million contribution from the ESF on August 26. Meanwhile, the Fed chipped in another $325 million by expanding the size of an existing $700 million swap line with the Bank of Mexico. That deal dated back to 1967 as part of the Fed's Bretton Woods–era lending network.

Meanwhile, Mexican authorities remained in the consultation stage with IMF staff. It was not until November 8 that they formally submitted their letter of intent to the executive board requesting an Extended Fund Facility (EFF) arrangement.[10] Thus, the initial emergency loan from the United States reached Mexico a full 86 days before their authorities had even submitted a formal request for Fund assistance. Yet, despite the dire circumstances facing Mexico and the threat this posed to the global financial system, submission of the letter did not lead to a speedy approval by the board. Rather, IMF Managing Director Jacques de Larosière informed the major commercial banks at a meeting that month in New York that the loan request would not be approved by the board until they provided him with "written assurances that they would increase their exposure by enough to cover a substantial fraction ($5 billion) of Mexico's scheduled interest payments for 1983."[11] This marked the beginning of the Fund's concerted lending strategy (discussed at length in chapter 4). Once banks agreed to increase their exposure to Mexico, the board scheduled the letter for consideration. Ultimately, the board approved the request on January 1, 1983—54 days after the letter was submitted and a full *142 days* after the Mexican moratorium began! This case clearly shows that although concerted lending may have been effective at promoting (or, perhaps more appropriately, coercing) private-market participation in the management of the debt crisis, it further slowed down an already slothful IMF. Fed and ESF financing was vital in enabling Mexico to begin meeting its obligations. The credit simultaneously protected US banks from suffering substantial losses, gave Mexico and the IMF time to hammer out a long-term financing deal, and allowed de Larosière to press the commercial banks to reschedule Mexican debt, making the burden less onerous.

Mexico was not the only Latin American economy in trouble in 1982. Once Silva Herzog's decision went public, commercial bank lending to other heavily indebted developing economies rapidly retrenched. Argentina and Brazil were both now firmly in the crosshairs of the debt

10. Boughton 2001, p. 307.
11. Ibid., p. 405.

crisis as banks began refusing to roll over their debts as well. Like Mexico, the government of Brazil had borrowed heavily from US banks to a tune of more than $21 billion as of 1982. This represented more than 6 percent of US financial institutions' total foreign claims and 31 *percent* of total bank capital. With the US financial system on the hook once more, Treasury was again called to action. At the General Agreements on Tariffs and Trade (GATT) ministerial meetings in October 1982, Brazilian Finance Minister Ernane Galveas met with US Deputy Treasury Secretary Timothy McNamar, where the two negotiated a rescue deal. The ESF would provide $500 million in immediate, short-term assistance to Brasilia.[12] By the end of November, Treasury added two additional bilateral credits, bringing the total commitment to $1.24 billion. These loans were kept secret until December 1 when President Reagan unveiled them amid the "fanfare" of a state visit to Brasilia.[13] Describing the loan as "government to government," Reagan indicated that Treasury's involvement should encourage commercial banks in the United States and beyond to roll over Brazil's debts while the country worked to reestablish solvency.[14] Days later, Treasury made it clear that its commitment was by no means maxed out. It was "standing by as necessary to be of further assistance" in rounding up short-term assistance to Brazil via the BIS.[15]

As was the case with Mexico, the ESF commitment to Brazil was intended to buy that government time to work out a long-term EFF financing program with the IMF and to negotiate a rescheduled debt deal with commercial banks. It was also a way to keep the severity of Brazil's crisis under wraps until these negotiations could get under way. In a November meeting of the Federal Open Market Committee (FOMC), Chairman Paul Volcker noted that Treasury's emergency packages to Brazil were intended "just to keep them afloat until the timing is right for them to go to the Fund and try to deal with the problem more openly, which is certainly going to have to be done. It is still a very uneasy situation."[16] Brazil did not formally enter into discussions with Fund staff regarding the loan program until the end of November. Those negotiations were completed on January 6 when Brazil formally submitted its letter to the executive board. In keeping with its concerted lending strategy, the board did not approve the request until commercial banks agreed to put up new money for Brazil. Ultimately, the IMF loan was not approved until March 1,

12. Aggarwal 1996, p. 462.
13. Boughton 2001, p. 339.
14. Weisman 1982.
15. Farnsworth 1982.
16. FOMC 1982b, p. 24.

1983—nearly *six months* after Brazil first requested official assistance.[17] By the time the dust had settled, the ESF had extended a total of six separate emergency credits to Brasilia—five bilateral loans and one multilateral package the United States pushed through the BIS—bringing Treasury's net contribution to $2.38 billion between October 1982 and February 1983.

Argentina was the third large Latin American economy that ran into problems rolling over its debts in 1982. In fact, strains in Argentina preceded those in Brazil. Although the United States considered coming to Argentina's aid, according to the Treasury's records, direct assistance was not provided in this case.[18] The ESF did not provide a credit despite the fact that the country was facing the same problems as Mexico and Brazil and despite the fact that its crisis threatened US banks at a time when systemic risk facing the US financial system was high. Given these conditions, why was Argentina passed over? Several factors likely played a role. First, US banks—while vulnerable to an Argentine default—were relatively less exposed to Argentina when compared to Brazil and Mexico.[19] After the Mexican moratorium, US policymakers knew all three countries were going to need assistance.[20] Treasury appears to have decided that assisting the two biggest threats to the US financial system—Brazil and Mexico—was the top priority. Argentina was left without a chair when the music stopped. As discussed in chapter 2, unlike the Fed's swap lines, ESF resources are finite. Consequently, Treasury had to weigh the prospect of overextending its limited financial resources. A report in the *New York Times* makes a similar implication, noting that although Argentina was in need of help, "[US] monetary authorities said the Brazilian request had a higher priority."[21]

Second, it is unclear if Argentine authorities ever directly requested Treasury assistance. Argentina, however, did seek emergency assistance from the BIS. That institution's annual report for 1983 reveals that Argentina approached the BIS in September 1982 to request a bridge loan. Negotiations successfully ended in January, resulting in a $500 million credit through that organization.[22] According to official Treasury

17. Boughton 2001, p. 338.
18. At the December 21, 1982, FOMC meeting, the committee openly discussed the possibility of extending a swap line to Argentina. It also debated whether or not the Fed or Treasury should aid Argentina should the country need assistance, which it viewed as likely. Ultimately, the committee balked at setting a precedent of opening Fed swap lines with countries outside of those it already had established relationships with (FOMC 1982c, 62).
19. Indeed, US bank claims in Argentina were roughly half as large as claims in each of the other troubled economies.
20. FOMC 1982a, p. 9.
21. Farnsworth 1982.
22. BIS 1983, p. 128.

records, the United States did not contribute to that multilateral package. However, the Federal Reserve may have been involved indirectly through a standing $1.85 billion swap line it maintained with the BIS. A 1982 Federal Reserve Bank of New York (FRBNY) report on foreign exchange operations documents that the BIS drew $124 billion from its swap line with the Fed around the time it provided the credit to Argentina. The report indicates that the BIS drawing was used in the multilateral package for Mexico. Yet, it also adds, "During the period, the U.S. monetary authorities provided or participated in the provision of short-term bridging credits to Brazil *and Argentina also.*"[23] Similarly, when discussing the 1982 BIS bridge loan to Argentina, James Boughton adds, "The BIS, *led by the United States,* granted a short-term stand-by credit in late January to serve as a bridge to the scheduled May drawing under the Fund agreement."[24] Thus, although Treasury's official position indicates that it did not provide direct assistance, it appears likely that the Federal Reserve provided indirect assistance to Buenos Aires by routing a loan through the BIS.

These three cases illustrate the factors that motivated US economic policymakers to act outside of the IMF as an ILLR by providing emergency liquidity to foreign governments in crisis. The IMF could not provide credits in a timely manner and employ the concerted lending strategy at the same time. Concerted lending was effective at forcing the hands of commercial banks to increase exposures to the heavily indebted countries. However, it had the adverse effect of delaying the disbursement of emergency financing. Due to the Fund's limitations, the United States stepped in as an ILLR by tapping the ESF and providing Mexico and Brazil with emergency, short-term loans. Moreover, the United States deliberately selected these two countries to protect the US financial system. Figure 6.2 compares the total adjusted claims of US banks in the five Latin American economies where those totals were highest.[25] In fact, the United Kingdom and Japan were the only two countries where US banks were more exposed at that time. US inaction would have forced both countries to wait several months for IMF financing, resulting in the suspension of debt servicing. This would have complicated, and potentially derailed, negotiations with the banks and allowed the crisis to spread more rapidly to other countries. The threat of contagion was both real and severe. Sachs

23. FRBNY 1983, p. 59. Emphasis added.
24. Boughton 2001, p. 335. Emphasis added.
25. Data are collected by the author from relevant Country Exposure Lending Surveys (CELS) via the Federal Reserve archive available at http://fraser.stlouisfed.org/publication/?pid=333.

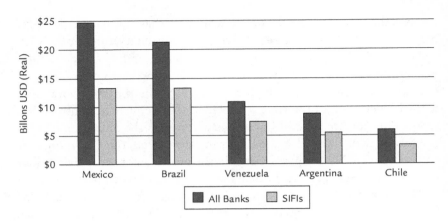

Figure 6.2
Adjusted Foreign Claims of US Banks, 1982

summed up the motivation behind US foreign bailouts during the initial year of the debt crisis in two words: "gut fear." He continued,

> At the end of 1983, the [Least Developed Country] LDC exposure of the nine U.S. [systemically important] banks was $83.4 billion, or 287.7 percent of bank capital. In Latin America alone, the exposure was 176.6 percent of bank capital . . . . It seemed obvious that if the largest debtor countries unilaterally repudiated their debt, then the largest U.S. banks could fail, with dire consequences for the U.S. and world economies.[26]

In short, without US involvement, its own banking system might have collapsed.

These cases illustrate how US ILLR actions can be viewed as an extension of the domestic lender of last resort mechanism in a world where the US financial system is global. That is, the provision of liquidity to a foreign economy is designed to protect the "general interest" of the US economy, in line with Walter Bagehot's ideal. Despite the clear and present risks these crises posed for the broader US economy, it is worth considering the argument that Treasury stepped in to protect the *private* interests of US banks. Indeed, banks had much to gain from any international rescue as this would allow the indebted governments to continue making interest and principal payments to these institutions.[27] To what extent did private banking interests play a role in the US decision to bail out Mexico and Brazil? Without first hand knowledge of all

---

26. Sachs 1988, p. 253.
27. Sachs and Williamson 1986.

potential backroom discussions, there is, of course, no way to know the answer with complete certainty. In chapter 5, I argued that the banking lobby should be expected to lobby Treasury for protection when the industry's interests are threatened. It is not difficult to imagine CEOs of major American banks calling contacts at Treasury or the Fed in order to make them aware of their exposure and even requesting that such credits be provided. Indeed, it seems likely that such conversations would have taken place during such extraordinary times. Moreover, bank lobbying for foreign bailouts would have been an important source of information for policymakers—helping them grasp the full extent of the financial system's exposure.

Yet, given the severity of the risks facing the heart of the US financial system, it seems incongruous to suggest that policymakers were motivated to provide foreign bailouts to protect bank profits and equity values in isolation. Without question, any bailout would benefit the banks since much of the money provided would be paid back to those institutions as interest payments. Yet such a result is unavoidable if foreign credits are the only way to protect the US financial system from catastrophe. FOMC transcripts indicate that protecting bank profits was not a top priority of policymakers—quite the opposite, in fact. This is evident in one telling exchange during a committee meeting in December 1982 that begins with Chairman Volcker explaining to the other members what needs to happen in order to steady the crisis:

CHAIRMAN VOLCKER: If we can get the Mexican and Brazilian situations stabilized, and Argentina is also big, I think we will have the whole situation stabilized because there's nothing else big enough and they'll never sell it to—

MR. BOEHNE: In other words, if there is a default in one of the smaller countries, the banks could eat it.

CHAIRMAN VOLCKER: Right.

MR. BOEHNE: Maybe they even should eat a little.

CHAIRMAN VOLCKER: Exactly.[28]

---

28. FOMC 1982c, p. 70. This is not the only example of Volcker's lack of love for the big banks. For instance, Volcker played an active role in assisting the Fund's efforts to make the concerted lending strategy succeed. Based on one account, "Although Volcker never explicitly said he would use his powers as a bank regulator to exact retribution from a bank that refused to follow his moral suasion, the implication was not lost on bank executives" (Blustein 2001, p. 188). In a 1984 FOMC meeting, Volcker went on record saying that he had not "made any great secret" of the fact that he thought banks ought to make interest-rate concessions to the indebted countries where there had been signs of improvement, something the banks opposed (FOMC 1984, p. 28).

2.2. Argentina, 1984

Although the world economy had absorbed the initial blow of the debt crisis by 1984, the storm had by no means passed. That year, the IMF was still employing concerted lending as a way to prevent commercial banks from turning their backs on the indebted countries. A byproduct of that strategy was the continued slothfulness of IMF lending and the need for bridge loans. Although Treasury did not go on record as assisting Argentina in 1983, it did so the following year. The loan caused a political uproar in the United States. The 1984 Argentine bailout, comprising two separate ESF credits, was the first foreign rescue by Treasury to generate serious political controversy. The ESF's credit to Argentina was tainted by the perception that US authorities were intervening not on behalf of the national interest but rather on behalf of big New York banks. The controversy culminated in congressional hearings on Treasury's potential abuse of power and waste of taxpayers' dollars.

In December 1983, following years of military rule, Raúl Alfonsín was sworn in as Argentina's first democratically elected president in nearly a decade. Despite regime change, Argentina was still on the hook for nearly $50 billion in external debts. The Alfonsín government was determined to deal with its inherited debt problem; however, it was equally determined to press for better terms than its predecessors in the ruling military junta. The government restarted negotiations with commercial banks and the IMF. It also decided to suspend interest payments until a better deal could be reached. As negotiations dragged on, the country's interest arrears to commercial banks were accumulating. This became problematic for US banks when interest payments reached nearly 90 days in arrears because of a peculiarity in US financial regulatory standards. In all other industrial economies at that time, banks could report interest arrears as income for up to one year. However, in the United States, the window was much shorter. US banks were required to publish their balance sheets on a quarterly—rather than annual—basis. Once interest went unpaid for 90 days, financial institutions could no longer report unpaid interest as income in their profit reports. Moreover, all unpaid interest that had previously been reported from their income or bank reserves would have to be deducted from their balance sheets. This problem, unique to the US banking sector, was coming to a head at the end of March 1984, just prior to when first-quarter reports would be published. It was in this context that the Treasury authorized a $300 billion loan to the Alfonsín government on March 30, one day before bank balance sheets would go public.[29]

---

29. US Senate 1984, p. 18.

The timing of the Treasury's response raised suspicions in Congress. Both houses held hearings on the matter later that spring. Treasury and Fed policymakers were hauled to Capitol Hill for testimony and questioning. In his opening statement, Senator Mack Mattingly of Georgia asked the question on the minds of many other members: "Was it Argentina's democracy or Citibank's profits that were most at risk at the end of March?"[30] Treasury officials vehemently denied the move was designed to protect bank profits. Treasury's Assistant Secretary for International Affairs, David C. Mulford, summed up his department's explanation for the loan in his Senate testimony as follows: "We were motivated by our desire to support the new democratic government of Argentina and to help ensure continued and effective functioning of the international monetary system, not to help U.S. banks avoid reporting earning losses for the first quarter of 1984."[31]

The strongest statement pointing to a real systemic threat came from Treasury Secretary Don Regan. Regan rejected the notion the rescue was intended to protect bank profits. Instead, he painted a rather dramatic picture of what would happen if Argentina failed to make its payments: "If you want to look over the cliff and see the chasm down below, that is the sort of thing that might happen."[32] However, during his Senate testimony, Anthony Solomon, now president of the FRBNY, sought to downplay the systemic threat posed by Argentina stating,

> I do not think that failure to arrange the Argentine package, with resulting nonpayment of interest, would, by itself, have had a significant adverse impact on the safety and soundness of the U.S. banking system . . . . The soundness of the U.S. banking system was not endangered.[33]

Similarly, a technical briefing paper by Congress from the Director for Congressional Liaison, commissioned for the hearings, noted that the overall "direct effect on U.S. banks' earnings would have been nominal."[34] FOMC meeting transcripts reveal a similar understanding. At one point Solomon notes, "I looked at the hit that the New York banks would take if

30. Ibid., p. 2.
31. Ibid., p. 11. This statement marks the only time the country's new democratic credentials were cited as a factor in Treasury's decision. Although regime change in Argentina may have played a part in Treasury's decision, neither Treasury nor the Fed had a problem assisting Brazil and Mexico fewer than two years prior. In 1982, neither country had impressive democratic credentials.
32. Kilborn 1984a.
33. US Senate 1984, p. 22.
34. US House 1984, p. 14.

the loans become nonperforming on March 31. It doesn't add up to a lot. [Bank name redacted] is the most vulnerable but the numbers still are not terribly large yet, although it has a definite impact."[35] So it seems unlikely that policymakers felt Argentina's failure to get itself out of arrears would have brought down the US banking system on its own. However, while policymakers downplayed the direct threat posed by Argentina, they raised the specter of contagion. Without the bridge loan, more dominos would surely fall. Allowing Argentina to effectively default on its loans could undo 18 months of careful debt management deals. Once again, US financial stability could be called into question.

For instance, Mulford noted that without ESF involvement, the bank syndicate (a consortium of banks that were involved in the debt negotiations) might have collapsed altogether. He explained that the banks were already resigned to an earnings hit; however, "the effect [of no ESF credit] would have been that some of the banks would have entirely withdrawn from the business with Argentina and therefore there would have been less credit available."[36] He added that small banks were the most likely to pull out, leaving the big banks "stuck" with increased exposures. The ultimate goal, according to Mulford, had been to "keep the syndicate functioning, keep all the banks participating and increasing . . . their exposure."[37] Echoing this statement, a paper commissioned by the Congressional Liaison noted that although the direct effects may have been negligible, the "indirect effect of Argentina not paying interest . . . might have been *systemically significant*," adding that it could have resulted in "sharp contractions in credit and capital flows within the U.S. and internationally. *There is no precise way of estimating these psychological market reactions.*"[38]

The combination of the substantial risks lurking in the system and the uncertainty about how markets would react to major US banks subtracting millions of dollars from their current and past earnings reports appears to be what ultimately led the Treasury to act. In that same FOMC meeting prior to the ESF credit's approval, Chairman Volcker also cited fears about uncertainty. He worried that the "psychological reaction it will have on the banks' attitudes or on the market, and indeed on Argentina, remains to be seen."[39] Similarly, Argentina's Latin American neighbors were equally concerned about how banks would respond to the situation. In fact, it was a group of Latin American economies that first approached

35. FOMC 1984, p. 27.
36. US Senate 1984, p. 112.
37. Ibid., p. 113.
38. US House 1984, p. 14. Emphasis added.
39. FOMC 1984, p. 25.

Treasury about providing a loan. Mexican officials approached counterparts in Argentina, Brazil, Colombia, and Venezuela about the possibility of the group collectively lending money to Buenos Aires in a good-faith effort to convince the United States to make its own contribution. The motivation for this was fear among Argentina's neighbors—fear that Buenos Aires' failure to make its interest payments might, again, turn the banks against them or result in credit downgrades for all heavily indebted Latin American economies. In the end, the group contributed an additional $300 million alongside the same commitment by the United States.[40]

The congressional hearings allowed legislators to air their grievances with Treasury, but ultimately no actions were taken to constrain Treasury's ability to use the ESF. In fact, later that same year, the United States provided a second, larger ($500 million) credit to the Alfonsín government and another the following year. The 1984 bailout of Argentina is a useful case for this study. On one hand, it fits a "typical" case based on my argument: US bank exposure was substantial and systemic risk was elevated. Yet charges made by some in Congress that the loan was designed to protect bank balance sheets rather than protect the broader US financial system reveal how entangled the "private" and "public" financial interest pathways are. Indeed, on the surface, they are observationally equivalent. Based on the case-study evidence, the direct threat posed by Argentina was not sufficient to bring down the US financial system. However, the potential for contagion raised the specter of systemic risk from foreign financial shocks once again. Although the IMF was in negotiations with Argentina when US financing was released, the executive board did not approve Argentina's loan request until late December 1984. Once again, the United States stepped in as an ILLR to bridge this gap and prevent the situation from spiraling out of control. In 1982, Treasury acted to minimize the consequences of an unfolding crisis. In 1984, its actions appear consistent with one recent study's contention that it is most desirable for an ILLR to provide "timely, immediate disbursements to *prevent crises* rather than cure their consequences."[41]

2.3. Poland, 1989

Treasury's ESF credit to Poland in 1989 is a curious case. US banks were not heavily invested in the country. For example, US bank claims in Poland

---

40. Kilborn 1984b.
41. Fernandez-Arias and Levy-Yeyati 2010, p. 15. Emphasis added.

represented little more than one-tenth of 1 percent of their total foreign portfolio. Additionally, although the Polish economy was struggling and in need of major reforms, it was not facing a 1982-style debt crisis nor was it facing the kind of currency crash that would define the emerging market crises of the next decade. This was not a situation that was calling for US ILLR efforts. Perhaps the most curious fact about the Polish rescue, however, was the fact that Congress pushed for the assistance while Treasury resisted—precisely the opposite of the Argentine loan five years earlier. More so than any other cases considered here, the Polish rescue of 1989 deviates the most from the argument I have presented.

The congressional push for an ESF loan began in the fall of 1989 just a few months after Poland became the first Eastern Bloc country to hold democratic elections that summer. With Poland's Solidarity movement pushing for further reforms, the formation of an incipient democracy in the Soviet Union's backyard was signaling the end of the Communist stranglehold on Eastern Europe. Keen to aid the United States' new democratic friend, Congress considered a package of economic and financial assistance for Warsaw as well as neighboring Hungary.[42] Some legislators wanted a portion of the funds to come from the ESF. The George H. W. Bush administration's first reaction was to resist the request. Treasury's public position was that Poland was not facing a situation that warranted tapping the ESF. Since 1976, the ESF had operated as a provider of short-term bridge loans to economies facing financial crises and this did not qualify. During congressional hearings on the matter, a House member asked Treasury's representative, Deputy Assistant Secretary for Trade and Investment Policy William Barreda, if Treasury had the authority and the willingness to lend to Poland. Barreda replied that although the administration supported a fund for Polish stabilization, the money ought to come via congressional appropriation, not the ESF. Providing funds for Poland via the ESF would be "a totally different use of the Fund. That is much closer to foreign aid . . . . We think, therefore, it should be appropriated."[43]

Throughout some intense questioning, Barreda noted another reason the administration had reservations about the proposed loan. At the time of the hearings in October, Poland was in negotiations with IMF staff working on the terms for a standby arrangement; however, an agreement was yet to be reached. Barreda explained that the administration was uncomfortable providing a bridge loan to Poland without an IMF

---

42. The specific title of the legislation was H.R. 3402—The Polish and Hungarian Democracy Initiative of 1989.
43. US House 1989a, pp. 148–149.

program in place since this would not meet Treasury's standard of having an "assured source of repayment" in hard currency in place.[44] Although this statement was consistent with Treasury's informal standard, it was disingenuous to suggest such an exception could not be made. In 1982, Treasury had looked the other way when lending to Brazil and Mexico despite the fact that neither government had submitted a letter of intent to the IMF. Sensing Barreda's recalcitrance, one obviously frustrated member of Congress asked, "Do we have the authority to legally mandate the use of those funds?" To which Barreda replied, "I can't touch that one," and when pressed further admitted, "I don't know if you do or not."[45]

On December 22, 1989, Poland completed its negotiations with IMF staff and submitted its letter to the executive board. That same day, the ESF authorized a $200 million loan to Poland as part of a $500 million multilateral package.[46] The credit was made despite the fact that Poland's economic troubles did not represent a real threat to the US financial system. Treasury's decision suggests either the Bush administration bowed to congressional pressure or changed its own mind on the subject. Regardless of the answer, this case shows that ESF resources have been used for reasons other than preserving financial stability.

2.4. Mexico, 1995

Nineteen ninety-four was supposed to be a banner year for Mexico's economy. The country had spent the last decade implementing a liberal economic adjustment program, which included restructuring its external debt, reining in the budget deficit, slowing inflation, privatizing state-owned enterprises, and reducing trade barriers. However, the biggest piece of good news came at the end of 1993 when the US Congress approved the North American Free Trade Agreement (NAFTA). The deal was slated to take effect on January 1, 1994. Mexico would now have special access

---

44. Similarly in a letter to Congress, David Mulford, then Under Secretary of the Treasury, advised: "I would like to advise you that the Treasury Department is willing to consider the use of the [ESF] as part of a multilateral bridge loan for Poland, in circumstances consistent with the existing legislation, policies and practices guiding the use of the ESF. Such bridge loans must have an assured source of repayment which is generally provided by funds of the [IMF] and World Bank" (US House 1989b, p. 25187).

45. US House 1989a, p. 167.

46. Six months later, the ESF chipped in $20 million as part of a broader $280 million multilateral loan package for Hungary. Although the issue of using the ESF on behalf of Hungary was not discussed during the hearings, the overall assistance package being considered by Congress targeted both Poland and Hungary. It is unclear if Congress pushed for ESF funds to be used on behalf of Hungary.

to the world's most lucrative market, a fact that would encourage foreign investment south of the US border.[47] As it happened, what was supposed to be a new beginning for Mexico turned out to be the country's most tumultuous year because it nearly defaulted on its external debt obligations a dozen years earlier. On New Year's Day, 1994, an insurgent group known as the Zapatistas led a political uprising in the state of Chiapas in opposition to NAFTA. A short three months later, the PRI presidential candidate, Luis Donaldo Colosio, was shot and killed while at a campaign rally. A sense that the country's political system was spiraling out of control combined with a large current account deficit caused many foreign investors to divest of their Mexican investments. As capital flowed out of Mexico, the government spent down $11 billion of its foreign exchange reserves to defend the peso's fixed exchange rate. Eventually, a loss of investor confidence in the peso forced the government of Mexico to devalue on December 20. Mexico was in the midst of a full-blown financial panic and in serious need of an ILLR.

Despite the devaluation, top US economic officials still had not realized with what they were dealing. Deputy Treasury Secretary Larry Summers remained convinced that the Mexican problem was a temporary liquidity crunch that could be fixed by activating existing standing swap lines between the Fed and US Treasury with the Bank of Mexico.[48] However, after two more weeks of volatility in Mexico and continued fears that the peso remained under attack, Mexican officials approached the IMF for assistance. Between $40 billion to $50 billion in external debt was coming due in the short term, and it appeared unlikely to be rolled over. Worse yet, the Mexican government was quickly running out of dollars to make these payments. Mexico's foreign exchange reserves—which had stood at $28 billion in December 1993—were almost gone after the government burned through them in an unsuccessful effort to defend the peso. Summers, in consultation with the IMF, decided that Mexico needed a package of at least $25 billion in assistance. Otherwise, it was likely to default, causing the crisis to further spiral out of control. Yet the IMF could not provide the full amount Mexico needed due to its access limit policy. As Boughton explains, "It looked unlikely that the Fund could lend

47. Whitt 1996.
48. As part of NAFTA, the United States, Canada, and Mexico also agreed to the North American Framework Agreement (NAFA) which was, in short, a trilateral swap network between the central banks of the three countries as well as the US Treasury. In the agreement, Mexico would have drawing rights to up to $6 billion from the United States: $3 billion from the Fed, $3 billion from Treasury (Pastor 2001, p. 116). In addition, in 1994 Treasury had three times extended short-term bilateral credits to Mexico via the ESF. However, in no case were these facilities drawn upon prior to their expiration.

Mexico more than 100 percent of its quota (about $2.5 billion) in 1995, and no other country was expected to offer very much, so the bulk of the $25 billion would have to come from elsewhere."[49]

The Mexican crisis and the Fund's problem of resource insufficiency were causing growing concern within the Clinton administration. The crisis threatened the United States in myriad ways: job losses from declining exports, increased inflows of immigrants, the financial repercussions of a crashing peso, defaults that would likely follow, and the potential for social and political unrest in a border country. According to David Lipton, at the time an assistant secretary at Treasury, the administration felt the Fund program was "too small" and "inadequate both from the standpoint of the financing and the policy adjustment."[50] Summers argued that the nature of this new crisis required a "massive and fast" response, which the IMF was unable to provide.[51] The figure the administration settled on was $40 billion—enough to cover nearly all of Mexico's short-term debts.[52] Thus, with the IMF seemingly incapable of acting as an ILLR, the administration sought $40 billion in loan guarantees from Congress. Meanwhile, Summers dispatched Lipton to Mexico to negotiate supplemental policy reforms.[53] By the end of the month, it became clear that congressional action was unlikely as critics on the Hill charged that the administration only wanted to bail out Mexico's creditors. Treasury made the decision on January 30—in concert with the Fed—to provide an unprecedented $20 billion ESF credit to the Mexican government.[54] This still left a sizable shortfall in Mexico's financing needs, but it was all that could be safely provided from the ESF's limited resources.[55]

Meanwhile, IMF Managing Director Michel Camdessus privately made the decision to ask the executive board to approve a $12

49. Boughton 2012, pp. 469–470.
50. Lipton 2014.
51. Greenspan 2007, pp. 156–160.
52. Boughton 2012, p. 473; Henning 1999, p. 62; Rubin and Weisberg 2003, p. 14.
53. Lipton 2014.
54. Although Treasury was the key actor in the Mexican bailout, the Fed played a key background role without which Rubin would have been unable to make such a large commitment. The Treasury's loan was not made official until three weeks later on February 21. Unlike ESF bridge loan commitments during the 1980s debt crisis, the 1995 Mexican rescue was intended to supplement the IMF loan. Although the ESF had roughly $25 billion in resources, only about $5 billion of this was in US dollars—the currency Mexico needed. Consequently, the Fed agreed to a warehousing arrangement whereby Treasury could essentially swap its foreign exchange (German marks, Japanese yen, etc.) for dollars. The Treasury could then use those dollars from the Fed and swap them with Mexico for pesos. In short, what this entailed was a three-step currency swap between the three parties (FOMC 1995).
55. Boughton 2012, p. 475.

billion Mexican financing package. This was nearly seven times the size of Mexico's quota—an unprecedented request at the time. According to Lipton, Camdessus's decision was made independently. As he put it, "We had no indication that the IMF was preparing to provide such huge financing for Mexico."[56] On February 1, the board considered Mexico's request for a $12 billion standby arrangement, a much larger package than had initially been expected.[57] Karin Lissakers, the US executive director on the board, acknowledged the ESF pledge but indicated that this was not enough. She added that although the request was unprecedented, the global financial system had changed dramatically since the 1980s debt crisis and required a different kind of response:

> The growing reliance on securitized international private financial flows means that the number of creditors has grown enormously. The days when [former] Managing Director de Larosiere and Federal Reserve Chairman Volcker could call together in one room six central bankers and twelve commercial bankers to solve a large problem are over. Therefore, we cannot speak to a few institutional leaders. We have to speak to an unidentifiable collection of thousands, if not millions, of investors—investors who can move with the flick of a button and transfer amounts of money that swamp this institution and potentially could swamp the resources of individual governments that stand behind this institution.[58]

In the end, the board voted to approve the request. However, the decision was not without controversy. In particular, a number of executive directors from Europe strongly objected to the unprecedented size of the request. They also chafed at the fact that they had only been given a matter of hours to review the program details before voting. Indeed, following the vote, several directors requested to have their yea votes changed to abstentions.[59] Ultimately, Camdessus was able to ram through a program several times the size of Mexico's quota, but the backlash among some on the board reveals how such herculean efforts by the Fund have their limitations. Moreover, on its own, the IMF's $12 billion rescue remained woefully shy of Mexico's financing need. Complementary action by the United States was necessary, in this case, to fill as much of Mexico's financing gap as possible in the hopes of shocking markets and bringing the panic under control. In retrospect, Peter Kenen has described the Mexican bailout as

---

56. Lipton 2014.
57. Treasury also drummed up an additional $6.2 billion in contributions from the Bank of Canada and the BIS (Boughton 2012, p. 473).
58. EBM 1995, pp. 53–54.
59. Copelovitch 2010, p. 226.

having "all the features of a Bagehot-style lender of last-resort operation" based on the speed with which the United States and IMF acted and the overwhelming overall size of the collective bailout.[60]

If the Fund's resource insufficiency generated the need for US action, a number of factors undergirded US interests behind the bailout. In his memoir, Treasury Secretary Rubin sums up the US motives behind the rescue this way: "We weren't proposing intervention for the sake of Mexico, despite our special relationship, but to protect ourselves."[61] A review of FOMC transcripts reveals the central bank was willing to help the Treasury bailout to Mexico given the substantial financial risks posed by the peso crisis. In discussions, the FRBNY president, William McDonough, described the Mexican situation as being "unique, not just unusual" and that "there was very serious systemic risk involved."[62] At the time of the crisis, Mexico was the third-largest locale for cross-border claims of US banks. On its own, it totaled about 6 percent ($23 billion) of their total foreign portfolio. Moreover, the exposure of US banks represented only a portion of total US financial exposure. As of 1994, US residents held nearly $17 billion in Mexican debt securities and had invested almost $35 billion in Mexico's equity markets.[63] To make matters worse, it was not just Mexico that was in trouble. Policymakers were also fearful that the crisis could spread elsewhere, specifically Argentina, which was facing financial problems of its own. Indeed, the FOMC debated whether the institution should provide assistance to Buenos Aires if it came to that. McDonough noted that the Argentine government "had better policy" and was the "next deserving case" for assistance.[64] In fact, the following year Treasury tapped the ESF to provide $250 million in loan guarantees on behalf of Argentina as conditions there worsened. Together, the US financial system had roughly $100 billion in exposures to these two countries as reported in Figure 6.3. The economist Rudi Dornbusch, who was called to testify before Congress about the Mexican bailout, pointed to these same risks at the proceedings:

> The lender of last resort does not come in to reward poorly managed debtors but rather to avoid the spillover effects of a credit system connected by confidence or

60. Kenen 2001, p. 22.
61. Rubin and Weisberg 2003, p. 4.
62. FOMC 1995, p. 10.
63. US Treasury 1994.
64. FOMC 1995, p. 10. Ultimately, the committee seemed to lean away from providing assistance to Argentina. They had accepted helping Mexico because it was "unique," and if they provided assistance to Argentina, as McDonough put it, "God knows where you decide the line gets established" (FOMC 1995, p. 10). In the end, the ESF ended up providing a $250 million credit to Argentina later that year as part of a multilateral package; however, the Fed had no involvement in that loan.

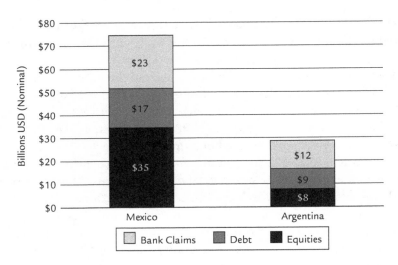

Figure 6.3
US Financial System Exposure to Mexico and Argentina, 1994

contagion. A Mexican default and collapse will spill over to our own economies and bring down other economies, most immediately Argentina.[65]

The Republican-controlled Congress had a swift negative reaction to Treasury's use of the ESF to rescue Mexico. Many legislators felt that the administration had performed an end-run around Congress by using the Treasury's special "slush fund." Others pointed to the new Treasury Secretary's ties to the financial industry. As it had done years earlier with the Argentine rescue of 1984, Congress quickly hauled Treasury and Fed officials to Capitol Hill to question their motives. In one hearing, Representative Steve Stockton of Texas charged, "One benefactor of the Mexican bailout would be a firm called Goldman Sachs which Rubin was a part of. It was the number one underwriter of bonds to Mexico . . . . It raises some very serious questions."[66] Rubin, of course, strongly denied these charges and argued the loan package was designed to protect Main Street rather than Wall Street's bottom line. He pointed to the threat the Mexican crisis posed to US jobs first, immigrant flows second, and financial risks third. Referencing the motives of Rubin and other officials at Treasury, Lipton noted that "these were a bunch of people who had been involved in one way or another in the Latin American Debt Crisis and its resolution. They believed that creditors take their lumps."[67]

65. US House 1995a, p. 401.
66. US House 1995a, p. 144.
67. Lipton 2014.

Of all ESF rescues, this is one of the most difficult cases in which to tease out the primary motivations that led to the decision by Treasury and the Fed to help the United States' besieged neighbor to the south. While the financial threats were real and potentially systemic if the crisis were allowed to spread, the range of spillovers that threatened the US economy in light of Mexico's troubles was broad. Thus, although concerns about financial spillovers played an important part in motivating the rescue, it is equally unlikely that financial factors *alone* determined the outcome. Indeed, Lipton indicated that fears concerning political tumult in Mexico were a major consideration as well. Asked whether Mexico was viewed as a "special case," he acknowledged, "We basically had that discussion. We asked ourselves whether we would do this for anyone else and it was basically our view that Mexico was unique."[68] As it turns out, it was only unique until the Asian financial crisis a few years later.

2.5. Thailand, 1997

Following the Mexican rescue in 1995, the use of the ESF to provide foreign bailouts became less common. When it was used, it was typically as a backup plan in the event that IMF resources were not sufficient to address a country's financial needs. Its declining use is attributable to several factors. First, congressional restrictions that were imposed limited its use in 1996 and 1997. In the summer of 1995, Senator Alfonse D'Amato led a push in Congress to restrict Treasury's ability to use "taxpayer dollars" to fund foreign bailouts. D'Amato was successful in his efforts. Both Houses of Congress passed the bill requiring congressional approval for all ESF credits larger than $1 billion and with maturities longer than 60 days unless the president assured Congress in writing that vital US economic interests and the stability of the global financial system were at risk.[69] The law was enacted in August that year. The second factor that contributed to the ESF's declining use for foreign rescues was a set of reforms the IMF implemented, based on terms agreed to at the G-7 Halifax Summit (discussed in chapter 4). In short, these reforms—most notably the establishment of the emergency financing mechanism (EFM) procedure—were designed to enable the IMF to address its two chronic weaknesses as ILLR: resource insufficiency and unresponsiveness. The EFM would

68. Ibid.
69. For more on the congressional response to the Mexican bailout, see Henning 1999, pp. 66–70.

allow the Fund, in extreme circumstances, to respond more swiftly and with more resources when a financial crisis demanded such a response.

The Asian financial crisis was the first true test of the IMF's new approach to crisis management. Thailand was hit first. In the summer of 1997, Thailand's currency, the baht, collapsed after investors pulled out and speculators bet against the Thai central bank's ability to defend its pegged exchange rate. In late July 1997, Thailand had nearly exhausted its supply of foreign exchange reserves in an unsuccessful defense of the baht. The government was forced to approach the IMF for assistance. Less than a month later, the IMF approved a nearly $3 billion standby arrangement for Thailand, though "no one believed that this amount alone would suffice."[70] Despite the Fund's new powers embodied in the EFM, its limitations as an ILLR remained apparent. Reports at the time noted that "it appears increasingly likely that Thailand may need a 'bridge loan' of roughly $1 billion" before the IMF makes the funds available. Initially, the United States indicated it would chip in as it had with Mexico several years earlier. Reports quoted Secretary Rubin saying "the United States is prepared to participate in a short-term, multilateral bridging facility."[71] Yet, this lip service was not backed up with action. Why did the United States decide against providing bridging resources to Thailand? Several factors appear to have played a role in the decision.

First, from an economic and financial perspective, the risk Thailand posed to the US financial system was moderate. Aggregate financial exposure—including total US bank claims and residents' holdings of debt securities and equities—was about $13 billion, or one-sixth the US economy's financial exposure to Mexico three years prior. More important, the Clinton administration believed that the Thai crisis was an isolated event. The perception at the time was that Thailand did not pose an immediate risk to other more systemically important economies in the region. As Laura Tyson, then the chair of the Council for Economic Advisors, explained, "Thailand is a very small economy. It doesn't have a lot of links and it's not exactly in your back yard . . . . The U.S. chose not to intervene in Thailand, thinking it was not going to spill over. Why would it? The contagion effects were not apparent to anybody."[72]

Second, Treasury felt the IMF was better prepared to deal with the Thai crisis on its own than it had been when faced with the Mexican crisis two years prior. There was no reason to act unilaterally when the Fund could handle the problem multilaterally. For instance, Lipton noted

70. Boughton 2012, p. 508.
71. Sanger 1997.
72. *Commanding Heights* 2002.

that "from a financial standpoint [an ESF credit on behalf of Thailand] wasn't necessary. The IMF was using its lending capacity; at that point they could lend a sufficient multiple of quota to handle the problem."[73] Third, the proposed ESF contribution to Thailand was reportedly quite small. James Steinberg, then Deputy National Security Advisor in the Clinton administration, explained that while the State Department and the National Security Council (NSC) felt it was symbolically important from a political perspective for the United States to have some "skin in the game"—even if the contribution was not substantial—Treasury "saw little economic value for the small, additional, bilateral piece that was being advocated by some" and that it "wouldn't make a difference."[74]

Finally, and perhaps most important, the administration felt constrained by the domestic political climate at the time. As noted above, in the aftermath of Mexico, Congress had imposed temporary restrictions on Treasury's ability to use ESF resources for foreign credits. When the Thai crisis erupted, those restrictions were still in place (though they were only months away from expiring). The congressional backlash to Mexico had a chilling effect on Treasury's willingness to tap the ESF on behalf of Bangkok. Steinberg explained that Rubin et al. were in "never again" mode. The fear was that bailing out Thailand would lead to additional congressional restrictions on Treasury's autonomy over ESF resources. Thus, providing a largely unnecessary rescue in this case "would risk the ability to use the ESF in the future." President Clinton was persuaded to "preserve the tool."[75] Despite Rubin's early insinuation that Treasury would act to support Thailand, in the end the administration balked.[76] As it turned out, the IMF's contribution was not enough to prevent the crisis from spreading to others in the region.

2.6. Indonesia and South Korea, 1997

What became known as "the Asian flu," a financial crisis spread around the region over the course of the fall and winter of 1997, infecting Indonesia

73. Lipton 2014.

74. Steinberg 2014. Lipton echoed Steinberg saying that the arguments from State and NSC were to essentially "do it [provide a credit to Thailand] for symbolic purposes. Show we care" (Lipton 2014).

75. Steinberg 2014. Lipton noted similar fears at Treasury that a Thai rescue might "have even led to the ESF becoming completely unavailable for the Secretary of the Treasury" (Lipton 2014).

76. In his memoir, President Clinton admitted that in retrospect "not making at least a modest contribution to the Thai package" was a mistake, adding, "Rubin and I didn't make too many policy errors. I believe this was one of them" (Clinton 2004, pp. 806–807).

and then South Korea. Both countries watched as tens of billions of dollars quickly flowed out of their economies, placing intense pressure on their currencies and raising the prospect they might default on their external debts. Late that year, both countries had agreed to substantial aid packages from the IMF. Invoking the EFM, the Fund responded swiftly and with immense resources: $8 billion for Indonesia in November 1997; $15 billion for Korea in December. The Korean package was, in fact, the largest single commitment the Fund had ever made. It was almost 20 times larger than Korea's quota. In terms of speed, the program was approved just one day after Korea's letter was submitted to the board.

With the expiration of the D'Amato amendment in September 1997, Treasury was again free to make commitments to foreign governments without congressional constraints. It did just that, pledging $3 billion for Indonesia and $5 billion for Korea in early December.[77] In the case of Indonesia, the funds were to be used only if IMF financing was inadequate.[78] The money promised to Korea would only be released "to fill any gaps in [Korea's] financing needs between the release of IMF installments." Treasury's initial commitment to Korea was "at the low end of expectations" and paled in comparison to its bailout of Mexico two years prior.[79] Shortly after the initial tepid commitment to Korea, markets were not responding as hoped and it appeared the initial response had failed. Once again, a Korean default seemed imminent. Recognizing that the major commercial banks held the majority of Korea's short-term debt, the United States, in consultation with the IMF and G-7, attempted to revive the "concerted lending" strategy. This time, the Federal Reserve took the lead. Edwin Truman—the director of the Fed's Division of International Finance—spearheaded the effort. As described in one account of the crisis, Truman, "better than any other senior U.S. policymaker, appreciated the art of twisting bankers' arms to save countries from financial crises."[80] The plan was put into action in late December 1997. The FRBNY president, William McDonough, called executives from the six largest US banks to the New York Fed and applied pressure, informing them,

My advice to my colleagues in Washington is, there should be no additional public-sector money for Korea unless you guys reschedule the debt. That's my position. It doesn't mean it will be followed . . . . But I wanted you to know that, because the flow

77. See IMF (2003, p. 113) and Copelovitch (2010, p. 273) for a more detailed discussion of the "second line of defense."
78. Stevenson 1997a.
79. Stevenson 1997b.
80. Blustein 2001, p. 188.

of funds is such that we're talking about a Korean default next week if this matter is not resolved.[81]

The Fed urged its European counterparts to apply similar pressure on their banks. On Christmas Eve 1997, a group of major US banks agreed to negotiate with Korea to reschedule the government's debts. British banks soon followed suit.[82] Even with the concerted lending plan in action, Treasury felt the financing package was too small. Rubin authorized the ESF to make yet another $1.7 billion credit available to Seoul just days before the New Year. This was part of a broader, multilateral rescue package coordinated by the G-7, designed to be announced alongside a second $9.5 billion IMF commitment.[83] In total, Korea now had access to a massive $55 billion line of credit.[84] Yet, unlike Mexico, bilateral credits pledged outside the Fund (including ESF resources) were only to be used as a "second line of defense" if IMF financing proved insufficient. At the time, however, this seemed a distinct possibility. Ultimately, neither Korea nor Indonesia drew on the pledged ESF resources.

On one hand, the decision to limit the US commitment to a "second line of defense" can justifiably be viewed as a weak response when compared to the Mexican rescue. The temporal proximity to the congressional backlash to that massive 1995 bailout likely tempered the Clinton administration's response. Indeed, even after the relatively tepid commitments to Indonesia and Korea were made public, many of the usual suspects in Congress once again placed the ESF in their crosshairs. For example, during the crisis, the IMF was seeking to increase member quotas as its resources were under considerable strain. Charging that the White House had once again acted to bail out big Wall Street banks, some Republicans in Congress were threatening to tie new IMF appropriations to the reimposition of constraints on the ESF.[85] In short, larger, up-front credits to Indonesia or Korea may have resulted in even more forceful limits on ESF credits and complicated the administration's ability to get Congress to approve an increase in the United States' IMF quota. Viewed in this political context, the decision to act as an ILLR alongside the IMF in these cases indicates the administration believed American interests were

81. Ibid., p. 196.
82. Copelovitch 2010, p. 273.
83. G-7 1997; Stevenson 1997b.
84. Besides IMF credits, an additional $10 billion came from the World Bank, $4 billion from the Asian Development Bank, $6.7 billion from the United States, $10 billion from Japan, as well as smaller contributions from Australia, the United Kingdom, Canada, France, and Germany (Pollack 1997).
85. Stevenson 1998.

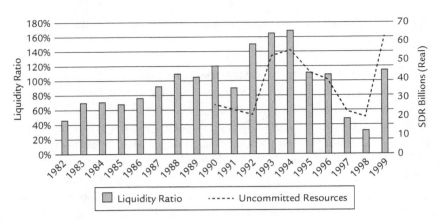

Figure 6.4
IMF Liquidity Ratio, 1982–1999

sufficiently threatened by the Asian crisis to demand action. This, despite the fact that these actions might result in new constraints on the ESF.

Why did the United States choose to pledge ESF resources on behalf of Korea and Indonesia? First, like the Mexican case, the United States tapped the ESF as a way to supplement an IMF credit—to augment the overall size of the financing package and convince a heterogeneous group of investors that there was sufficient liquidity to backstop the crisis. Even though the size of IMF's commitment to Indonesia and Korea was unprecedented, Lipton noted that Treasury believed it was still not large enough (especially after the failure of the initial Korean loan). What was needed was "overwhelming financial force," which led to the second line of defense concept and its ultimate multilateralization.[86] Steinberg echoed this, noting the administration wanted to send a message that "the full faith and credit of the [United States] is behind this and there is no point in running on Korea . . . . It's all about what you can do to crush the Bears; to crush the short-sellers."[87] On its own, there was no way the IMF could have pledged $55 billion. It had already promised loans in many multiples of borrowers' quotas, and the potential for pushback from the executive board if additional funds were requested would grow.

More important, the Fund's increasingly large rescue packages were placing severe pressure on the institution's resources. Figure 6.4 depicts the IMF's liquidity ratio from 1982 through 1999. This represents the liquidity position of the Fund and is calculated by dividing the institution's

86. Lipton 2014.
87. Steinberg 2014.

net uncommitted usable resources by its liquid liabilities.[88] A lower liquidity ratio indicates that the Fund's resources were under growing strain at that time. The figure also reports the IMF's net uncommitted usable resources (in SDRs, which are special drawing rights) from 1990 through 1999.[89] Although the IMF was relatively flush with resources during the first half of the 1990s, the cumulative effect of fighting the Mexican and Asian crises was substantial. Indeed, in 1997 and 1998, the IMF's liquidity ratio was lower than it had been during the initial years of the 1980s debt crisis. The possibility that the world economy's primary financial fire brigade might run out of water contributed to Treasury's decision to supplement the Fund's ILLR actions. According to Steinberg, "There was concern [within the administration] about IMF resources." He added, "If you look at any one crisis, Korea was one that could significantly impair [the Fund's] financial resources. So there was some question as to how many fires the IMF could put out."[90]

If IMF resource insufficiency provided the *need* for unilateral ILLR actions, US economic and geopolitical interests provided the motivation. By December 1997, the contagion effects of the crisis, which had escaped the administration earlier that year, had crystallized.[91] On their own, the crises in Korea and Indonesia did not represent a systemic threat to the US financial system. Indeed, systemically important US banks held only about 6 percent of total foreign claims in these two countries. Combined, these claims represented about 12.7 percent of their total capital. Thus, a full-scale default on their obligations was not sufficient to bring down a major US bank. However, uncertainty about how far the crisis could spread without a strong response from the United States and IMF was high.

At the Fed, which from the outset of the Asian crisis was deeply involved in crafting the US response, top brass worried about the possibility of the

---

88. "Net uncommitted usable resources" accounts for the IMF's total resources *minus* nonusable resources (i.e., gold, funds committed to borrowers). In short, this measures the resources available to meet new loan requests by IMF members. The IMF's total liquid liabilities largely reflects credit extended by the IMF. That is, the more members borrow from the IMF, all else equal, its liquid liabilities should increase. It may seem odd that the IMF's liquidity ratio can exceed 100 percent. However, when the IMF's net uncommitted usable resources are greater than its liquid liabilities, this can occur.

89. Liquidity ratio and net uncommitted usable resources data are taken from relevant IMF annual reports. Annual reports did not regularly report uncommitted resources data prior to 1990.

90. Steinberg 2014.

91. Rubin summed up Treasury's motivation for contributing to the multilateral rescue in a speech at Georgetown University in January 2001, stating, "These countries face the risk of default . . . which could readily result in deep and prolonged distress in these countries, possible contagion effects for emerging and developing countries around the world, and potentially serious impacts on the industrialized countries, including our own" (Rubin 1998).

crisis spreading across the Atlantic to Latin America. At an FOMC meeting in November 1997, prior to Korea's troubles, the group discussed the worst-case scenario (which it had shared with the White House via its Greenbook forecast). Specifically, it noted that if the "storm clouds" over Korea "darkened further . . . the spread of contagion to Latin America may intensify."[92] At the following month's meeting, Vice Chairman McDonough presciently warned that "the next country we have to worry about is Brazil."[93] Steinberg notes in meetings on the crisis, "There was a lot of worry about Brazil and other emerging markets . . . . Every day you have a meeting asking, 'Who's next?'" He then added that there was also "a lot of focus on Mexico."[94] In a conversation about the crisis with British Prime Minister Tony Blair, President Clinton remarked, "If Brazil goes south we are all going to suck eggs big time."[95] If the response to Korea was not sufficiently large to prevent contagion across the Atlantic, economies where US financial interests were far more at risk could be the next to fall. More than 10 percent of systemically important US banks' foreign claims were concentrated in Brazil and Mexico. More worrisome, these combined claims represented 21.5 percent of their total capital. Add in US investments in stocks and bonds in these two Latin American economies and the US financial system was exposed to a tune of $167 billion, as presented in Figure 6.5. Thus, US ILLR actions during the Asian crisis were part of a strategy that aimed to contain the crisis and prevent it from spreading to systemically important markets that would have posed a clear and present danger to the stability of the US financial system.

Finally, geopolitical factors also weighed heavily in the US decision to act. South Korea's strategic importance to the United States was evidenced by the 37,000 US troops stationed there to deter a North Korean attack.[96] Indeed, existing accounts of the administration's debates over whether or not to come to Korea's aid reveal that some of the strongest supporters of the bailout were at the Department of State, the Department of Defense, and the NSC.[97] Indeed, Steinberg pointed out that although these groups

92. FOMC 1997a, p. 19.
93. Ibid.
94. Steinberg 2014.
95. National Security Council and Records Management Office 2016, p. 209.
96. Pempel 1999.
97. Steinberg was one of the most vocal bailout proponents within the administration as was his boss, Sandy Berger, who worried about the kind of "mischief" North Korea might attempt if the South Korean economy collapsed (Blustein 2001, p. 138). In his memoir, President Clinton acknowledges the role geopolitics played in the decision as well. Indeed, Clinton admits that Defense and NSC both lobbied for a US contribution to the Thailand bailout because that country was the United States' "oldest ally in Southeast Asia." Treasury, however, did not support putting US funds into the Thai package and their position held (Clinton 2004, p. 807).

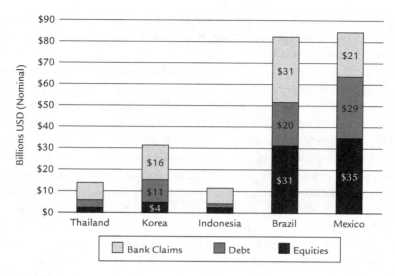

Figure 6.5
US Financial System Exposure in Five Emerging Markets, 1997

had advocated for a package for Thailand, the effort was relatively weak, and what won out was Treasury's assertions that Thailand was not systemically important enough for a unilateral rescue and fears about additional restrictions on the ESF. However, by the time the crisis had spread to Korea, Steinberg indicated that the diplomats at State and the NSC had gained the upper hand within the administration. As he put it,

> We [at the NSC and State] didn't push hard enough in Thailand . . . . By the time we
> got to Korea, now we're on top. Because now Indonesia has gone, and now you have
> a treaty ally . . . at that time the Secretary of State [Madeline Albright] says, "We're
> going to do something."[98]

2.7. Declining Use: The ESF Is Put Out to Pasture

Concerns at the Federal Reserve and within the Clinton administration regarding the fragility of the financial situation in Brazil turned out to be well founded. Later in 1998, Brazil's currency—the real—was attacked by speculators, necessitating an IMF program. Once again, Treasury stepped in with $5 billion in loan guarantees from the ESF. However, after

98. Steinberg 2014.

Brazil, the ESF's role in ILLR actions fell into disuse.[99] Several notable things changed at the beginning of the twenty-first century that contributed to the declining use of ESF resources for international bailouts. First, the IMF's push for additional resources was ultimately successful as the Eleventh General Quota Review was adopted in January 1998.[100] This included the creation of the New Arrangements to Borrow (NAB). In December 1989, the Fund held just under $99 billion in total assets; in December 1999, total assets stood at $217 billion.[101] With additional resources, the problem of resource insufficiency attenuated somewhat, reducing the need for supplemental ESF credits. Barry Eichengreen and Richard Portes observed that the combination of enhanced IMF resources and domestic political opposition to bailouts in the United States meant that the ILLR role and the responsibility for managing "future Mexicos" was placed "squarely on the shoulders of the IMF."[102] Another notable change was the election of President George W. Bush, who, like Reagan decades earlier, assumed office with a belief in the efficiency of the market. Bush's Treasury Department emphasized "limiting official involvement" in foreign financial crises.[103] Under Bush's tenure, the ESF was only used once on behalf of a foreign government—a very short-term $1.5 billion credit to Uruguay, which did not capture any headlines.[104] A final reason why Treasury got out of the business of providing credits to foreign governments is the remarkable era of financial stability that defined the 2000s. According to data collected by Luc Laeven and Fabian Valencia, debt defaults and currency crashes became increasingly rare between 2000 and 2007.[105] With few countries needing to be rescued, rescuers were no longer in high demand. And it was not just US ILLR mechanisms that were getting rusty. By 2007, outstanding loans from the IMF had declined to historically low levels. Some scholars openly wondered about the relevance of the IMF in such a stable global financial system.[106] In a world without financial crises, an ILLR no longer appeared necessary.

---

99. While the ESF's international use has all but vanished since 2002, the funds were tapped by Treasury during the 2008 financial crisis to guarantee investments in money markets and mutual funds.

100. IMF 2013.

101. Boughton 2012, p. 743.

102. Eichengreen and Portes 1997, p. 2.

103. Roubini and Setser 2004, p. 200.

104. The ESF's foreign activities during the Bush administration are most well known for a loan that never happened in 2003 in the lead-up to the Iraq War. In an attempt to gain Turkey's permission to use its military bases as a launch site for attacks against Iraq, Bush promised $8.5 billion from the ESF (Entous 2003). Ultimately, Turkey refused and the loan was never made. Nonetheless, the proposal indicates the administration viewed the purpose of the ESF somewhat differently from its predecessors.

105. Laeven and Valencia 2008.

106. Helleiner and Momani 2007.

3. CONCLUSIONS

The details behind these specific US ILLR actions largely fit with the argument of this project. In most cases, the analysis presented here reveals that the IMF's ability to deal with the crises on its own was called into question by US economic officials. During the 1980s, the Fund's concerted lending strategy slowed down its ability to respond to crises as they unfolded. IMF assistance to Mexico (1982), Brazil (1983), and Argentina (1984) arrived *months* after those respective crises began. Thus, US rescue efforts were based, in part, on the need to provide immediate assistance to these countries while they waited for the IMF to approve and disburse their assistance. During the 1990s, the case studies show that US policymakers were most worried about the overall size of the financing packages. Even though the IMF extended historically large loans to Mexico (1995) and Korea (1997), US officials still worried that this was not enough to calm markets. Additionally, during the Asian crisis, the IMF's total resources were under considerable strain, adding to the institution's problem of resource insufficiency.

Besides policymakers' fears about the IMF's limitations as an ILLR, US financial interests were clearly threatened in most of these cases. This was especially true in the cases of Mexico and Brazil (1982, 1983) when defaults on the part of these two economies would have clearly raised the specter of bankruptcy for multiple systemically important US financial institutions. The nonrescue of Argentina in 1983, which does not conform to my argument, appears to have been the result of Treasury focusing its finite resources on the two most pressing threats to US financial stability: Brazil and Mexico. In other cases I explore, there does not seem to be as clear an existential threat to the US banking system. For instance, even the rescue of Argentina in 1984 raised the eyebrows of some in Congress who suggested the act was about protecting banks' profits, not the public interest. Similarly, the ESF credits to Mexico (1995), Indonesia (1997), and Korea (1997) do not fit as neatly with my argument that bailouts are most likely when the public interests and the private interests of the banks coincide. In these cases, again, systemic risk, as I measure it, was relatively low even though SIFI bank exposure to these individual countries was elevated. However, the case studies suggest that policymakers' calculation of "systemic risk" included something my own measure may not fully capture: the threat of contagion. In each of these three cases, policymakers seemed to act not only because of the existing crisis at the time; they acted, in part, out of fear that inaction would lead crises to spread to other, more systemically important economies. Thus, concerns about systemic risk were on the minds of policymakers in each of these cases—it was just a broader conception of risk than my measure may account for.

Finally, the case studies show that policymakers used ESF resources for reasons outside of financial interests. In particular, the rescue of Poland in 1989 clearly does not fit my model. In this case, the decision to intervene appears to have been driven by congressional pressure and geostrategic calculations related to the end of the Cold War. The ESF rescue of Poland is closer to foreign aid than to an ILLR action. Similarly, although the rescue of Korea in 1997 was motivated by financial considerations, Korea's position as a key US ally in the region also played a role in the decision to provide additional support. The Mexican bailout in 1995 was motivated by myriad concerns including financial exposures, immigration flows, and sociopolitical unrest in a border country. In short, the case studies show that although these decisions largely comport with my argument, individual cases are always far more complex than a statistical model.

CHAPTER 7

The United States as an ILLR during the Great Panic of 2008–2009

The attitude is "don't show me anything east of a [New York] 212-area code." If you lend to [those banks], it could be a career-ending experience.

Anonymous banker (*The Financial Times*, 2007)

In a way, we [Europe] became the thirteenth Federal Reserve district.

Anonymous European central banker (*The Globalist*, 2013)

I guess I'm worried about this for all of the considerations that President Hoenig and President Lacker have just been talking about. I don't know where we draw the lines.

Charles Plosser, Federal Reserve Bank President, Philadelphia (FOMC 2008i)

By the early 1980s, the central bank currency swap network that the Fed so brilliantly developed to protect the dollar and the stability of the Bretton Woods monetary system in the 1960s had faded into obscurity. While the Treasury's Exchange Stabilization Fund (ESF) rose to prominence by extending bailouts to a developing world rife with financial crises during the late twentieth century, the financial seas in the world's wealthiest economies were remarkably calm during those decades. A system of official emergency credit lines between advanced industrial central banks was no longer needed to stabilize their currencies. International financial liberalization opened up new sources of private credit for governments and floating exchange rates made balance of payments crises in developed economies seem a thing of the past. Accordingly, in the fourth quarter of 1998, the Fed announced that

> owing to the formation of the European Central Bank and in light of fifteen years of disuse, the bilateral swap arrangements of the Federal Reserve . . . were jointly deemed no longer necessary in view of the well-established present-day arrangements for international monetary cooperation. Accordingly, the respective parties to the arrangements mutually agreed to allow them to lapse.[1]

Central bank swaps had fallen out of fashion. They seemed a relic of a bygone era when financial crises were not just relegated to developing and emerging economies. Yet, only a decade after their fall from favor, central bank currency swaps would once again become all the rage.

In late 2007, the Federal Reserve was compelled to reach back into its bag of tricks and dust off the old technique. What began as a housing crisis related to concerns over the rising number of foreclosures in the US real estate market quickly matured into a full-blown, five-alarm global financial crisis in 2008 as global dollar funding markets seized up. In the midst of the storm, the Fed willingly acted as an ILLR by establishing new swap arrangements with 14 foreign central banks. It also provided billions of dollars in liquidity directly to dozens of foreign banks with US affiliates through several additional domestic liquidity facilities. So, what explains the Fed's decision to act as an ILLR and provide an unprecedented amount of liquidity to the global economy during the Great Panic of 2008? And why did the Fed act as an ILLR on behalf of a select group of foreign economies while it passed on helping others facing similar circumstances?

While select foreign economies no doubt benefited greatly from the Fed's decision to provide dollar liquidity to foreign jurisdictions during the global financial crisis, their interests were not the target of the actions. Consistent with my argument in chapter 5, here I show that the goal of protecting US national financial interests was the primary motivation behind the Fed's efforts. More precisely, I explain that the international dimensions of the crisis threatened US financial stability in two key ways. First, systemically important US banks and money market funds were directly exposed to foreign financial institutions that were blocked from frozen dollar-funding markets. Thus, without an international lender of last resort (ILLR), the US financial system was facing an existential threat from a wave of potential foreign defaults. Moreover, the International

---

1.. Treasury and Federal Reserve 1998, p. 9.

Monetary Fund (IMF) was incapable of providing the volume of liquidity that the global financial system needed. Once again, Fund resources were too limited. Second, the seizure of global credit markets was severely impairing the transmission of the Fed's interest-rate cuts to the real economy. Only by providing dollars to a global economy desperate for liquidity could the Fed ensure that the US economy got the stimulus it desired by cutting rates to historically low levels. In support of the argument, this chapter presents a variety of evidence, including case-study analysis of the financial risks facing the US economy from foreign sources, statistical analysis of the Fed's swap line selection, and chronological process tracing drawing from a review of Federal Open Market Committee (FOMC) transcripts during the crisis.

1. BACKGROUND: "A NOVEL ASPECT" OF THE GREAT PANIC OF 2008

The global dollar shortage that suddenly began in the summer of 2007 and led to the Fed's decision to open up swap lines with more than a dozen foreign central banks had its roots in a near decade-long development. Since 2000, banks around the world—especially European and Japanese institutions—had dramatically increased the stock of foreign currency assets on their balance sheets. According to one study, the outstanding volume of banks' foreign assets grew from $10 trillion at the beginning of the decade to $34 trillion by the end of 2007.[2] The primary form these investments took was in US dollar-denominated claims on nonbank entities, including loans to corporations and hedge funds as well as holdings of US mortgage-backed securities and other structured finance products. These assets typically represented medium- to long-term investments.

Of course, banks funding asset purchases in a foreign currency have to acquire the currency from somewhere. While US banks have significant dollar deposits to draw on, European and other foreign banks do not. Consequently, as these institutions expanded their holdings of dollar claims, they had to find dollar funding from external sources to fill the "dollar gap." Broadly speaking, banks have three methods of obtaining foreign exchange on wholesale markets in order to purchase an asset denominated in that currency. First, they can directly convert domestic currency into a foreign currency through a foreign exchange spot transaction. Second, they can utilize foreign exchange swaps. These work just

2. McGuire and von Peter 2009, p. 9.

like the central bank swaps being investigated here except they involve nonofficial participants (i.e., corporations or banks are the parties "swapping" monies). Finally, banks can borrow the foreign currency directly from other banks in the interbank market, from central banks, or from nonbank entities such as money market funds. Prior to the crisis, foreign banks could—and did—employ each of these methods to finance their voracious appetite for dollar-denominated asset purchases.

It is important to note that in most cases, these types of dollar funding are short-term in nature. Yet, as discussed above, most of the banks' dollar claims were medium- to long-term. This created a maturities mismatch between foreign banks' assets and liabilities. Foreign banks regularly rolled over their debts, borrowing from one short-term source to pay off other short-term loans as they matured. That is, they borrowed to make the initial investment—and then borrowed more to pay off the first debt when it came due, doing the same for each successive debt thereafter. Meanwhile, their own dollar claims matured at a much slower pace. Initially, this was not a problem because debts could simply be rolled over. Once the original investment matured, or so the theory went, the bank would cash out, pay off its last dollar debt once and for all, and do with its profit what it wished. In sum, they were borrowing short while lending/investing long in a foreign currency.

Filling the dollar-funding gap through borrowing short on the wholesale market works fine so long as the wholesale market is well lubricated. However, if the funding markets were ever to seize up, filling the gap would become a problem. Like the fictitious Bedford Falls savings and loan discussed in the introductory chapter, foreign banks' dollar-denominated assets were tied up for many months or years in mortgage investments. But their liabilities were much shorter-term. If enough lenders (depositors) demanded repayment at once, and banks could not liquidate their assets, they would be forced to default. In other words, conditions were ripe for a liquidity crisis. Illiquidity became a very real problem beginning in 2007 when the US subprime crisis erupted. In August 2007, markets began to seize up based on the fear that counterparties might soon become insolvent due to their ownership of collateralized debt obligations (CDOs) that were contaminated by subprime mortgages increasingly likely to go into default.[3] As market participants grew more and more reluctant to lend to one another, it became more costly and difficult for foreign banks to acquire the dollar funding they needed in wholesale markets to roll over their debts.[4] A scarcity of dollar-denominated credit

3. Schwartz 2009a, p. 191.
4. Baba and Packer 2009; Coffey, Hrung, Nguyen, and Sarkar 2009; Goldberg, Kennedy and Miu 2010; McGuire and von Peter 2009; Taylor and Williams 2008.

in the international financial system—what Fed Chairman Ben Bernanke understatedly referred to as "a novel aspect of the current situation"—was developing.[5] This raised the very real possibility that a foreign bank (or banks) could be forced to default on their obligations to a US financial institution.

As the crisis unfolded, it became clear that resource insufficiency severely constrained the IMF's ability to stabilize the global economy. Fund quotas had not been increased since the Eleventh General Quota Review in 1998. Meanwhile the size of the global financial system, measured in cross-border capital flows—had nearly tripled in the decade that passed. Between 2000 and 2007, US banks' foreign claims and US residents' holdings of foreign debt securities had doubled. Simply put, the Fund was incapable of providing the emergency liquidity the global financial system needed. Similarly, the Treasury's ESF, which had become the primary US ILLR mechanism in the 1980s and 1990s, did not have the financial capacity to respond to global needs. The Fed was the only actor capable of responding to the crisis by virtue of its ability to act quickly, to make decisions independently—and most important—to create dollars. At its full development, the twenty-first-century version of the Fed's swap network included lines ranging in size from $15 billion up to four unlimited lines. At the peak of their use, the swap lines alone provided nearly $600 billion in liquidity to foreign central banks in need. Alongside the swap lines, US-based dollar auction facilities contributed additional liquidity to foreign banks into the hundreds of billions of dollars. By comparison, the IMF possessed roughly $250 billion in lendable resources in 2008—roughly one-third of the liquidity global financial markets needed at the peak of the crisis. Also problematic was that the epicenter of the 2008 crisis was located in the advanced industrial economies. For reasons of appearance, these countries would have been reluctant to approach the Fund for help even if it was a capable ILLR. Resolution of the situation required US involvement as a global financial crisis manager.

It was in this context that the US central bank, uniquely positioned to act as an ILLR, given the dollar's international role and its monopoly on issuing the currency, extended an emergency $20 billion swap line to the European Central Bank (ECB) and a $4 billion line to the Swiss National Bank (SNB) in December 2007. The two initial swaps were summarily expanded. New lines were eventually extended to eight other central banks in advanced economies. The Fed's extraordinary actions culminated in two sequential moves in October 2008, just weeks after

5. Wessel 2009, p. 140.

the collapse of the major US investment bank Lehman Brothers further jammed already sticky credit markets. First, it announced that swap lines with the ECB, SNB, Bank of England (BOE), and Bank of Japan (BOJ) would be unlimited in size. Second, it extended $30 billion swap lines to four emerging market economies: Brazil, Mexico, South Korea, and Singapore. This brought the total number of participating beneficiaries to 14. Alongside these actions, the Fed also initiated a suite of domestic liquidity facilities in the United States, which collectively provided hundreds of billions of dollars to foreign (primarily European) banks with US branches. Indeed, the majority of emergency credit provided to financial institutions via the Term Auction Facility (TAF), the Term Securities Lending Facility (TSLF), and the Commercial Paper Funding Facility (CPFF) went to foreign institutions.[6]

Table 7.1 presents a timeline that identifies (1) the size of the swap line [in billions USD; ∞ = unlimited line, exp = swap allowed to expire], (2) when new swap arrangements were opened [**bold**], (3) when existing swap arrangements were increased [*italics*], and (4) when swap agreement expiration dates were extended [gray box]. Each column is representative of the date at the top; each row is representative of a different central bank partner (see the key below the table). Figure 7.1 reports aggregate drawings on the swap lines by participating foreign central banks from their inception until their expiration. It also reports the total number of participating central banks. As the figure shows, drawings peaked in December 2008 at nearly $600 billion. Figure 7.2 disaggregates the data by reporting the share of outstanding swap drawings by partner central bank at the end of each quarter.[7] Figures 7.3 and 7.4 present total monthly lending by two of the Fed's domestic liquidity facilities: the TAF and TSLF, respectively.[8]

---

6. The TAF was launched in December 2007 alongside the central bank swap lines. It provided 28- to 84-day loans to commercial banks (depository institutions) in the domestic market that were having difficulty borrowing in wholesale markets. The TSLF was introduced in March 2008, and it was designed to meet the needs of financial institutions ("primary dealers") that did not qualify for credit under the TAF including investment banks (nondepository institutions). In normal times, these institutions raised funding by offering securities, including mortgage-backed securities, as collateral. When markets for these securities collapsed, the Fed allowed primary dealers to swap toxic securities for US Treasury securities, which they could then use as collateral to obtain funding in wholesale financial markets. The CPFF was introduced in October 2008 as the market for commercial paper (discussed below) dried up. In short, the Fed, via the CPFF, made loans through the purchase of commercial paper issued by financial and nonfinancial firms. At one meeting, Bernanke humorously referred to these, and other primarily domestic liquidity facilities, as "the various credit facilities for which even I do not know all the acronyms anymore." See FOMC 2008j, 26.

7. As the figure reveals, only 10 of the 14 central banks actually used the swap lines and the ECB alone accounted for at least half of their use during the program's entire existence.

8. TAF and TSLF data are publicly available on the Federal Reserve's website at http://www. federalreserve.gov/newsevents/reform_taf.htm#data and at http://www.federalreserve. gov/newsevents/reform_tslf.htm. The author and an assistant first coded the institutions'

Table 7.1 US FEDERAL RESERVE SWAP TIMELINE, 2007–2010 (TOTALS IN BILLIONS USD)

	12.12 2007	3.11 2008	5.2 2008	6.30 2008	9.18 2008	9.24 2008	9.26 2008	9.29 2008	10.13 2008	10.14 2008	10.28 2008	10.29 2008	2.3 2009	6.25 2009	2.1 2010
ECB	20	30	50	55	110	110	120	240	∞	∞	∞	∞	∞	∞	exp
SNB	4	6	12	12	27	27	30	60	∞	∞	∞	∞	∞	∞	exp
BOJ	—	—	—	—	60	60	60	120	120	∞	∞	∞	∞	∞	exp
BOE	—	—	—	—	40	40	40	80	∞	∞	∞	∞	∞	∞	exp
BOC	—	—	—	—	10	10	10	30	30	30	30	30	30	30	exp
RBA	—	—	—	—	—	10	10	30	30	30	30	30	30	30	exp
SR	—	—	—	—	—	10	10	30	30	30	30	30	30	30	exp
DN	—	—	—	—	—	5	5	15	15	15	15	15	15	15	exp
NB	—	—	—	—	—	5	5	15	15	15	15	15	15	15	exp
RBNZ	—	—	—	—	—	—	—	—	—	—	15	15	15	15	exp
BCB	—	—	—	—	—	—	—	—	—	—	—	30	30	30	exp
BDM	—	—	—	—	—	—	—	—	—	—	—	30	30	30	exp
BOK	—	—	—	—	—	—	—	—	—	—	—	30	30	30	exp
MAS	—	—	—	—	—	—	—	—	—	—	—	30	30	30	exp

Key: ECB = European Central Bank, SNB = Swiss National Bank, BOJ = Bank of Japan, BOE = Bank of England, BOC = Bank of Canada, RBA = Reserve Bank of Australia, SR = Sveriges Riksbank, DN = Danmarks Nationalbank, NB = Norges Bank, RBNZ = Reserve Bank of New Zealand, BCB = Banco Central do Brasil, BDM = Banco de Mexico, BOK = Bank of Korea, MAS = Monetary Authority of Singapore.

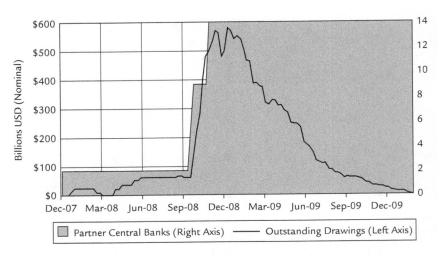

Figure 7.1
Federal Reserve Swap Line Credits Outstanding, 2007–2009

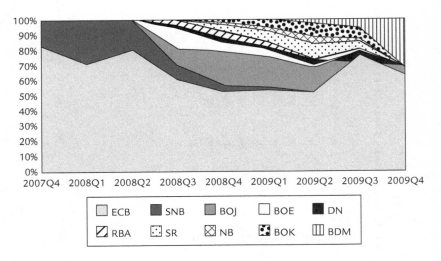

Figure 7.2
Quarterly Share of Outstanding Swap Drawings by Partner Central Bank

Never before in its history had the Fed provided this amount of international liquidity in such a condensed period of time. Indeed, the Fed's actions in 2008–2009 make its swap line program during the 1960s and

country of origin and then calculated the aggregate monthly borrowing totals reported in the figures. To be clear, these figures report total loans by month, not outstanding credit as reported in the swap figures.

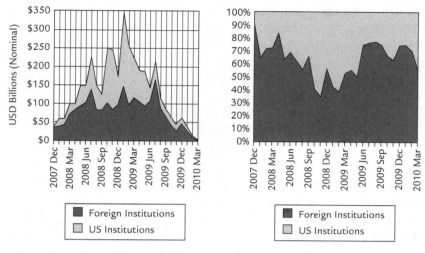

Figure 7.3
TAF Lending by Month, 2007–2010

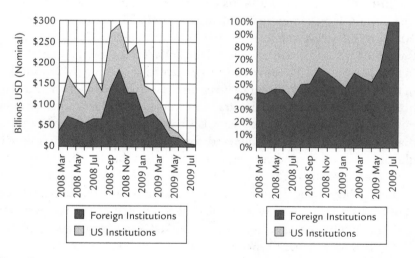

Figure 7.4
TSLF Lending by Month, 2008–2009

the ESF's largest foreign bailouts look tiny by comparison. What motivated the Fed to act in such an unprecedented way? In the following section, I argue that the Fed was compelled to act as an ILLR during the crisis in order to protect systemically important US banks and money market funds from the threat of foreign defaults. Indeed, I show that the foreign central banks most likely to receive Fed swap lines operated in jurisdictions where US financial institutions were most exposed. In short, swap lines were provided to jurisdictions that posed the greatest risk to the stability of the US financial system. Moreover, I will show that these risks were systemic in nature. Thus, as was the case with ESF rescues during the 1980s and 1990s, the Fed was acting not simply to protect the financial interests of the private financial institutions, but also to protect the stability of the broader US financial system—the broader *public* interest.

2. US FINANCIAL INTERESTS AND THE FED'S ILLR ACTIONS

In the fall of 2008, the US financial system was severely exposed to the threat of foreign bank defaults in light of frozen global dollar-funding markets. The risks facing US financial institutions were not just troubling; they were also systemic and existential. In particular, the two components of the US financial system most at risk were its major banks and money market funds. After that brief lull in foreign lending by US financial institutions during the 1980s after the international debt crisis early that decade, it picked up again during the 1990s.[9] It exploded during the 2000s. What drove the foreign lending boom among US banks during the 2000s was the growing demand for dollars from foreign banks looking to invest in the lucrative mortgage-backed securities (MBS) market in the United States. In order to invest in these assets, foreign institutions borrowed huge volumes of dollars from wholesale credit markets, a large portion of which came from major US banks via the interbank funding market. Although foreign demand for short-term dollar funding was global, it was most concentrated in Europe where banks were borrowing heavily to invest in MBS.

Besides borrowing directly from US banks in the interbank market, foreign banks wanting to invest in dollar-denominated assets also acquired dollars by issuing what is known as asset-backed commercial paper (ABCP). ABCP is simply another type of short-term debt instrument—an IOU— which firms can issue to raise funds. Typical maturities range from 30 to 180 days. While US banks purchased some of the foreign ABCP, the biggest player in the market during these years was US money market funds. Money market funds are those "safe-as-a-savings-account" investments where millions of middle-class US residents stash away their hard-earned cash. Risk associated with money market investments is low. The return, while modest, is typically better than a standard savings account at your corner bank. So, in short, millions of middle-class US residents invested their savings in

---

9. See Figure 4.5 in chapter 4.

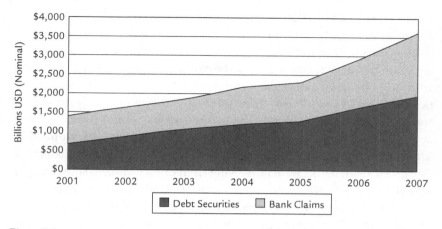

Figure 7.5
US Foreign Debt Securities and Bank Claims, 2001–2007

money markets; those funds, in turn, used the money to invest it in short-term debt securities (ABCP) issued by major domestic and foreign financial firms. Besides ABCP, money market funds also loaned tens of billions of dollars to foreign financial firms via various other instruments, including certificates of deposit (CDs) and corporate notes. One study examines the mid-2008 holdings of the largest 15 prime money markets using data drawn directly from portfolio holdings reports. It finds that these prime funds placed *half* of their dollar portfolios in foreign banks with a total estimated value of $1 trillion.[10] When the assets of the Institutional Money Market Fund Association's European US dollar funds are included—another $180 billion—McGuire and von Peter estimate that prime fund exposure to European banks *alone* was about $1 trillion.[11] To put this in perspective, this means that European banks alone relied on US money market funds for one-eighth of their total $8 trillion in dollar funding.

Together, US bank and money market lending was the lifeblood of the global, dollar-dependent financial system that expanded dramatically during the decade that preceded the crisis. To illustrate the impressive buildup of foreign assets by US banks and money market funds, Figure 7.5 reports US foreign debt securities and bank claims from 2000 through 2007.[12] In aggregate, US holdings of foreign debt securities nearly tripled

10. Baba et al. 2009.

11. McGuire and von Peter 2009, p. 67. Baba et al. (2009) say that these 15 prime funds account for about 40 percent of the total prime funds' assets, meaning that the numbers would increase if the other 60 percent were accounted for.

12. Bank claim data are from the Bank for International Settlements consolidated banking statistics, immediate borrower basis available at http://www.bis.org/statistics/consstats.

from $700 billion in 2000 to just under $2 trillion in 2007. Foreign bank claims grew more than two-fold from roughly $700 billion to nearly $1.7 trillion during that period. Thus, trillions of dollars in foreign, dollar-denominated purchases required to be paid back rather quickly were made with other people's money. This put foreign banks in a rather precarious position: if credit markets were to freeze and they were no longer able to roll over their loans, a colossal gap in international dollar funding would appear. Of course, it was not just the foreign banks that were vulnerable. The parties that lent to these banks were equally (if not more) exposed. Because foreign banks were borrowing from one short-term source to pay off existing short-term debt as it matured, if wholesale markets jammed, their ability to continue servicing maturing dollar liabilities would come into question. To put it plainly, if foreign banks were cut off from private dollar funding, they would be forced to default on maturing obligations to US banks and money market funds.

How capable were US financial institutions of weathering a broad-based default on the part of major European banks? The amount of capital US banks held in reserve relative to their European lending was quite small. Figure 7.6 presents all US banks' claims on just the Eurozone and United Kingdom in relation to their Tier 1 capital stock.[13] In 2007, US bank claims on the Eurozone and United Kingdom alone were nearly twice the amount (193 percent) of their total capital. The picture was even starker if we focus just on the nine systemically important financial institutions (SIFIs) that in 2007 held claims on Eurozone and UK sources equal to 430 percent of their Tier 1 capital![14] Thus, a broad-based default on the part of major European banks alone was sufficient to render the

htm. Debt securities data represent aggregate long-term (maturities greater than one year) and short-term (maturities less than one year) debt securities together and include commercial paper, CDs, and other forms of foreign debt issuances, such as straight debt and zero-coupon debt. Calculations were made by the author with data collected from the US Treasury's Annual Cross-US Border Portfolio Holdings (ACBPH) report available at http://www.treasury.gov/resource-center/data-chart-center/tic/Pages/fpis.aspx. The 2002 debt securities data are interpolated because no ACBPH report was released that year.

13. Tier 1 capital, sometimes referred to as core capital, refers to the sum of a financial institution's common stock and disclosed reserves or retained earnings. In chapters 4, 5, and 6, my references to capital referred to *total* capital, which also includes additional reserves, subordinated debentures, and other legitimate components of an institution's capital base. However, beginning largely after the Basel I agreement was reached in 1988, Tier 1 capital became the standard measure of a bank's core financial strength. I relied on total capital data because the Country Exposure Lending Surveys (CELS) reports only published total capital data until late 1998. Beginning in 1999, CELS began only reporting Tier 1 capital.

14. Totals in the figure were calculated by the author using data from 2007 CELS reports. Unfortunately, due to changes in how foreign bank claims are reported in the CELS reports, I am unable to present a consistent picture of SIFI exposure to Europe from 2000 to 2008.

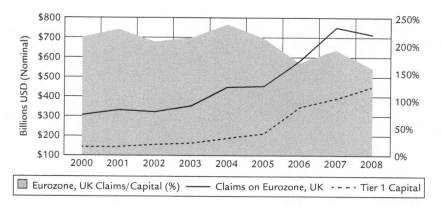

Figure 7.6
US Banking System's Exposure to Eurozone and United Kingdom, 2000–2008

small number of systemically important US banks (which held nearly all of this foreign debt) insolvent. Similarly, US money market funds were also facing an existential crisis. Although data on capital held by these institutions are unavailable to the public, these institutions hold even less capital in reserve than major banks.[15] To make matters worse, deposits in money markets are at far greater risk to panic runs than traditional bank deposits. Unlike money in a bank, money market investments are not insured by the Federal Deposit Insurance Corporation (FDIC). Consequently, if global credit markets froze, the possibility of a worst-case scenario, depicted in Figure 7.7, would emerge. As a consequence of frozen credit markets, European borrowers would default on their obligations to money market funds. This would in turn generate fears that a prime fund might actually "break the buck,"[16] sparking a run on money market investments among millions of middle-class US investors. A run would complete the vicious cycle by causing money markets to collapse under the panic. This further threatened the US financial system because lending by these funds represented a vital artery of credit (to a tune of $1 trillion) for US financial institutions.[17] Thus, their potential collapse would have resulted in the drying up of a critical source of domestic funding for US financial institutions at a time when banks themselves were also incredibly reluctant to lend. How plausible is this counterfactual story? How real was the threat of foreign bank default? And, even if such a default had occurred, would this really have caused a run on the market?

15. Norris 2013. This is in part a consequence of lax regulation. For instance, at the time of the crisis, money markets were not required to hold any capital in reserve.
16. This is a circumstance when the net asset value of a money market fund drops below $1.
17. Baba et al. 2009.

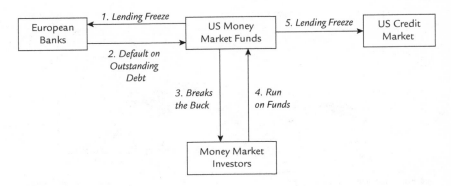

Figure 7.7
Money Market Fund Worst-Case Scenario

Although it is impossible to answer these questions with complete certainty, there are salient examples from the crisis that offer strong support to the veracity of these counterfactual claims.

First, how real was the threat of foreign bank default? In the summer of 2007, when international dollar scarcity was just beginning to become a real problem, two German banks nearly did just that. Indeed, there is little doubt they would have defaulted on their dollar debt were it not for the multiple government-led bailouts they received. According to estimates, IKB Deutsche Industriebank and Sachsen Landesbank had each provided credit guarantees three times larger than their equity capital as a means of issuing ABCP.[18] Viewed as a low-risk investment, most ABCP was sold to money market funds prior to the crisis through ABCP "conduits"—special entities set up by banks for this purpose. Like many other foreign banks, a majority of the assets IKB and Sachsen conduits used to guarantee the ABCP they issued was the US residential MBS they had accumulated. Table 7.2 is a reconstructed balance sheet of Sachsen Landesbank ABCP conduit Ormand Quay in July 2007.[19] The sheet reveals two important facts that are indicative of the financial structure of conduits at this time. First, nearly 80 percent of Ormand Quay's assets were of the MBS variety, meaning the conduit was significantly exposed to subprime risk. Second, Ormand relied exclusively on the short-term ABCP market to finance its dollar investments and lending activities.

---

18. Acharya and Schnabl 2010, p. 3. Commercial paper is a promissory note with a fixed maturity between one and 270 days. ABCP is a collateralized form, meaning that the issuer provides another asset to guarantee the debt.

19. Adapted from Acharya and Schnabl 2010.

Table 7.2 ORMAND QUAY (SACHSEN ABCP CONDUIT)
BALANCE SHEET, JULY 2007

Assets—*Guaranteed by Sachsen Landesbank*		**Liabilities**—*Short-Term Debt, Maturity < 1 Month*	
Residential Mortgage-Backed Securities	*$6.3 bn*	Asset-Backed Commercial Paper	*$11.3bn*
Commercial Mortgage-Backed Securities	*$2.7 bn*		
Consumer Loans	*$0.5 bn*		
Other	*$1.8 bn*		
Total:	**$11.3 bn**	Total:	**$11.3 bn**

As information about the increasingly toxic nature of assets linked to US subprime mortgages became available, money markets became very reluctant to extend these short-term loans to banks for fear that the counterparty's MBS might be infected with the subprime virus. As the ABCP market dried up, banks that backed the conduits became their sole provider of capital.[20] So long as the banks that backed the entities had sufficient dollars, calamity could be forestalled. Yet, the extent to which European banks could finance the conduits' losses was in doubt. If the backing bank itself were to run out of dollars, the only recourse for the conduit would be to sell off its assets to pay its debts. Of course, as the subprime crisis unfolded, once valuable AAA-rated MBS now had little appeal to markets. In short, these assets had become effectively illiquid. In July and August 2007, conduits backed by IKB and Sachsen were unable to issue sufficient commercial paper to roll over their short-term debt. The two financial institutions were unable to fund the conduits on their own. In the end, both avoided default (in the short term) only when a consortium of state-owned and private banks as well as the German federal government came to their rescue with nearly €12 billion in emergency loans and guarantees.[21]

But what would have happened if IKB, Sachsen, or any other European bank had been unable to pay off a maturing debt obligation to a US money market fund? Again, one need not look far in answering this counterfactual.

---

20. Fitch Ratings 2007, p. 3.
21. Ram 2007. Ultimately, the €3.5 billion in loans and €8 billion in guarantees to IKB were not enough as the bank eventually defaulted on $7 billion in debt and was sold off to a US private equity firm (Schwartz 2009b, xiii). Sachsen was initially given a €17.3 billion credit line but was soon bought out by the German bank LBBW and subsequently merged and dissolved.

During the week of September 15, 2008, shares in the Reserve Primary Fund, one of the oldest and largest money market funds in the world, fell below $1 to $0.97. For only the second time in history, a money market fund "broke the buck." What led to this nightmare scenario was the fact that the Reserve Fund had a $785 million position in Lehman Brothers' commercial paper. When Lehman collapsed, those holdings lost all their value. The Reserve Fund would have to "eat" the losses. Investors panicked. In a very short period of time, $300 million was withdrawn from the money markets as people sought to insulate themselves from any further losses.[22] For a time, the whole prime funds system appeared to be on the edge of disaster. An artery that provided $1 trillion credit to the US economy, including the teetering banking system, was frozen. There is little reason to believe that a default on the part of a European or any other foreign institution would have resulted in a different outcome. These two cases provide a window into what very well would have happened had the Federal Reserve not stepped in and acted as an ILLR by providing swap lines of unprecedented size to 14 foreign central banks.

Thus, it is likely that the primary motivation for the Fed's dramatic provision of liquidity was to prevent just such a worst-case scenario from unfolding where a foreign financial institution defaulted on its obligations to a US money market fund or major bank. Amid the subprime panic, financial institutions all but stopped lending to one another. To address the credit shortage in the domestic market, the Fed introduced a suite of liquidity facilities including the TAF, TSLF, and the CPFF. Yet, as noted above, the Fed permitted foreign banks with affiliates operating within the United States to borrow from these facilities, and, ultimately, these foreign banks gobbled up the majority of the dollars the facilities provided.[23] However, banks and other financial institutions not operating within the United States did not have access to these programs. This left them vulnerable. Since foreign central banks were unable to create the dollars that these institutions needed, it raised the possibility that some might default on their external, dollar-denominated liabilities with calamitous consequences for the US economy. As Figure 7.8 depicts, the Federal Reserve globalized its lender of last resort mechanism when it provided dollars via swap lines to selected partner central banks. Those monetary authorities, in turn, took the dollars and provided them to banks within their jurisdiction. Those banks, then, were able to use the newly acquired dollars to continue servicing their obligations to US banks and money market funds, thereby insulating the US financial system from foreign default.

22. Serchuk 2009.
23. A fact that, as I will discuss, raised concerns among some members of the FOMC.

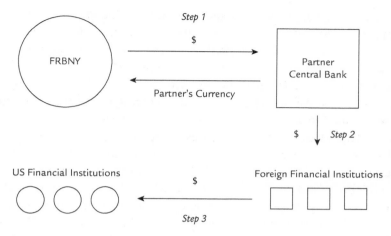

Figure 7.8
How the Fed's Swap Lines Protected the US Financial System

Thus, the Fed's actions were entirely consistent with a classic Bagehot-style effort to stabilize a financial system amid a panic—with one notable exception: Because US financial institutions managed global portfolios, the Fed was forced to act as a *global* lender of last resort in order to protect the stability of the domestic financial system.

3. AN EMPIRICAL MODEL OF FED SWAP LINE SELECTION

If the claim that the Fed acted as an ILLR in order to protect the US financial system is correct, then we would expect a positive statistical relationship between foreign exposure of major banks and money market funds and swap line selection. Major commercial financial institutions are a well-organized, well-financed political lobby. It is highly likely they recognized the substantial threat that the global dollar shortage posed to their profits and, in some cases, their very survival. I anticipate that these institutions pressed US economic officials to provide emergency liquidity to foreign jurisdictions where their portfolios were most at risk. However, as I argued in chapter 5, it is overly simplistic to portray the Fed policymakers as mere puppets of private financial actors. Policymakers are individuals, operating inside state institutions, with their own interests over policy. One of the Fed's primary roles is to maintain the stability of the US financial system and contain systemic risk in financial markets. Thus, I anticipate that policymakers should be most sensitive to financial institutions' pleas for protection when the health of the entire system is threatened. As I have already explained, in the fall of 2008, the threats facing the US financial system were existential. In short, during the Great Panic, the interests of major private financial institutions and the Fed's interest in upholding its public mandate were in close alignment. If my argument is correct, the Fed should have been most likely to deploy its resources on behalf of foreign economies where systemically important US banks and money market funds were most exposed.

In order to test this argument, I estimate an empirical model of the Federal Reserve's swap line selection against a sample of all countries that had accepted the IMF's Article VIII by 2008. This has historically been the Fed's "red line" for swap line selection. Thus, it is unreasonable to include nonsignatories in the sample since there is essentially no way the Fed would have provided liquidity lines to these countries.[24] The key explanatory variable in the model accounts for US financial system exposure in 2007, just before the crisis erupted. It combines cross-national variation in the foreign claims of SIFIs and US residents' holdings of foreign debt securities into one measure. As discussed in chapter 5, SIFIs lie at the core of domestic banking systems. As such, they are viewed as having more "systemic importance"—defined as "the damage a bank's failure inflicts upon the rest of the system"—than smaller banks.[25] Foreign debt securities data include commercial paper and negotiable certificates of deposits. These account for US money market fund exposure to foreign jurisdictions. In sum, the key covariate in the model accounts for cross-national variation in the exposure of the US financial system as a percentage of total SIFI foreign claims and residents' foreign securities holdings. A higher percentage equates to greater US financial system exposure. This variable is discussed in detail in the appendix.[26] As exposure to a foreign jurisdiction increases, I anticipate that the likelihood of a Fed swap line should increase.

Additionally, I follow Lawrence Broz in including several control variables drawn from two federal reports on the swap program.[27] These reports point to four factors that contributed to the Fed's selection

24. This decision is in line with Mahoney and Goertz's (2004) "possibility principle," which, simply put, states that when selecting negative cases, researchers should exclude cases where—based on either theory or evidence—a positive value on the outcome of interest does not seem possible.

25. Craig and von Peter 2010, p. 22.

26. Once again, SIFI claims data were gathered from the CELS. These data are available at http://www.ffiec.gov/e16.htm. Data on US foreign debt securities holdings were gathered from the US Treasury's Annual Cross Border Portfolio Holdings report available at http://www.treasury.gov/resource-center/data-chart-center/tic/Pages/fpis.aspx.

27. Broz 2015; CRS 2009, p. 49; GAO 2011, p. 118.

Table 7.3 FEDERAL RESERVE SWAP LINE REGRESSION
RESULTS, 2008

	Model 1		Model 2	
Intercept	−3.513***	(1.290)	−3.407	(2.3297)
Share of world GDP (%)	−2.048	(1.379)	−5.647*	(1.8235)
Inflation	−0.324	(0.340)	−0.259	(0.4404)
Share of US trade (%)	−1.054+	(0.573)	−2.289*	(1.0772)
Global financial center	0.474	(1.384)	−3.491	(8.0470)
US financial system exposure (%)	10.627*	(4.497)	19.099*	(7.4864)
Dollar liquidity shortage			0.009	(0.0468)
N	63		33	
AIC	28.947		26.415	

Heteroskedastic and Autocorrelation Consistent (HAC) standard errors in "( )": $+ p < 0.10$, $* p < 0.05$, $** p < 0.01$, $*** p < 0.001$.

process: the economic size of the partner, its record of sound economic management, its importance as a major US trading partner, and whether it was a major financial center. To account for these factors, I control for a country's share of world GDP, the level of inflation (as a proxy for sound economic management), a partner's share of US trade, and whether or not the partner is home to a global financial center. Finally, in a second model, I also include a measure of dollar scarcity.[28] This controls for the extent of the "dollar shortage" facing foreign jurisdictions. As I explained earlier, the crisis resulted in the seizure of global dollar-funding markets because of fears of counterparty risk. However, some jurisdictions were hit harder by the dollar "shortage" than others. A lower score on this measure indicates a more intense shortage of dollar liquidity. Allen and Moessner find that increased dollar scarcity is associated with a higher probability of receiving a swap line.[29]

Results for two logistic regression models are presented in Table 7.3.[30] As expected, the measure of US financial system exposure is positively signed and statistically significant in each model.[31] Thus, jurisdictions most likely to receive a swap line from the Fed were those where systemically important US banks and money market funds were more exposed. No other covariates appear to explain variation in swap line selection. For instance, although the coefficient on the share of trade with the United

28. Data were obtained by the author from Allen and Moessner 2010.
29. Allen and Moessner 2010.
30. All models are fitted by using the R package Zelig (Imai, King, and Lau 2007, 2008).
31. These results are consistent with Aizenman (2009) and Broz (2015), who each find US bank exposure correlates with swap line selection.

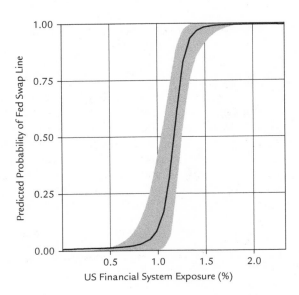

Figure 7.9
US Financial Exposure and Swap Line Predicted Probability

States is statistically significant, it is negatively signed. Thus, increased trade with the United States is associated with a diminished probability of receiving a swap line. It is also worth noting that a shortage of dollar liquidity is not associated with an increased likelihood of a swap line when US financial exposure is accounted for.

To further illuminate the magnitude of the effect of financial exposure on swap line selection, Figure 7.9 displays simulated Model 2 predicted probabilities of receiving a swap line (with 90 percent confidence intervals) as financial system exposure increases from 0 percent to 2.5 percent. Although this may seem like a limited range, a 1 percent increase in this measure accounts for roughly an additional $50 billion in foreign exposures. As the figure indicates, the effect of financial exposure on the probability of a swap line is substantial. For countries where the US financial system was exposed at less than 0.5 percent, the probability of receiving a swap line is essentially 0. However, at 1.5 percent, the probability of receiving a swap line is nearly 1. This comports with a simple survey of the data. Of the 14 jurisdictions where financial exposure was highest, 13 received liquidity lines. Only India (1.1 percent exposure) was passed over.[32] Conversely, only one country where US exposure was

32. A 2012 Bloomberg report sheds some light on why India was not selected for a swap line in 2008. Four years later, in November 2012, India reportedly asked the Fed to open

below 0.5 percent—New Zealand (0.21 percent)—received a swap line. In short, consistent with my argument, the models show that the Fed was most likely to act as an ILLR on behalf of partners where the US financial system was exposed to significant counterparty risk.

4. THE INTEREST-RATE THREAT AND THE FED'S ILLR ACTIONS

As the evidence indicates, stabilizing the US financial system was a fundamental motivation behind the Fed's unprecedented ILLR actions in 2008–2009. Yet, another risk facing the US economy likely played a role in the Fed's decision. Besides protecting banks and money market funds from foreign default, the swap program represented an indirect way of bringing down rising interest rates that the Fed did not have direct control over. As domestic credit markets in the United States tightened during the panic, the Fed aggressively cut short-term interest rates in the hopes of stimulating the economy. Between October 31, 2007, and December 16, 2008, the central bank slashed the federal funds rate on nine separate occasions from a high of 4.5 percent to a target rate of 0.25 percent or below. Despite these unprecedented efforts, interest rates on many contracts were not falling. Indeed, some began climbing. This had to do with a trend that developed nearly 20 years prior to the crisis. Beginning in the early 1990s, a wide variety of financial products, including corporate and consumer loans, started to be linked to the London Interbank Offered Rate (Libor). Hence, if Libor rose, so did rates on any financial product linked to it. The Libor index is tallied daily by the British Bankers' Association, which polls an elite group of 16 major banks to see at what rate a bank could borrow dollars from other banks. Unlike the federal funds rate, which is under the direct control of the Fed, Libor is more independent of the US monetary authority. What made the Libor link especially threatening during the financial crisis was the fact that the vast majority of adjustable-rate mortgages (ARMs) in the United States were also indexed to Libor. During the 2000s, it had become commonplace for banks to issue what are referred to as "hybrid ARMs"—mortgages that begin with a fixed interest rate for the first two or three years and then reset (monthly, semi-annually, or annually) based on the rate to which they were indexed.[33] Libor is not

a dollar swap line with the Reserve Bank of India. However, the Fed rebuffed the request, reportedly because the rupee was not a fully convertible currency (Agrawal and Goyal 2012). See Helleiner (2014, p. 46) and Prasad (2014, pp. 208–209) for brief discussions of other requests for swap deals that were reportedly rebuffed by the Fed.

33. Schweitzer and Venkatu 2009.

the only rate to which ARMs have been indexed. Indeed, there are three other indices that have been used.[34] However, in the decade leading up to the crisis, Libor became the index of choice. At the time of the financial crisis, some 60 percent of prime hybrids and virtually all of subprime hybrids were indexed to Libor.[35]

Libor began showing signs of strain as early as the summer of 2007; the trend continued and worsened after Lehman collapsed. As banks panicked, interbank lending sputtered to a halt and the rates banks charged one another for dollars rose rapidly. Since Libor reflects the rates banks are charging each other for credit, the financial market skittishness caused the index to spike. Between September 15 and October 15, 2008, the one-month dollar Libor rate nearly doubled from roughly 2.5 to 4.5 percent. Consequently, many US homeowners with prime ARMS and virtually all homeowners with subprime ARMs ready to reset during the fall of 2008 were about to experience a significant hike in their monthly payment. How significant is this? One report gives us a pretty good guess. The authors estimate the spread between monthly payments of ARMs linked to US Treasury rates—the second most popular index for ARMs at the time, and one more sensitive to changes in the federal funds rate—and those linked to Libor. They conclude that for a typical subprime borrower, having a Libor-indexed loan as opposed to a Treasury-indexed loan equaled a roughly $100 monthly payment increase for every $100,000 of remaining principal. For prime borrowers, the figure was about $50 per month. According to an internal Citibank report from October 6, 2008, the Libor spike was predicted to bring about a "10 [percent] increase in defaults for outstanding non-delinquent ARMs at reset, which translates to roughly 1.8 [percent] increase in cumulative loss."[36] And this was for Citibank alone. The trend was the same across other major banks as well. Libor was threatening to bring about a second wave of foreclosures as more ARMs prepared to reset at even higher and more unsustainable interest rates. As Figure 7.10 depicts, a vicious cycle was emerging where initial subprime losses caused interbank lending to seize up and Libor to rise, which was poised to cause more subprime losses and feedback into credit markets. The US monetary authority had a clear interest in doing whatever it could to indirectly bring Libor rates under control to prevent this vicious cycle from fully developing.

---

34. Others indices include the one-year constant-maturity Treasury yield, the Eleventh District Cost-of-Funds Index, and the Federal Housing Finance Board national average contract interest rate.

35. Parulekar et al. 2008, p. 1.

36. Ibid., p. 1.

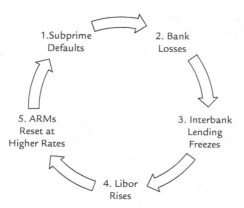

Figure 7.10
Libor/ARM Default Vicious Cycle

It was in this environment that the Fed opened and expanded its swap program, which I contend was partially aimed at bringing Libor rates back in line with Treasury rates. As stated previously, Libor first began showing strains in the summer of 2007. This was visible due to movements in the TED spread, which measures the difference between Libor and short-term Treasury rates. As discussed earlier, the TED spread, which typically averaged around 40 basis points, spiked several times during the crisis. The first spike was in August 2007, when it reached 240 basis points. That month the Fed first approached the ECB about the possibility of opening up a swap line between the two central banks. The second TED spread spike was on December 12, 2007, when it reached 220 basis points. On that same day, the Fed opened its first two swap arrangements with the ECB and SNB. The third spike was in March 2008, when the spread hit 203 basis points. That month marked the first wave of swap line increases. Then, when Lehman filed for bankruptcy, the spread peaked at an astounding 457 basis points. Again, this large spread meant that resetting Libor-linked ARMs would experience substantial mortgage payment increases. Following Lehman's collapse and the major TED spread spike, the Fed's swap program entered its dramatic 40-day period of expansion.[37]

How did the swaps function as a method for the Fed to rein in a wild Libor rate? Because Libor reflects risk and tension in the international interbank lending market—specifically lending in dollars—swaps provided an alternative means of getting dollars in the hands of foreign banks that needed them. A purely domestic injection of liquidity would only

37. Spread according to Bloomberg Financial, available at http://www.bloomberg.com/apps/ cbuilder? tickerl=.TEDSP:IND, on July 21, 2010.

have had a marginal effect on Libor, since huge volumes of dollars are also lent outside of the United States. Indeed, of the 16 banks that were polled daily to determine the rate, 13 were non-US institutions. Consequently, easing the domestic interbank lending market would not have been sufficient to bring Libor rates, and hence ARM rates, down. Foreign banks had to be included as well, which is why the swap program was the perfect backdoor method to rein in Libor. Foreign central banks could now deliver liquidity to dollar-starved banks through auctions. This relieved demand in the frozen interbank market. As demand for dollars *between* banks shrank (because demand was now met via the swap lines) the rates banks charged each other for dollars fell. When the Fed made four of the swap lines unlimited in size and increased the total number of central banks participating to 14, Libor fell from its mid-October high faster than it had risen to that point. It dropped from roughly 4.5 to 1.5 percent by mid-November 2008. The TED spread, for its part, closed from 457 basis points to 210 basis points in the same period. And, although still elevated, these declines represent dramatic improvements in a very short period of time. The swaps had both a practical as well as a psychological effect on markets, helping to bring Libor under control. As Naohiko Baba and Frank Packer explain,

> Financial markets reacted well to the announcements of both the increases in the absolute amounts of the swap lines and the increase in numbers. In particular, the approval of unlimited dollar swap facilities for selected central banks on October 13 was greatly welcomed. Many market participants reported that the expended swap facilities improved term funding conditions.[38]

As Libor fell, resetting ARMs now faced rates considerably closer to the Treasury rates the Fed had more control over. If the Fed viewed swap lines as a way to prevent Libor-indexed ARMs from experiencing significant monthly payment increases, they proved to be an effective tool.

5. TRANSCRIPT ANALYSIS OF FOMC MEETINGS

In the preceding sections, I presented circumstantial and statistical evidence to support my assertion that the Fed was motivated to act as an ILLR in order to ensure the stability of the US financial system and to bring down interest rates, which, indirectly, would stabilize the housing

---

38. Baba and Packer 2009, p. 11.

market. Here, I draw on a new resource—transcripts from FOMC meetings during the crisis—to further assess the veracity of my argument. This allows us to see what policymakers actually said during the critical moments in which the decisions to act as the ILLR were made. Not only does this provide another way to test my argument, it also allows us to uncover alternative motivations not yet considered. There is another reason why transcript analysis is important for this study: The Fed's actions were composed of *multiple* decisions that took place within a dynamic of changing conditions over a period of many months. None of the analysis presented here has accounted for this effectively. By comparison, the transcript analysis is presented chronologically. The final composition of the swap program and other liquidity facilities was not the result of a single decision by the Fed. Rather, it was the outcome of multiple, successive decisions by the monetary authority. First, there were the initial decisions by the Fed to open the swap lines with the ECB and SNB as well as allowing foreign banks operating in the United States to have access to the TAF. Next, the Fed made the decision to incrementally increase the size of the initial two swap lines and the TAF. Third, after the Lehman bankruptcy filing, the Fed ramped up its ILLR actions by rapidly expanding the swap program—increasing the size of credit lines and the number of participating central banks through new agreements with eight additional advanced economies. Finally, in late October 2008, the FOMC made the unprecedented decision to extend $30 billion swap lines to four select emerging market economies (EMEs). This section reviews how events that unfolded over time led the Fed to initiate and expand its ILLR actions.

5.1. The Initiation of the Swap Lines and the TAF, August 2007–December 2007

While the Fed's swap program did not fully mature until the fall of 2008, its origins can be traced back to more than a year before Lehman's collapse. In mid-August 2007, billions of dollars in short-term dollar-denominated borrowing by European banks were days from coming due. Meanwhile, money market funds and US banks had significantly retrenched lending to European institutions.[39] This raised the prospect that foreign banks, on a widespread basis, would face difficulty rolling over their short-term

---

39. As both the interbank market and money markets seized, foreign banks in need of dollars first turned to the foreign exchange swap market. Yet, as Baba et al. (2008) show, this shift in demand drove up the cost of borrowing on the FX swap market.

dollar debt. The tightening became clear in the interbank credit market, evidenced by spikes in the TED spread.[40] For a decade, the TED spread averaged about 40 basis points; in August 2007, it reached 220 basis points.[41] Around this time the Fed began expressing serious concerns about strains in money markets. Indeed, as early as mid-August, it is clear the Fed was aware of the severity of the risks facing US money market funds. In an August 16 FOMC conference call, members were briefed by William C. Dudley (manager of the FOMC's System Open Market Account). Dudley noted that strains in credit markets raised the risk that "money market mutual funds could suffer losses on certain asset-backed commercial paper programs that have weak backstops. *This could conceivably cause some funds to 'break the buck.'* "[42]

Also in August 2007, the Federal Reserve first began considering the prospect of opening up swap lines with the ECB and, potentially, other central banks. According to David Wessel, it was actually the Fed that first approached the ECB about the plan.[43] However, Wessel says that the ECB refused the idea at the time in large part because it wanted to "pin the Great Panic" on the United States. Accepting the credit line was akin to accepting a portion of the blame for troubling circumstances developing in the markets.[44] Bernanke first proposed the possibility of opening up a temporary swap line with the ECB and SNB to the entire FOMC in the group's September 18 meeting. By that time, conditions had improved since August, and so the chairman admitted that it was "a relatively close call as to whether such a facility is needed at this juncture."[45] Ultimately, after minimal discussion, the swap proposals were not put to a vote during the meeting.[46]

By December, sentiments in Europe had apparently changed. In a December 6 conference call with the committee, Bernanke once again raised the prospect of opening up a $20 billion swap line with the ECB and possibly a smaller one with the SNB as well.[47] The chairman noted

---

40. As discussed above, this index measures the difference between Libor rates and short-term US Treasury rates.

41. Schwartz 2009a, p. 202.

42. FOMC 2007a, p. 4. Emphasis added.

43. This is interesting in its own right since it contrasts with how ESF credits were made. According to officials I spoke with at Treasury, that institution was never the first mover. Rather, countries in need of financing came to ask for the Treasury's help. This does not appear to have been the case with the Fed's swap lines in 2007.

44. Wessel 2009, p. 141.

45. FOMC 2007b, p. 44.

46. The decision to hold off was likely not just a function of improving conditions but also because the ECB and SNB were still lukewarm on the idea at this time.

47. According to Bernanke's comments during the meeting, the ECB (which had met the same day) had informed the Fed on December 6 that they were now interested in the swap

that the "problem" with dollar funding in Europe was once again reverberating in the US economy. The unusually elevated demand for dollars was, as Bernanke put it, creating "problems for our monetary policy implementation," as it tended to push the federal funds rate to open higher in the United States. The swap lines would allow the ECB and SNB to provide dollars to financial institutions in their jurisdiction through credit auctions and, thus, would ease growing strains in the market. In addition to the direct benefit the Fed's provision of liquidity would have on markets, Bernanke also hoped they would have an important psychological impact, adding, "I think it will send a good signal, and particularly I think the international cooperation aspect of this would be well received."[48] Support for the measure was not unanimous, however. Governor William Poole raised doubts about the necessity of the lines, pointing out that the ECB held a considerable sum of dollar reserves. "What does a swap give them," Poole asked, "that they don't already have on deposit at the [Federal Reserve Bank of New York] or their holdings of Treasuries?" Poole wanted to know why the ECB could not simply self-finance the dollar shortage rather than relying on the United States. [49] In response, a Fed economist (tapped to answer the question by Bernanke) acknowledged the ECB's roughly $200 billion in reserves but added that "pursuing some sort of a cooperative arrangement with the ECB would provide us with more advance information about what the ECB is planning to do . . . . So we see some advantages arising from cooperation and coordination as opposed to their injecting the reserves just on their own."[50] Thus, at least initially the swap lines appear to have been motivated not only by a desire to reduce spillovers from European dollar-funding strains but also as a means to foster coordination and information sharing between the United States and European central banks. In his memoir of the crisis, Bernanke explained that the ECB swap line's "purpose would be to help insulate US markets from financial turbulence in Europe."[51] The FOMC approved both swap lines with a 9–1 vote with Poole being the lone dissenter in each case.

At this same meeting, the TAF was established to provide liquidity to banks in the domestic US market, which were also facing difficulties

line. The Swiss, however, had not yet made a formal request, although Bernanke noted it was possible they would soon follow suit (FOMC 2007c, pp. 13–14).

48. FOMC 2007c, p. 14.

49. McGuire and von Peter estimate that in mid-2007 the euro area, SNB, and BOE had a combined total of $294 billion in reserves, a total far smaller than their lower-bound estimate of the dollar funding gap (p. 20). In these cases, there were ultimately not enough dollars to go around.

50. FOMC 2007c, p. 18.

51. Bernanke 2015, p. 157.

finding the credit they needed.[52] The facility was designed to address funding pressures in the United States at the same time the swaps would address funding pressures in Europe. Eligible borrowers were depository institutions determined to be in "generally sound financial condition," which included foreign-owned banks with branches operating in the United States.[53] As it became evident that the majority of the TAF's credit was going to US branches of foreign banks, concern and confusion were expressed at FOMC meetings. One Federal Reserve Bank (FRB) president inquired about the benefits of lending to European banks via the TAF as opposed to allowing the ECB and SNB to provide dollars from the swap lines at their own auctions.[54] At another meeting a different FRB president expressed concerns about the "optics" of a liquidity facility that was lending primarily to foreign institutions, noting he was concerned about "political vulnerability" and "worried about a backlash."[55]

However, William Dudley, manager of the Fed's System Open Market Account, explained that giving foreign banks access to the TAF was a condition the ECB imposed on the Fed in exchange for accepting the swap line.[56] The reason for this condition, according to Dudley, had to do with the ECB's "sense of what their responsibility [was] in terms of providing dollar liquidity to their institutions . . . . They were less willing to do something in which they were taking responsibility for the problem and saying that they were going to get the dollars and supply them to those banks."[57] In other words, the ECB felt that becoming the sole provider of dollars to European banks would equate to taking responsibility for the crisis. So the decision to provide credit to foreign banks via the TAF *as well as* the swap lines appears to have been the results of a preference for blame sharing at the ECB.[58]

---

52. The FOMC did not vote to approve the TAF as it was established by the Federal Reserve Board under the authority granted by Regulation A ("Extensions of Credit by Federal Reserve Banks").

53. FOMC 2007c, p. 8.

54. FOMC 2008a, p. 14.

55. FOMC 2008d, p. 21.

56. Dudley explained, "Regarding the foreign institutions issue—the choice between dollar balances from us versus dollar balances from foreign central banks—I think it was a little more complicated than that because, if I remember how we got to the foreign exchange swaps, they were essentially more or less conditional on our doing the TAF. They were willing to do the swaps if they could get the auctions in tandem with our term auction facilities. So my judgment would be that we probably didn't really have a choice of getting dollars to those foreign banks through the ECB if we hadn't done the [TAF]" (FOMC 2008a, p. 14).

57. FOMC 2008a, p. 15.

58. This echoes Wessel's (2009) account of the ECB's initial rejection of the swap lines in the summer of 2007.

5.2. Incremental Expansion of Liquidity Facilities, March 2008–August 2008

In March 2008, as the New York investment bank Bear Stearns flirted with bankruptcy due to its exposure to bad mortgage investments, conditions in the wholesale markets significantly worsened. Vice Chairman Timothy Geithner provided a colorful label for what was happening: an "adverse dynamic margin-spiral-downward-self-feeding thing."[59] The cause of the spiral, Bernanke concluded, was the continued withdrawal of money market funds and "other, less sophisticated investors" from credit markets as fears about exposures to vulnerable banks like Bear grew.[60] Of course, the very decision by money market funds to pull out of the market only pushed the vulnerable financial institutions closer to the edge. This point was echoed by one governor whose "real concern" was that many of the money markets "that hold between $3 trillion and $4 trillion will just walk away."[61] Foreign banks were especially susceptible to tightening credit conditions. At one meeting, a Fed researcher informed committee members of the unfolding problem facing European banks backing "conduits" (like Ormand Quay discussed above) that had financed billions of dollars in MBS investments by selling ABCP to US money market funds:

> As the conduits that issued the ABCP encountered difficulty rolling their paper over, many of these banks, *fearful of damage to their reputations, elected to purchase assets from the conduits or extend credit to them, which proved in many cases to be a significant source of balance sheet pressures. This list is dominated by European banks.*[62]

One member observed that as credit dried up in London and across Europe, there was a growing possibility that a major financial institution would fail as "liquidity and solvency [were] becoming intertwined." Dudley echoed this sentiment, warning that "if the vicious circle were to continue unabated, the liquidity issues could become solvency issues, and major financial intermediaries could conceivably fail."[63]

---

59. FOMC 2008d, p. 15.
60. Ibid., p. 17.
61. Ibid., p. 83.
62. FOMC 2008A, p. 161. Emphasis added. Materials presented at that FOMC meeting identify the following three foreign banks as being most exposed to the liquidity strains facing ABCP conduits: HBOS (United Kingdom), HSBC (United Kingdom), and Fortis (Belgium), responsible for $42, $33, and $26 billion in outstanding ABCP, respectively (FOMC materials 2008, 240).
63. FOMC 2008b, pp. 22, 7.

As the committee worried about the exposure of US institutions to increasingly illiquid European counterparts, it also lamented that the dollar shortage was blunting the stimulative impact of aggressive rate cuts. Members recognized that the liquidity crisis "impairs the monetary policy transmission mechanism" such that "mortgage rates have risen . . . even with Treasury rates going down."[64] The Fed was clearly aware of the "ominous" link between Libor and ARMs. One member explained to the group, "The LIBOR-OIS spread has widened, so *borrowers tied to LIBOR rates have seen those rates rise* more than 25 basis points since the last meeting."[65] At another meeting, an FRB president relayed concerns from his district about a "second wave of foreclosures" among option ARM mortgage borrowers.[66] By the end of April, it is clear the committee understood that the swap lines and other liquidity facilities were "associated with a decline in . . . LIBOR."[67] Consequently, Geithner lobbied other members to vote in favor of expanding the swap lines and TAF in order to

> [take] another shot at trying to get [Libor] down . . . because—to use a technical term—[it is] screwing up the transmission mechanism of US monetary policy now. We're not sure how much effect we can have. There is a plausible case that increasing the size of the swaps will help on that front.[68]

It was within the context of these discussions that the FOMC voted unanimously to renew (once) and expand the size of its swap lines (three times) with the ECB and SNB. At the same time, the Fed increased the size and lengthened the maturity on TAF loans, and it introduced several additional domestic liquidity facilities that also began to lend to foreign banks operating within the United States.

5.3. Rapid Growth of the Swap Program: September 15, 2008–October 28, 2008

The day after Lehman Brothers filed for bankruptcy, the FOMC held an emergency meeting. Chairman Bernanke opened the meeting with a

---

64. FOMC 2008b, p. 5; FOMC 2008c, p. 57.
65. FOMC 2008d, p. 56. Emphasis added. Fed staff materials during the crisis also echoed this concern: "Amid poor liquidity, rates on six-month and one-year Libor—reference rates for a wide variety of contracts, including floating-rate mortgages—rose over the intermeeting period" (Blue Book 2008, p. 11). OIS stands for "overnight indexed swap." The Libor-OIS spread is similar to the Libor-TED spread. Both are used to measure stress in money markets.
66. FOMC 2008e, p. 37.
67. FOMC 2008d, p. 7.
68. Ibid., p. 15.

request. He wanted the Committee to grant the Fed's Foreign Currency Subcommittee (FCS) the temporary authority to authorize swap lines with foreign central banks as needed, without preset limits.[69] This way, the Fed could respond to changing conditions immediately, without needing to call an FOMC meeting for approval. Although central bank swaps were already an incredibly effective ILLR mechanism, Bernanke wanted to move them as close as possible to Bagehot's ideal of automatic and unlimited lending. Before his request went to a vote, Dudley briefed those in attendance on what had transpired in the hours since the Lehman shoe had dropped. Money market funds, he explained, were hemorrhaging money and suffering from a serious liquidity problem as panicked investors withdrew their investments.[70] Breaking the buck, he explained, was a very real risk as "the capital resources of . . . the [money market funds are] often quite modest, so their ability to top up the money funds and keep them whole is quite limited."[71] The bloodletting from the money markets meant that the commercial paper market, already dealing with a lack of liquidity, had entered a deep freeze. Dudley went on to explain that stresses in the market were greatest in Europe. The lack of liquidity across the Atlantic raised the prospect of a European bank default and was "having a feedback effect on people's willingness to do business with one another in the broader market."[72]

After Dudley's briefing of the committee on the market's dramatic turn for the worst over the past 24 hours, discussion turned back to approving Bernanke's request for transferring swap authorization authority to the FCS. Making the case for the chairman's request for authority to authorize credit without limit, Dudley warned that any "notions of capacity" could be tested by markets. It was better, he felt, to "provide a backstop for the entire market." He then added, "If the program is open ended, the rollover risk problem goes away. If I lend you more dollars today, I don't have to worry about getting those dollars back because I always know that the facility is there."[73] In other words, the only way that money markets

---

69. The FCS consisted of the chairman of the Federal Reserve (Bernanke), the vice chairman of the FOMC (Geithner), and the vice chairman of the Board of Governors (Donald Kohn).

70. Specifically, Dudley pointed to the Reserve Fund, which, as discussed above, ultimately did "break the buck" after Lehman's collapse triggered investors to withdraw their savings in a race for the exits. Governor Rosengren also warned about another money market fund, backed by State Street Global Advisors—a massive asset management firm in Boston, Massachusetts—which paid out $20 billion to terrified investors on September 15, that on its own did not "have sufficient capital to make people whole" (FOMC 2008f, p. 7).

71. FOMC 2008f, pp. 3–5.

72. Ibid., pp. 4, 10.

73. Ibid., pp. 11, 17.

and banks both at home and abroad would continue to lend to each other, thereby preventing the collapse of the US and global financial systems, was if some ILLR was willing to provide dollars without limit. The only actor capable of doing this was the Fed. Ultimately, the committee unanimously approved Bernanke's request to give complete swap authorization authority to the FCS through January 30, 2009.[74] Over the course of the next 40 days, the swap program grew from two participating foreign central banks to 10 and from an aggregate total of $67 billion to unlimited in size.[75]

5.4. Swap Lines for Four Emerging Markets: October 29, 2008

Although the FOMC had granted full authority to the FCS to authorize swap agreements with foreign central banks as needed, Bernanke still brought such proposals before the full committee for a vote on several occasions.[76] One such occasion came on October 29, when the FCS wanted to include four EMEs in the swap program. Historically, the Fed had only opened swap lines with other advanced industrial economies—Mexico, being the one notable exception. Before taking such an unprecedented step, Bernanke wanted the FOMC's blessing. In the days after Lehman's demise, the global financial system had not healed itself. A major, historic money market fund, the Reserve Fund, broke the buck. The result was a "wholesale flight out of prime institutional money market funds" and even further tightening in the commercial paper market.[77] During a conference call earlier that month, Bernanke painted the grim picture: "It's more than obvious that we have an extraordinary situation. It is not a single market . . . . Virtually all the markets—particularly the credit markets—are not functioning . . . . It's creating enormous risks for the global economy."[78]

Within the context of this global economic tailspin, a number of EMEs approached the Fed, interested in establishing swap lines with the US

---

74. Ibid., p. 18.

75. Most of the conversations related to the expansion of the swap program during this period took place among the FCS and, consequently, there are no publicly available records to review. However, at one meeting after the FOMC granted swap authorization authority to the FCS, Dudley remarked, "All of the foreign central banks that have obtained dollar swap lines in response to dollar funding pressures in their home markets have decided, *with some encouragement on our part*, to seek an increase in the size of these swap line authorizations" (FOMC 2008g, p. 4; emphasis added). Thus, it appears that just as the Fed initiated swap discussions with the ECB and SNB in August 2007, it also initiated talks to increase the size of the lines.

76. In each case, the FOMC voted unanimously to increase the size of the program.

77. FOMC 2008g, p. 30.

78. FOMC 2008h, p. 12.

ILLR. Among the countries that had asked for help, the FCS felt that four were deserving: Brazil, Mexico, Singapore, and South Korea. The FCS had proposed that the lines be $30 billion in size and come with additional "safeguards" that were not included as part of the agreements with the industrialized countries. In particular, even after authorization of the lines, the FCS would cap individual drawings at $5 billion and would not permit drawings without the approval of the FCS. Thus, the Fed could ensure that the credits were being used "in a manner consistent with the purposes of the swap agreement." A Fed economist, Nathan Sheets, explained that these four EMEs were appropriate candidates for three reasons. First, they were all large economies with "significant financial mass"; thus, "a further intensification of stresses in one or more of these countries could trigger unwelcome spillovers for both the US economy and the international economy more generally."[79] Second, these countries had all pursued "prudent" economic policies in recent years. Third, the FCS felt that the swap lines would help diffuse financial pressures facing these countries.[80] Later, the members were also informed that the dollar had strengthened considerably against the currencies of major trading partners and that "effective exchange values of the currencies of Brazil, Mexico, and Korea were particularly hard hit."[81]

The proposal raised some concerns among the committee. Charles Plosser, the president of the Reserve Bank of Philadelphia, wondered why these countries should not go to the IMF for assistance, adding "I just don't know where this ends." The exchange that followed once again highlights the inadequacy of the Fund as an ILLR during the crisis:

CHAIRMAN BERNANKE. President Plosser, a couple of things. The IMF has very limited resources. They're not remotely able to meet the needs of—

MR. PLOSSER. We don't know what the needs are yet, do we?

CHAIRMAN BERNANKE. Well, the resources are very limited . . .

MR. SHEETS. Just to put some numbers on IMF lending capacity— total IMF lending capacity is about $250 billion. To get even that high they have to call in some special arrangements that they have with a variety of countries. The maximum capacity is $250 billion. So the $120 billion that we're proposing today would be essentially half of what the IMF could do. In that sense I really see what

79. Later, Sheets referred to these four EMEs as being "systemically important" (FOMC 2008i, p. 33).

80. FOMC 2008i, p. 10. Bernanke also added that both the Treasury and State Departments had been consulted and each agreed that if EMEs were going to be included, this was the proper group.

81. FOMC 2008i, p. 52.

we're proposing as our taking off the IMF's hands some of the largest potential liquidity needs, which then allows them to focus on a whole range of additional countries.[82]

Another concern expressed was that there was a risk these countries would not pay the Fed back in full. However, Sheets pointed out that because each of these countries held substantial dollar-denominated assets in reserve at the New York Fed, this was not a concern. In the event an EME defaulted on a swap, Sheets explained, "We can take other assets on the books . . . to extinguish those liabilities." Geithner echoed this point, saying that the Fed could "take assets from their accounts to cover any loss," adding that the swaps were "a mechanism to help them transform the composition of their dollar reserves in a way that might be more effective in responding to lender-of-last-resort needs in dollars, rather than having to sell Treasuries . . . in a period of panic or distress to meet that cash need." Another member suggested that rather than accepting local currency as collateral, the Fed should require US Treasury bonds. In other words, the EMEs should have to put up their dollar reserves in order to get access to dollar swaps. However, several members spoke up saying that such a condition would "stigmatize" and "insult" these countries.[83]

Finally, some committee members were also worried that approving these swaps would open Pandora's Box by sending a signal that Fed swaps were available for all EMEs. When asked if other EMEs had asked for help, Sheets replied in the affirmative and listed the countries (which have been redacted from FOMC transcripts). Bernanke interjected: "But we have not encouraged that." Sheets quipped, "We have done everything we possibly can to discourage it . . . . We're not advertising."[84] In the end, the FOMC again unanimously moved to authorize the four EME swap lines. However, the committee did not agree to authorize the FCS to increase or authorize additional EME lines, preferring to set the bar for additional countries high and require full FOMC approval. In the end, the committee did not add new countries to the swap program or increase any existing swaps in size. The committee renewed all lines two more times in 2009 before it allowed the lines to expire in February 2010.

6. CONCLUSIONS

This chapter began with a question: What motivated the Fed to provide an unprecedented amount of liquidity to the global financial system

82. Ibid., pp. 36–37.
83. Ibid., pp. 19, 21.
84. Ibid., p. 30.

during the Great Panic of 2008? This chapter argues that the primary reason the Fed was motivated to act as an ILLR during the crisis was a desire to protect the stability of the US financial system from the threat of a foreign default. Alongside this was a secondary desire to improve the transmission of the Fed's interest-rate cuts to the real economy—a transmission that was impaired by the shortage of global dollar liquidity. In support of the argument, this chapter presents a variety of evidence. First, it reconstructs the unprecedented level of systemic risk facing the US financial system from foreign—primarily European—banks. Major US banks and, especially, money market funds were facing an existential crisis in the fall of 2008 and winter of 2009. Statistical analysis bears this out as increased exposure of the US financial system to a foreign jurisdiction is strongly associated with the probability of receiving a Fed swap line. The chapter also explains the unfortunate relationship between global dollar scarcity and a rising Libor rate. This was threatening to further intensify the US housing crisis by causing ARMs to reset at higher rates, despite interest-rate cuts at the Fed.

Finally, a chronological review of FOMC transcripts provided additional support for my argument as well as new details about the monetary authority's ILLR actions. Concerns about the effect that an elevated Libor had on the transmission of the Fed's interest-rate cuts were clearly a contributing factor in the Fed's decision to provide liquidity to Europe during the second stage of the program. Members discussed the link between growing strains in interbank market lending, rising Libor rates, and financial contracts like ARMs that were being adversely affected by these changes—despite their institution's aggressive rate cuts. FOMC members were also informed that preliminary evidence from the swap lines suggested that providing additional liquidity to Europe had a chance of bringing Libor down. However, discussions about the dollar shortage's effects on monetary policy implementation fell by the wayside after September 15, when the focus—for obvious reasons—shifted to preventing a total collapse of the US and global financial systems.

If the transcripts reveal anything, it is that, from beginning to end, fears about financial exposure were the primary driver behind the Fed's decision to act as an ILLR. In particular, FOMC minutes reveal that policymakers were most concerned about the retrenchment of money market funds in the commercial paper market and the direct effect this was having on dollar funding in Europe. Meeting after meeting, throughout the crisis, these concerns were shared and directly linked to the "liquidity backstop" that the Fed ultimately provided to the market. The committee worried that money market funds would "walk away" from international funding markets and leave European banks with unfunded dollar-denominated assets; that foreign banks would be unable to finance these assets; that depositors would panic and withdraw investments en masse; that major prime funds would "break the buck"; that the international, trillion-dollar commercial paper market dependent on these institutions would disappear; that illiquid commercial banks at home and abroad would turn into insolvent ones. In sum, all of the evidence strongly supports the assertion that the chief motivation behind the Fed's ILLR actions was an interest in protecting the stability of the US financial system from existential risk.

CHAPTER 8

Conclusions

The situation in Europe poses significant risks to the US financial system and economy and must be monitored closely. As always, the Federal Reserve remains prepared to take action as needed to protect the US financial system and economy in the event that financial stresses escalate.

> Ben Bernanke (Testimony before the Joint Economic
> Committee, US Congress, June 7, 2012)

We are right now involved with bailing out Europe and especially bailing out Greece. And we're doing this through the Federal Reserve. The Federal Reserve does this with currency swaps . . . . So this is placing the burden on the American tax payers, not by direct taxation, but by expanding the money supply.

> Rep. Ron Paul (Speech before the US House of Representatives, May 11, 2010)

Financial markets are prone to breakdown. In times of crisis when capital is no longer being effectively or efficiently allocated within an economy, it is the responsibility of the lender of last resort to swiftly provide as much liquidity as is necessary to stem the panic and prevent otherwise healthy institutions from failing. Today, national financial markets are imbedded within a much larger *global* financial market. For more than 50 years, the incremental process by which finance has become globalized has meant that the lines separating national financial markets from one another have grown increasingly blurry over time. The capital controls of Bretton Woods that once divided national systems gave way to a transatlantic financial market in the 1960s. This gave way to a truly global banking system in the 1970s and 1980s, which was then joined by the global portfolio investment market in the 1990s. The 2000s witnessed exponential growth across a range of global capital markets tied to the US housing sector. In this environment, crises in one locale are now rarely contained within national borders. Typically, the effects of financial crises spill over state boundaries and inhibit the ability of financial markets to distribute capital *internationally*. In such circumstances, the provision of international liquidity becomes necessary to stabilize markets. However, without a formal international lender of last resort (ILLR), it is unclear where the provision of this public good is to come from.

The International Monetary Fund (IMF) is most commonly associated with the ILLR role. Yet, as I have shown here, it is a misconception to conclude that the Fund has exclusively performed this function since its creation. In fact, time and time again, the United States has implemented unilateral ILLR actions by providing emergency liquidity directly to foreign jurisdictions in crisis when policymakers believed a multilateral response via the IMF was either too slow or too small. In short, this book shows how the globalization of finance has resulted in the *globalization of the US lender of last resort mechanism*. Over a 50-year period, the United States has repeatedly adapted to the changing nature of the international financial system. It has responded to unexpected and sometimes unprecedented crises that the existing structures of international financial governance were ill equipped to address. In this concluding chapter, I summarize the contributions of this book to the literature on international financial crisis management. This is followed by a consideration of the United States as an ILLR moving into the future. Finally, I discuss the policy implications of my research and offer a few closing thoughts.

1. CONTRIBUTIONS

Until very recently, a survey of existing analyses on the political economy of international financial crisis management would turn up a bevy of studies on the IMF with only a select few articles or chapters focusing on the role of any other actors. It should come as no surprise then that in the popular academic imagination, the IMF has conventionally been viewed as the de facto ILLR. It is the Fund that typically provides international financial "bailouts" to countries in distress. Although work on this subject has generated many important findings about the nature of IMF lending, the fixation on the Fund has painted an incomplete picture of how international financial crises are managed. In particular, scholars have for too long overlooked how the United States has responded to such situations and how US actions are directly related to the Fund's limitations as an ILLR. I have argued that in order to understand US ILLR actions, we must also understand the IMF's limitations as a financial crisis manager. Created in a world without capital mobility and designed to manage crises that developed slowly in the current account, the Fund falls short of Walter Bagehot's ideal-type lender of last resort that provides liquidity automatically and without limit. The changing nature of global finance has repeatedly called into question the IMF's ability to manage international crises as they develop. I have documented how, at different points in history, the problems of resource insufficiency and unresponsiveness—embedded in the IMF's multilateral character—have rendered the institution an ineffectual ILLR. Although US policymakers would prefer to allow the IMF to manage the problem and not put national resources at risk, situations sometimes arise where the Fund's inability to stem a panic would threaten vital US economic interests. In such cases, the United States tends to step in and act as an ILLR unilaterally in order to defend its economy from potentially destabilizing foreign shocks.

Besides highlighting the overlooked role of the United States as an ILLR, this project also contributes to the literature on international financial crisis management by making the case for why the United States is ideally positioned to act as an ILLR in the first place. The recent fixation on the role of the IMF led scholars to ignore not only the empirical role the United States has played in this regard, but also the theoretical reasons as to why the United States is in fact better positioned to perform the ILLR function. US actions during the 2008 financial crises clearly illustrate this point. The Federal Reserve is the closest thing in the international system to a Bagehot-style ILLR by virtue of its ability to act quickly and independently and, most importantly, to create the world's most global currency—the dollar. In lieu of the creation of a new global currency unit like John Maynard Keynes's "bancor," the United States will maintain this unique capability so long as the dollar remains the world's top currency. For the foreseeable future, this is a position it is likely to hold. Because of the inertia associated with monetary dominance, top international currencies tend to maintain their preeminent position for years—even after their issuer has ceased to be the world's top economic power. Thus, the United States should maintain its capacity to act as an ILLR despite relative economic decline vis-à-vis the rest of the world for years to come.[1] Indeed, despite the decline in the relative size of the US economy over the past few decades, several recent studies have shown that since 2008 the US financial system and the dollar have actually increased their structural

---

1. For more on the lag time between economic decline and top currency transition, see Krugman (1992), Eichengreen and Flandreau (2008), and Eichengreen (2011). For a broader dicussion of why the dollar is likely to maintain its dominance see Drezner (2010).

dominance in the global economy.[2] This bodes well for the longevity of US ILLR capabilities.

Finally, another contribution of this project is uncovering the motivations behind US ILLR actions. First, my empirical analyses acknowledge and consider the role that systemic conditions play in determining state action. Much prominent analysis in international political economy explains the international economic policy choices of states by focusing exclusively on domestic-level variables. This comes at a cost: neglecting the fact that systemic conditions external to the state could also influence decision making. Within the context of this study, I focused carefully on two potential causal pathways linking the US financial system and ILLR actions: protecting private financial interests, or protecting the broader, *national* financial interests. The distinction is an incredibly important one, yet the ability to distinguish between the two is admittedly quite hard. The difficulty in disaggregating policymakers' motivations is obvious in the primary source data I presented in this study (for instance, when members of Congress charged that a foreign bailout was designed to protect Goldman Sachs' profits while Treasury officials claimed it was intended to prevent financial instability from reaching the US banking system). Although numerous studies investigating variation in IMF lending have found statistical correlations between US bank exposure on one hand and larger loans and easier terms from the Fund on the other, researchers have typically made no distinction between the two potential causal pathways that may be driving the observed outcome. In this book, I have relied on primary historical documents as well statistical analysis to, as best as possible, distinguish between these two pathways. By accounting for the systemic risk facing the US financial system from foreign crises, I placed each potential bailout decision within the broader global risk climate. As my empirical results indicate, systemic context matters. US officials are most likely to provide foreign bailouts when both private and public interests converge. Thus, at the domestic level, US foreign rescues reflect a joint product model where two outputs are produced by the same process. In this case, the joint outputs are protecting the private financial interests of major banks while also protecting the stability of the national financial system.

Similarly, at the international level, US ILLR actions fit with traditional notions of hegemonic stability pioneered by Charles Kindleberger. Without question, this book supports the claim that the world's leading economy does in fact regularly provide the global public good of financial

---

2. Cohen and Benney 2014; Oatley et al. 2013; Winecoff 2015.

stability. Yet, as I have argued here, US officials are not motivated to rescue foreign economies for benevolent reasons. Rather, their actions are both defensive and self-interested. This is evidenced by the fact that both the US Treasury and the Federal Reserve have historically been quite picky about whom they rescue. That is, they have a strong propensity to respond to those economies in crisis where the US financial system is most exposed and tend to ignore those countries where direct risks are minimal. Thus, coincidentally, at the interstate level, US foreign rescues also reflect a joint product model where both the US and global financial systems are simultaneously stabilized.[3]

2. THE FUTURE OF THE UNITED STATES AS AN ILLR

Is the United States likely to continue acting as an ILLR in the event of future international financial crises? The 2008 financial crisis, the relative economic decline of the United States, and the recent debt crisis in Europe have led some to question the United States' ability and willingness to stabilize the global financial system in the face of future crises.[4] One very prominent scholar of international relations, G. John Ikenberry, noted in a recent book that

> in previous postwar economic crises, the United States played a role—directly or indirectly—in stabilizing global markets. The most recent financial crisis was unique in that the United States was the source of the instability. Whether it can return to the position of global economic leader remains uncertain.[5]

Ikenberry is correct that the United States was the source of instability. Yet he ignores the fact that the Fed also played the role of international stabilizer by providing unprecedented global liquidity via its swap program. Ikenberry's concern about the future of the United States as a global "economic leader," however, is echoed frequently in the post-2008 public sphere. For example, another prominent scholar of international relations recently wrote, "The hegemon is supposed to be the lender of last resort in

---

3. I am indebted to Jeffry Frieden for bringing the joint product model point to my attention.

4. Such assertions are reminiscent of similar premature claims that were made about US decline and ILLR capabilities by very prominent scholars in decades past. See Kindleberger 1986, p. 9 and Eichengreen 1995, pp. 238–239. These arguments are discussed in more detail in chapter 2.

5. Ikenberry 2011, p. 299.

the international economy. The United States, however, has become the borrower of first resort—the world's largest debtor."[6] One newspaper columnist raised similar questions about US ILLR capabilities post-2008:

> In 1995, the U.S. Treasury single-handedly rescued Mexico when its peso and economy collapsed. Two years later, acting through the International Monetary Fund, Washington played a crucial role in stabilizing the Asian financial crisis. And as late as the spring of 2009, a freshly inaugurated Obama arrived at a summit in London like a white knight, marshaling support for a synchronized international stimulus to avert a global meltdown . . . . In one international crisis after another, the U.S. has long been front and center in leading the way out. But not this time. As countries with economies as small as Australia's stepped up Thursday to pledge money for Europe's bailout fund, President Obama made no such commitment.[7]

Such comments are representative of a decline narrative as it relates to US ILLR capabilities. The economic decline of the United States, the narrative says, limits the ability and saps the willingness of US officials to provide global public goods like international liquidity in times of crisis. As it relates to Europe's debt woes, the assertion is that *if* the United States still had the ability, surely it would have bailed out Europe when it was in the darkest days of the debt crisis.[8] The apparent lack of a US response is interpreted as evidence of the country's declining economic capabilities. How accurate is this position? Is the United States no longer able to provide international liquidity in times of crisis? And, if so, does this not run counter to my contention that, by virtue of the dollar's key role in the global financial system, the United States will retain its ILLR capacity for many years to come?

On at least two counts, the decline narrative is wrong. First, although the United States has not contributed to Europe's new "bailout" funds, it provided ample financial assistance to Europe via new unlimited currency swap lines with the Federal Reserve. While the Fed's swap program was allowed to expire in February 2010, the US monetary authority reopened "precautionary" swap lines with the European Central Bank (ECB) on May 9, 2010. The Fed also reopened swap lines with Canada, Japan, Switzerland, and the United Kingdom. It was around this time that the earliest signs of debt troubles in Europe were appearing. Indeed, the events leading up to the reopening of the swap lines looked eerily similar to the events in the summer of 2007. The dollar Libor rate was rising daily,

6. Layne 2012, p. 210.
7. Parsons and Lee 2011.
8. For another column with a similar perspective, see Cooper (2011).

Table 8.1 FED SWAP LINE TIMELINE, 2010–2012

	05/09/ 2011	12/21/ 2010	06/90/ 2011	11/30/ 2011	12/13/ 2012	10/31/ 2013*
Bank of Canada	$30 bn	$30 bn	$30 bn	$30 bn	$30 bn	$30 bn
Bank of England	∞	∞	∞	∞	∞	∞
Bank of Japan	∞	∞	∞	∞	∞	∞
European Central Bank	∞	∞	∞	∞	∞	∞
Swiss National Bank	∞	∞	∞	∞	∞	∞

*Swap lines effectively made permanent and reciprocal.

rates on commercial paper were increasing, and markets were getting worried. In practice, these swap lines work exactly the same as those open between December 2007 and February 2010, as discussed in chapter 6. Table 8.1 lists the partners and the size of the swaps (∞ = unlimited). Each column indicates the date on which the five lines were extended.[9] In October 2013, the swap lines were extended indefinitely, making them effectively permanent.

These new swap lines went largely unused until the winter of 2011 as global credit conditions began to worsen on fears of the exposure of major European banks to bad sovereign debt. At that time, the ECB—along with other partner central banks—ramped up their borrowing. Around that same time, fears began to increase that the IMF did not have enough resources to put out the European fire were it to spread from countries like Greece and Portugal to larger economies in the region. These fears emerged despite the fact that the Fund had substantially increased its resources in the years following the 2008 crisis. At the end of 2011, the IMF had roughly $400 billion at its disposal; however, $168 billion of that had already been committed to member countries—$66 billion to Greece, Ireland, and Portugal alone. If countries like Italy or Spain (economies roughly eight and five times the size of Greece, respectively) required IMF assistance, the institution's capability to meet the needs of its members would have been called into question. Despite its increased financial war chest, global financial conditions were once again pointing to the problem of resource insufficiency. Moreover, if the crisis spread to the major economies of Europe, the US financial system would once again come face-to-face with the potential for a systemic crisis at home. It was within this context that European borrowing from the Fed began to pick

9. For more information, see http://www.newyorkfed.org/markets/liquidity_swap.html.

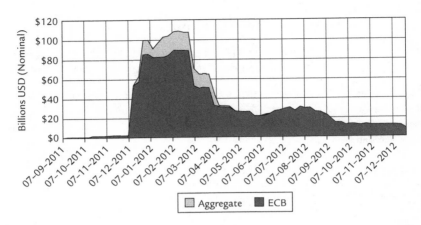

Figure 8.1
Federal Reserve Swap Line Credits, 2011–2012

up again. Figure 8.1 presents the weekly outstanding balance of the Fed's swap program, plotting ECB borrowing as well as aggregate borrowing (including all five partners) from the US central bank. As the figure shows, borrowing from the Fed topped $100 billion in late 2011. Thus, the decline narrative ignores the fact that the United States *did* act as an ILLR during the European crisis in a substantial way.

Yet some may still suggest that had these events unfolded at the height of US economic might, the United States would have provided direct assistance to Greece. This hints at the second problem with the decline narrative: Waning US economic power does not explain the difference between the US reaction to the European crisis and its reactions to the major financial crises in the past. In fact, the narrative ignores another very important contrast between the Mexican and East Asian crises on one hand and the Greek crisis on the other: the degree to which the US financial system was threatened by the countries engulfed in crisis. When systemic risk is elevated, US officials should be most likely to respond to crises in countries where the US financial system is most exposed because intervening in these cases will have the greatest likelihood of preventing destabilizing spillovers. When the US Treasury put together a multibillion-dollar rescue package for Mexico in 1995, around 6 percent of major American banks' foreign claims were concentrated in Mexico. Two years later, in 1997, when the Asian financial crisis erupted, US banks were exposed to South Korea and Indonesia to the tune of 5 percent of total foreign claims. By contrast, the degree to which US banks were exposed to Greece in 2011—the epicenter of the European crisis—was minuscule. For example, in the fourth quarter of 2011, claims against the

Greek financial system represent roughly one-quarter of 1 percent of total US bank foreign claims.

This helps explain why the United States aimed its assistance at the ECB rather than Greece directly. The United States has rarely, if ever, acted as an ILLR for charity's sake. Its motives are self-interested: to protect the US financial system from serious instability that might spill over from financial crises abroad. A May 2010 Fed statement describing the swaps explained, "These facilities are designed to help improve liquidity conditions in US dollar funding markets and to prevent the spread of strains to other markets and financial centers."[10] On its own, the threat from Greece simply did not merit a direct response. Of course, if Greece were to have defaulted in a disorderly fashion, this could have caused significant losses to banks in France, Germany, and other major economies in the Eurozone. These are economies where US financial institutions had much larger exposures. Interbank lending, which was already tight in light of the European problem, would have likely been further squeezed. In short, systemic risk conditions would have been similar to those in the fall of 2008.[11] In such an event, the Greek crisis could have become much more of a US problem. This is precisely what the Fed's liquidity lines were put in place for. They were designed to provide dollars to European banks so that they could continue to meet their obligations to US financial institutions as dollar-funding markets tightened. As the Federal Reserve regional president Charles Plosser explained when the new lines were opened, the Fed was doing what was necessary to "protect our financial institutions."[12] Similarly, Fed Chairman Ben Bernanke explained to congressional leaders that the situation in Europe "was basically a European problem but with ramifications ... [for] our banks and our banking system if there was no intervention."[13] In other words, the US response to the European debt crisis was quite consistent with its past ILLR actions. It might be tempting to conclude that the United States is no longer a capable ILLR, but that conclusion would be wrong.

However, the United States' ILLR capabilities are not immune to degradation. The most prominent threat does not come from a rising economic

10. Federal Reserve Press Release, May 9, 2010, http://www.federalreserve.gov/newsevents/press/monetary/20100509a.htm.

11. Indeed, in testimony before a House subcommittee, one Fed official explained that there was the possibility for a worst-case scenario where financial strains "could lead to a replay of the freezing up of financial markets that we witnessed in 2008" (Aversa 2010).

12. Hilsenrath 2010.

13. Quote is from Senator Richard Shelby of Alabama, paraphrasing what Bernanke told the Senate Banking panel after a closed-door meeting regarding the reopening of the swap lines. See Felsenthal and Somerville (2010).

rival or the specter of US decline, however. It comes from Congress. The Federal Reserve's foreign lending in 2008–2009 and again in 2010–2011 raised the ire of many on Capitol Hill. This is important because the Fed's authority is derived from Congress. Thus, it must "maintain congressional support to protect itself from legislative challenges."[14] In recent years, there have been a number of efforts to curtail the Fed's political independence and impose increased transparency on the institution. As part of the Dodd-Frank financial overhaul law, for instance, the Fed's ability to provide liquidity to specific banks in trouble was constrained.[15] Beginning in 2009, Ron Paul (R-TX) launched the most prominent effort to rein in the Fed's powers with his "Audit the Fed" movement. Paul and his supporters sought to pass legislation that would curtail the Fed's powers to provide liquidity during crises. For example, a report on the Federal Reserve Transparency Act of 2014 summarizes the movement's intended reforms. Among other things, it would enable the Government Accountability Office (GAO) to audit "any of the Federal Reserve's transactions involving a foreign central bank, the government of a foreign country, or a non-private international financing organization."[16] The US House of Representatives passed this bill in September 2014. However, sister legislation did not pass in the Senate. Nonetheless, this is exemplary of the kind of action Congress may take if the political climate surrounding the Fed continues to worsen.

The possibility of such scrutiny, especially during times of crisis, could cause the Fed to think twice about providing assistance to foreign jurisdictions in crisis. Indeed, one need only look to the Treasury's use of Exchange Stabilization Fund (ESF) funds for foreign rescues after Congress voted to increase scrutiny of that ILLR mechanism in 1995. Without question, the heightened political attention on US emergency foreign lending in the 1990s dampened the Clinton administration's appetite for providing global liquidity. Increased political attention today could have a similar chilling effect on the Fed's desire to act as an ILLR in the future. As I argued in chapter 2, a key reason the United States has been so well positioned to manage international financial crises over the last 60 years is because its ILLR mechanisms are *independent* of Congress. To be most effective, the lender of last resort must be able to act quickly and without reservation or fear of reprisal. The threat of increased political scrutiny and, perhaps, even curtailed powers is a far greater threat to

14. Broz 2015, p. 325.
15. Harrison 2015.
16. Congressional Budget Office 2014.

the United States' ILLR capability moving forward than relative economic decline.

3. POLICY IMPLICATIONS

A central theme of this book has been to raise questions about the adequacy of the IMF as the world's de facto ILLR. The historical narrative of this project highlights that, almost since its inception, the Fund has been afflicted with two chronic institutional flaws. The Fund has consistently found itself playing catch-up to the winds of change in global finance rather than anticipating these changes and adapting in order to better function as a global financial crisis manager. The story of the IMF's evolution as the de facto ILLR has been one of *reaction* rather than *preemption*. Of course, it is a bit unfair to criticize the Fund for not being able to predict the future. The problem is not so much the institution's lack of foresight, but rather its relative lack of flexibility. As I discussed early in this book, the Fund was not designed by its makers to function as an ILLR. Its lack of independence and inability to create liquidity are part of the institution's DNA.

The process of playing catch-up began in the 1960s with the creation of the General Arrangements to Borrow (GAB). Although this increased the Fund's access to lendable resources, it also exacerbated the problem of unresponsiveness through its cumbersome borrowing procedures. As debt crises rocked the developing world decades later, the Fund's unresponsiveness became especially acute as it implemented its concerted lending strategy. In addition, it was once again short on resources, seeking quota increases from member countries in 1980, 1983, and 1990. When demand for Fund credit outpaced its lending capacity, the Fund was forced to seek special supplementary loans from surplus economies.[17] In the aftermath of the Mexican peso crisis of 1994–1995, the IMF introduced the Emergency Financing Mechanism (EFM). This was designed to provide speedier loan approval. After the Asian financial crisis of the late 1990s, the Fund attempted to address the problems of resource insufficiency and unresponsiveness by creating two new mechanisms. The first was the Contingent Credit Line (CCL), which was designed to serve as "precautionary resources in the event of contagion from a crisis" and once again increasing quotas.[18] The second was the Supplemental Reserve

---

17. Boughton 2001, p. 44.
18. Bird and Rajan 2002, p. 6. The basic idea of the CCL was that a country could approach the Fund before a crisis to negotiate conditions in return for the promise of financing from

Facility (SRF), which was designed to provide "extra quick-disbursing resources to countries facing a crisis of confidence in financial markets."[19]

In the years since the 2008 global financial crisis, the IMF has once again sought to address its two chronic weaknesses. To minimize the problem of resource insufficiency, the Fund initially increased its lendable resource base by securing a number of large (temporary) bilateral commitments from some of its major shareholders. In 2010, the IMF agreed on quota reform that would permanently increase the institution's resources to roughly $660 billion—a deal that waited until late 2015 for US congressional approval. Besides increasing its aggregate resource base, the Fund changed the rules that limit how much individual countries can borrow in times of crisis. It did this by doubling both annual and cumulative access limits for member countries from 100 and 300 percent to 200 and 600 percent, respectively.[20] Without question, these adjustments are big improvements. They better position the IMF to address financial crises. Yet, despite these efforts, the fact remains that the IMF is still ill equipped to address a systemic global financial crisis on the order of 2008. As one scholar has explained, even with its increased lending capacity, "The IMF can hardly exert any systemic role in today's global financial system."[21]

The Fund has also taken steps to mitigate the problem of unresponsiveness. In particular, it introduced three new facilities designed to provide speedier financing to member states facing balance of payments crises: the Flexible Credit Line (FCL), the Precautionary and Liquidity Line (PLL), and the Rapid Credit Facility (RCF). The FCL is designed to provide countries with "strong fundamentals" with access to "large and up-front access to IMF resources with no ongoing conditions," while the purpose of the RCF is to provide "low access, rapid, and concessional financial assistance to [low-income countries]."[22] The PLL is quite similar to the FCL; however, it meets the needs of countries precluded from drawing on the FCL because of disqualifying economic vulnerabilities. At the time of this writing, three countries (Colombia, Mexico, and Poland) have used the FCL, while two countries (Macedonia and Morocco) have used the PLL. No member has yet to tap the RCF. Even the basic Stand-By Arrangement was overhauled after 2008 in order to make the workhorse facility more effective for members who may not qualify for an FCL

outside the IMF's quota-based resources in the event of a financial crisis. However, in practice the CCL proved to be very unpopular and, during the relatively calm 2000s, it was deemed unnecessary and allowed to "expire" as a facility in November 2008.

19. Boughton 2000, p. 277.
20. IMF 2009.
21. Lombardi 2012.
22. IMF 2012b; IMF 2012c.

arrangement "by providing increased flexibility to front-load access" intended to improve its "crisis prevention and crisis resolution" performance.[23] Of course, the effectiveness of these reforms remains to be seen. As one recent paper on the subject put it, "The recent strengthening of IMF resources and redesigning of instruments, while a move in the right direction, met the demand of only a few countries, and its effectiveness as a protective safety belt remains largely untested."[24] As has been the case with nearly all of its previous reforms, these changes may in fact be too little, too late.

By contrast, the United States has the ability to compensate for the Fund's institutional flaws through the provision of liquidity via the Fed or Treasury. Yet, as the evidence presented here has shown, US rescues are highly discretionary and selective. Typically, only countries where the United States has sizable financial interests find themselves on the receiving end of a US bailout. This paints an unflattering picture of global financial governance when it comes to equity and fairness. This is especially the case when paired with existing empirical research that has shown IMF lending tends to favor countries with close political and economic ties to the United States (and other advanced economies). The picture that emerges is an overtly two-tiered ILLR system. Countries of financial import to the United States are far more likely to receive swift or supplemental US bailouts as well as preferential treatment under an IMF arrangement. Countries where US interests are not so prominent, conversely, are left with less-responsive and less-robust ILLR mechanisms.

In light of the Fund's chronic flaws as an ILLR, the remaining risks facing the global financial system, and the global economy's tepid recovery, policymakers should consider the value of a permanent central bank swap regime. Such a system would be a revival of the system discussed in chapter 3 that existed from 1962 until 1998. Among six major central banks, such a system has already re-emerged. As noted above, in 2013, the Fed, Bank of Canada, Bank of England, Bank of Japan, ECB, and the Swiss National Bank made permanent their network of unlimited reciprocal central bank swap lines. However, this leaves out all emerging market economies that, arguably, are most vulnerable to financial shocks. This is especially true as the world's major central banks unwind years of unconventional monetary policy. One option is a reciprocal swap regime that includes all members of the newly empowered Group of 20 (G-20). A G-20 swap network, with the Fed at the center, would provide markets with

23. IMF 2009b, p. 3.
24. Fernandez-Arias and Levy-Yeyati 2010, p. 2.

confidence that the world's largest economies have access to a large volume of liquidity, which can be released at a moment's notice. Moreover, it could have the added benefit of helping to correct global imbalances by giving emerging market economies an added sense of security against financial crises, reducing their incentive to build up large stocks of foreign exchange reserves for self-defense.

Such a network today would work much like it did in the 1960s when the intended design was to create a system where short-term shocks could be addressed directly via central bank cooperation, while the IMF would work to correct longer-term imbalances. Of course, the likelihood of such a plan hinges on the political will of the countries involved, especially the United States. If recent history is any indication, the prospects do not look good. South Korea discovered this when it suggested just such a system in the spring of 2010, as it assumed the presidency of the G-20.[25] The proposal gained no traction and was essentially dead on arrival.[26] In the meantime, emerging market economies have been busy signing both multilateral and bilateral swap agreements with each other as a means of insulating their economies from financial tumult. On the multilateral front, the Chiang Mai Initiative (CMI) beefed up its East Asian crisis-management capabilities in 2012, including a doubling of its lending capacity to $240 billion.[27] In 2014, the BRICS economies—Brazil, Russia, India, China, and South Africa—created the Contingent Reserve Arrangement (CRA): a $100 billion swap network designed to provide dollars to participating countries in times of crisis. On the bilateral side, India and South Korea have both actively sought bilateral swap deals with willing partners since 2008. Indeed, in 2013, the Indian government commissioned a "task force" to investigate the benefits of signing more such agreements.[28] Then there is China. Since 2008, the People's Bank of China has negotiated more than 30 swap deals with partner central banks.[29] Although the primary function of these agreements is to promote trade settlement in China's currency, they can also function as emergency credit lines. For example, in in 2014 and 2015, Argentina tapped its swap line with Beijing to a tune of $2.3 billion to replenish its dwindling foreign exchange reserves.[30] This

25. As one South Korean official explained to the *Financial Times*, "Bilateral swaps are very effective, but they are negotiated individually at the moment. They are prisoners to circumstances" (Oliver 2010). In 2014, India's Finance Secretary similarly suggested that the IMF should study whether a G-20 swap network would address the threats facing emerging market economies (Sikarwar 2014).

26. Oliver 2010.

27. Grimes 2011. See also Adam and Sharp 2012.

28. *The Hindu* 2013.

29. Liao and McDowell 2015.

30. Devereux 2015.

is all part of an interesting trend that appears to be driven by financial insecurity. Because the IMF remains an imperfect ILLR and the United States is unwilling to provide *ex ante* assurances that it will come to the aid of emerging market economies when times get tough, vulnerable economies are looking to each other for help.

4. FINAL THOUGHTS

Given the events of the past decade, there are few issues more salient in the international political economy today than the management of international financial crises. Yet nearly all of the recent literature on the political economy of international financial crisis management has focused on IMF lending. Although important, this work has neglected the fact that for decades the United States regularly extended emergency loans to countries facing financial crises *outside* the Fund. Scholars of international political economy have failed to systematically investigate the political and economic determinants of bailouts that flow from one sovereign to another. This book takes the first step toward addressing these gaps by bringing the incredibly important role that the United States has played in managing international financial crises back into the discussion of the political economy of international bailouts. Indeed, I have shown that in many cases, the US role as an ILLR has been far more important than the IMF itself. In the end, one thing seems clear: So long as the IMF suffers from institutional inadequacies as an ILLR, so long as the United States retains this capacity, and so long as the US financial system has a global balance sheet, selective ILLR actions will remain a part of the US international economic policy toolkit. All that is missing is another crisis.

Appendix

CHAPTER 4: COX PROPORTIONAL HAZARD MODEL

In chapter 4, Figure 4.3 presents survival curve estimates of the probability a country's International Monetary Fund (IMF) loan request will still be waiting for approval after a given number of days. To create this figure, I first fit a cox proportional hazard model of IMF loan approval duration periods (the number of days that transpires between filing a letter of intent and the date on which the request was approved; dependent variable data are presented in Figure 4.2). The sample used includes 63 country requests for standby and extended fund facility arrangements from 1983 through 1987. These dates correspond with the IMF's use of the concerted lending strategy (McDowell 2016). I estimate a simple cox model where the foreign exposure of major American banks is the key covariate (same as the "Bank Exposure" variable discussed below) with year fixed effects and no additional controls. The coefficient for bank exposure is -17.1 (log hazard, nonexponentiated metric) and is statistically significant at the $p < 0.01$ level. This indicates that, at higher levels of bank exposure, borrowers were subject to longer waits for approval. To create Figure 4.3, I generated simulations using the R package Zelig to replicate estimates of survival rates at levels specified for covariates of interest while holding all other covariates at their means. Point estimates displayed are the median observation from the simulation at each day after the loan request, based on 1,000 sample replications. The results are in line with McDowell (2016).

CHAPTER 5: SELECTED VARIABLES
(SEE TABLE 5.1)

ESF Credit: The dependent variable is binary, taking on the values of 0 or 1 based on the presence or absence of an Exchange Stabilization Fund (ESF) credit for a country that appears within one year of a formal request for IMF assistance. ESF credits are not always immediately proximate to IMF requests. Thus, I use the one year (+/−) range. In some cases, ESF credits were many months in advance of IMF credits (bridge loans). In other cases, ESF credits were provided after an IMF loan was approved (supplemental loans). Cases where borrower countries received more than one ESF credit in a given year are also coded as 1. Thus, there is no distinction between the number of credits extended in a given year. Finally, of the 28 ESF credits included in the sample, 22 occur within one year of a request for IMF assistance. Thus, Treasury also extended six credits that do not coincide with a request from the borrower for IMF assistance as defined here. This raises a problem because including these six cases seems ad hoc in light of my sample selection procedures. Yet, excluding them may call into question my results with a number of cases excluded. In the analysis presented here, I estimate all models with these six cases included. However, as a robustness check, I estimated specifications excluding those six cases. The results of these separate tests were substantively unchanged with the financial interaction term remaining positive and statistically significant.

SIFI Bank Exposure: I measure US significantly important financial institution (SIFI) exposure as

$$ SIFI\ bank\ exposure_{i,t} = \left(\frac{SIFIclaims_{i,t-1}}{SIFIclaims_{t-1}} \right) * 100 $$

where $SIFIclaims$ is the total foreign claims of US SIFIs in country$_i$ at time$_{t-1}$ divided by the sum total of all foreign claims of US SIFIs in year$_{t-1}$. I then multiply this by 100 to yield a variable that accounts for country$_i$'s share of SIFIs' foreign portfolios in percentage terms. I construct this variable by using data I gathered from the US Country Exposure Lending Surveys (CELS). Specifically, I rely on consolidated, adjusted claims. Consolidated claims are the highest aggregate data type, which includes loans to both private and public (sovereign) sources. Adjusted claims, also referred to as "ultimate risk basis" data, assign claims to the country where the original risk lies, accounting for risk transfers between national banking systems. For instance, if a portion of a bank's loan to a foreign source is guaranteed by a foreign institution, the adjusted claims data will reflect this by sub-tracting the guaranteed claims from the total whereas unadjusted claims would not. Adjusted claims data are preferable to unadjusted because the latter can either over- or underestimate the extent of bank exposures. Indeed, as the Bank for International Settlements (BIS) explains on its statistics website, "The BIS consolidated international banking statistics on an ultimate risk basis are the most appropriate source for measuring the aggregate exposures of a banking system to a given country" (Avdjiev 2010). Because the CELS did not begin reporting bank capital data until 1982 and then changed how it was reported after 1998, I was forced to restrict the sample to ESF credits that occurred between 1983 and 1999. CELS reports from 1977 through 1996 are available at http://fraser.stlou-isfed.org/publication/?pid=333; reports from 1997 to present are available at http://www.ffiec.gov/e16.htm.

Systemic Risk: I measure systemic risk as

$$systemic\ risk_{i,t} = \frac{(\ SIFIclaims_{t-1} \mid IMF_t) - SIFIclaims_{i,t-1}}{SIFIcapital_{t-1}}.$$

were *SIFIclaims* is the sum total of consolidated adjusted foreign claims of US SIFIs in year$_{t-1}$ that requested a standby arrangement or extended fund facility loan from the IMF in year$_t$ (| *IMF$_t$*) less the consolidated adjusted foreign claims of banks to country$_i$ in year$_{t-1}$, divided by the total reported capital of money center banks in year$_t$ (*SIFIcapital$_{t-1}$*). To avoid double counting bank exposure to each country, I subtract SIFI claims in country$_i$ when calculating the numerator in the fraction. In other words, the model assumes that when deciding whether to provide an ESF credit to Argentina in 1984, US officials considered the concentration of bank claims to Argentina at that time within the context of the broader banking system's exposure to all other countries that were facing financial turmoil as indicated by approaching the IMF for assistance that year. Excluding Argentina's claims from the systemic context is appropriate since it is already factored into the model via the claim concentration measure. To put it differently, when estimating the likelihood that the United States will provide a bailout to Argentina in 1984, the attendant systemic risk variable will equal the total claims of SIFIs in all other countries (excluding Argentina) that asked for IMF assistance in 1984 over total SIFI bank capital in 1984.

Speculative Attack: Using monthly exchange rate and foreign exchange reserves data from the IMF International Financial Statistics database, I code this measure as 1 if the exchange market pressure

(EMP) index score is more than two standard deviations above the country mean (0 otherwise). I then annualized the data; the variable is equal to 1 if a speculative attack is present in any month of year t, and 0 otherwise. It is calculated as follows:

$$EMP_{i,t} = \frac{\Delta e_{i,t}}{\sigma \Delta_{ei}} - \frac{\Delta r_{i,t}}{\sigma \Delta_{ri}}$$

where e is the end-of-the-month US dollar exchange rate of country i and r is the end-of-the-month nongold reserves. A higher score on the index indicates increased pressure on a country's currency. I identify a speculative attack as:

$$EMP_{i,t} = 1 \text{ if } 2\sigma EMP_{i,t} + \mu EMP_1.$$

if 2 σEMP and μEMP are the country-specific mean and standard deviation of EMP, respectively. Consistent with Leblang (2002), the

Table A.1 SUMMARY STATISTICS

Variable	Obs.	Min	Max	Mean	Std.Dev.
ESF credit	179	0	1	0.16	0.36
GDP (log)	179	20.69	27.15	23.78	1.56
GDP per capita (log)	179	4.93	9.22	7.35	0.96
External debt service/exports	179	0.28	82.83	28.59	15.83
Current account balance	179	−300	78	−16.28	47.62
Reserves/GDP	179	0	0.29	0.05	0.05
GDP growth	179	−12.9	13.5	2.24	4.78
Speculative attack	179	0	1	0.55	0.49
Share of US trade	179	0	10.78	0.52	1.34
Latin America	179	0	1	0.46	0.5
Democracy (PolityIV)	179	−9	10	1.2	7.13
UN ideal point distance	179	1.47	4.4	2.92	0.56
US unemployment	178	4.5	9.7	6.75	1.5
US GDP growth	179	−1.98	7.19	3.05	2.2
Republican president	179	0	1	0.68	0.47
Year	179	0	16	7.06	4.83
Year^2	179	0	256	73.03	75.76
Year^3	179	0	4096	864.49	1146.15
SIFI bank exposure	179	0	10.05	0.92	1.88
Systemic risk	179	0.01	1.17	0.35	0.3

cut-off of two standard deviations above the mean is selected so that only extreme levels of exchange rate pressure are identified as speculative attacks. In my statistical models, observations were coded as 1 if $EMP = 1$ in the same year, or the year before, a country approached the IMF for a loan.

CHAPTER 7: VARIABLES (SEE TABLE 7.3)

US Financial System Exposure: I measure the exposure of the US financial system as

$$financial\ system\ exposure_{i,t} = \left(\frac{SIFIclaims_{i,t-1} + DEBTclaims_{i,t-1}}{SIFIclaims_{t-1} + DEBTclaims_{t-1}} \right) * 100.$$

were *SIFIclaims* is the total adjusted foreign claims of US SIFIs in country$_i$ at time$_{t-1}$ (December 2007) and *DEBTclaims* is the total US portfolio holdings of foreign debt securities in country$_i$ in year$_{t-1}$ (2007). These two measures are added together and then divided by the sum total of all foreign US SIFI claims and all US portfolio holdings of foreign debt securities. I then multiply this by 100 to yield a variable that accounts for country$_i$'s share of all US resident and SIFI foreign claims in percentage terms.

Table A.2 SUMMARY STATISTICS

Variable	Obs.	Min	Max	Mean	Std.Dev.
Swap line	63	0	1	0.22	0.42
Share of world GDP (%)	63	0.01	22.09	1.07	3.04
Inflation	63	−0.93	16.28	6.1	3.93
Share of US trade (%)	63	0	17.8	1.38	3.35
Global financial center	63	0	1	0.11	0.31
US financial system exposure (%)	63	0	21.78	1.09	3.44
Dollar liquidity shortage	34	−394.41	177.26	−10.31	91.86

BIBLIOGRAPHY

Abbott, Kenneth W., and Duncan Snidal. 1998. "Why States Act through Formal International Organizations." *Journal of Conflict Resolution* 42, no. 1: 3–32.

Acharya, Viral V., and Philipp Schnabl. 2010. "Do Global Banks Spread Global Imbalances: The Case of Asset-Backed Commercial Paper during the Financial Crisis of 2007–2009." NBER Working Paper, 16079. http://www.nber.org/papers/w16079. Accessed February 2011.

Adam, Shamim, and Andy Sharp. 2012, May 3. "Asia Doubles Reserve Pool to $240 Billion to Shield Region." *Bloomberg Business.* http://www.bloomberg.com/news/articles/2012-05-03/asia-set-to-double-reserve-pool-as-region-steps-up-cooperation.

Aggarwal, Vinod K. 1996. *Debt Games: Strategic Interaction in International Debt Rescheduling.* New York: Cambridge University Press.

Agrawal, Anoop, and Kartik Goyal. 2012, November 20. "US Hesitant on India's Currency Swap Proposal, Subbarao Says." *Bloomberg.* http://www.bloomberg.com/news/articles/2012-11-20/u-s-hesitant-on-india-s-currency-swap-proposal-subbarao-says. Accessed December 2012.

Ai, Chunrong, and Edward C. Norton. 2003. "Interaction Terms in Logit and Probit Models." *Economics Letters* 80, no. 1: 123–129.

Ainley, Michael. 1984. *The General Arrangements to Borrow.* Washington, DC: International Monetary Fund.

Aizenman, Joshua, and Jaewoo Lee. 2007. "International Reserves: Precautionary Versus Mercantilist Views, Theory and Evidence." *Open Economic Review* 18, no. 2: 191–214.

Aizenman, Joshua, and Gurnain Kaur Pasricha. 2010. "Selective Swap Arrangements and the Global Financial Crisis: Analysis and Interpretation." *International Review of Economics and Finance* 19, no. 3: 353–365.

Allen, William A. 2013. *International Liquidity and the Financial Crisis.* New York: Cambridge University Press.

Allen, William A., and Richhild Moessner. 2010. "Central Bank Co-operation and International Liquidity in the Financial Crisis of 2008–9." BIS Working Papers. No. 310. http://www.bis.org/publ/work310.pdf. Accessed April 2014.

Anderson, Robert B. 1960. "The Balance of Payments Problem." *Foreign Affairs.* April: 419–432.

Avdjiev, Stefan. 2010, June 8. "Measuring Banking Systems' Exposures to Particular Countries." http://www.bis.org/publ/qtrpdf/r_qt1006y.htm. Accessed August 2013.

Baba, Naohiko, and Frank Packer. 2009. "From Turmoil to Crisis: Dislocations in the FX Swap Market before and after the Failure of Lehman Brothers." *Journal of International Money and Finance* 28, no. 8: 1350–1374.

Baba, Naohiko, Robert N. McCauley, and Srichander Ramaswamy. 2009. "US Dollar Money Market Funds and Non-US Banks." *BIS Quarterly Review*, March: 65–81.

Bagehot, Walter. 1873. *Lombard Street: A Description of the Money Market*. London: Henry S. King and Company.

Bailey, Michael A., Anton Strezhnev, and Erik Voeten. 2015. "Estimating Dynamic State Preferences from United Nations Voting." *Journal of Conflict Resolution*, forthcoming.

Baring, Sir Francis. (1797) 1967. *Observations on the Establishment of the Bank of England*. Fairfield, NJ: A. M. Kelly.

Barro, Robert J. 2001. "Economic Growth in East Asia before and after the Financial Crisis." NBER Working Paper 8330. http://www.nber.org/papers/w14656. Accessed January 2011.

Bernanke, Ben S. 2015. *The Courage to Act: A Memoir of a Crisis and Its Aftermath*. New York: W. W. Norton.

Bird, Graham. 1996. "The International Monetary Fund and Developing Countries: A Review of the Evidence and Policy Options." *International Organization* 50, no. 3: 477–511.

Bird, Graham, and Ramkishen S. Rajan. 2002. "Regional Arrangements for Providing Liquidity in a Financial Crisis: Developments in Asia." *Pacific Review* 15, no. 3: 359–379.

Bird, Graham, and Dane Rowlands. 2004. "Does the IMF Perform a Catalytic Role? And What If It Doesn't?" *World Economics* 5, no. 1: 117–132.

BIS. 1983. "Fifty-Third Annual Report: 1st April 1982–31st March 1983." Basel, Switzerland.

Blue Book. 2008. "Monetary Policy Alternatives." FOMC. September 11. http://www.federalreserve.gov/monetarypolicy/files/FOMC20080916bluebook20080911.pdf. Accessed March 2014.

Blustein, Paul. 2001. *The Chastening: Inside the Crisis That Rocked the Global Financial System and Humbled the IMF*. New York: Public Affairs.

Bolton, Patrick, and David A. Skeel, Jr. 2005. "Redesigning the International Lender of Last Resort." *Chicago Journal of International Law* 6, no. 1: 177–201.

Boot, Max. 2002. "Doctrine of the 'Big Enchilada.'" *Washington Post*. 14 October.

Bordo, Michael D., and Harold James. 2000. "The International Monetary Fund: Its Present Role in Historical Perspective." *Greek Economic Review* 20, no. 2: 43–76.

Bordo, Michael D., and Anna J. Schwartz. 2001. "From the Exchange Stabilization Fund to the International Monetary Fund." NBER Working Paper 8100. http://www.nber.org/papers/w8100.pdf. Accessed April 2013.

Bordo, Michael D., Christopher M. Meissner, and David Stuckler. 2010. "Foreign Currency Debt, Financial Crises and Economic Growth: A Long Run View." *Journal of International Money and Finance* 29, no. 4: 642–665.

Boughton, James M. 2000. "From Suez to Tequilla: The IMF as Crisis Manager." *Economic Journal* 110, no. 460: 273–291.

———. 2001. *Silent Revolution: The International Monetary Fund, 1979–1989*. Washington, DC: International Monetary Fund.

———. 2002. "Why White, Not Keynes? Inventing the Postwar International Monetary System." IMF Working Paper. WP/02/52.

———. 2006. "American in the Shadows: Harry Dexter White and the Design of the International Monetary Fund." IMF Working Paper. WP/06/6.

———. 2012. *Tearing Down Walls: The International Monetary Fund, 1990–1999*. Washington, DC: International Monetary Fund.

Bremner, Robert P. 2004. *Chairman of the Fed: William McChesney Martin Jr. and the Creation of the Modern American Financial System*. New Haven, CT: Yale University Press.

Brooks, Stephen G., and William C. Wohlforth. 2005. "International Relations Theory and the Case against Unilateralism." *Perspectives on Politics* 3, no. 3: 509–524.

Broz, Lawrence. 1997. "The Domestic Politics of International Monetary Order: The Gold Standard." In *Contested Social Orders and International Politics*, edited by David Skidmore, 53–91. Nashville, TN: Vanderbilt University Press.

———. 2005. "Congressional Politics of International Financial Rescues." *American Journal of Political Science* 49, no. 3: 479–496.

———. 2011. "The United States Congress and IMF Financing, 1944–2009." *Review of International Organizations* 6, nos. 3–4: 341–368.

———. 2015. "The Politics of Rescuing the World's Financial System: The Federal Reserve as Global Lender of Last Resort, 2007–2010." *Korean Journal of International Studies*, 13, no. 2: 313–351.

Broz, J. Lawrence, and Michael Brewster Hawes. 2006. "Congressional Politics of Financing the International Monetary Fund." *International Organization* 60, no. 1: 367–399.

Calomiris, Charles W. 2000. "The IMF's Imprudent Role as Lender of Last Resort." *Cato Journal*, 17, no. 3: 275.

Calvo, Guillermo A. 1998. "Varieties of Capital-Market Crises." In *The Debt Burden and Its Consequences for Monetary Policy*, edited by Guillermo Calvo and Mervyn King, 181–202. New York: St. Martin's.

Capie, Forrest. 1998. "Can There Be an International Lender-of-Last-Resort?" *International Finance* 1, no. 2: 311–325.

Carter, David B., and Curtis Signorino. 2010. "Back to the Future: Modeling Time Dependence in Binary Data." *Political Analysis* 19, no. 3: 271–292.

Caskey, John P. 1989. "The IMF and Concerted Lending in Latin American Debt Restructurings: A Formal Analysis." *Journal of International Money and Finance* 8, no. 1: 105–120.

Clinton, Bill. 2004. *My Life*. New York: Knopf.

Coffey, Niall, Warren B. Hrung, Hoai-Luu Nguyen, and Asani Sarkar. 2009. "The Global Financial Crisis and Offshore Dollar Market." *Current Issues in Economics and Finance* 15, no. 6: 1–7.

Cohen, Benjamin J. 1971. *The Future of Sterling as an International Currency*. London: Macmillan.

———. 1982. "Balance-of-Payments Financing: Evolution of a Regime." *International Organization*. 36, no. 2: 457–478.

———. 1986. *In Whose Interest? International Banking and Foreign Policy*. New Haven, CT: Yale University Press.

———. 1998. *The Geography of Money*. Ithaca, NY: Cornell University Press.

———. 2002. "International Finance." In *Handbook of International Relations*, edited by Walter Carlsnaes, Thomas Risse, and Beth A. Simmons, 429–447. London: Sage.

———. 2013. "Currency and State Power." In *Back to Basics: State Power in a Contemporary World*, edited by Martha Finnemore and Judith Goldstein, 159–176. New York: Oxford University Press.

Cohen, Benjamin J., and Fabio Basagni. 1981. *Banks and the Balance of Payments*. London: Rowman and Allanheld.

Cohen, Benjamin J., and Tabitha M. Benney. "What Does the International Currency System Look Like?" *Review of International Political Economy* 21, no. 5: 1017–1041.

Commanding Heights: The Battle for the World Economy (film). 2002. "Episode Three: The New Rules of the Game." Public Broadcasting Service.

Congressional Budget Office. 2014. "Congressional Budget Office Cost Estimate: H.R. 24 Federal Reserve Transparency Act of 2014." https://www.cbo.gov/sites/default/files/113th-congress-2013-2014/costestimate/hr2400.pdf. Accessed January 2016.

Coombs, Charles A. 1976. *The Arena of International Finance*. New York: John Wiley and Sons.

Cooper, Richard N. 1968. *The Economics of Interdependence: Economic Policy in the Atlantic Community*. New York: Colombia University Press.

Copelovitch, Mark S. 2010. *The International Monetary Fund in the Global Economy: Banks, Bonds, and Bailouts*. New York: Cambridge University Press.

Cottarelli, Carlos, and Curzio Giannini. 2002. "Bedfellows, Hostages, or Perfect Strangers? Global Capital Markets and the Catalytic Effect of IMF Crisis Lending." IMF Working Paper. WP/02/193.

Cowan, Edward. 1963, December 10. "Roosa Defends Foreign Securities Tax Plan and Assails Wall St. Executives Who Oppose It." *New York Times*.

Craig, Ben, and Goetz von Peter. 2010. "Interbank Tiering and Money Center Banks." BIS Working Paper, No. 322. http://www.bis.org/publ/work322.pdf. Accessed July 2013.

Demirgüç-Kunt, Asli, and Harry Huizinga. 1993. "Official Credits to Developing Countries: Implicit Transfers to the Banks." *Journal of Money, Credit and Banking* 25, no. 3: 430–444.

Devereux, Charlie. 2015, January 12. "Argentina Said to Secure $400 Million More in China FX Swap." *Bloomberg*. http://www.bloomberg.com/news/articles/2015-01-12/argentina-said-to-secure-400-million-more-in-china-fx-swap.

de Vries, Margaret G. 1988. *Balance of Payments Adjustment, 1945 to 1986: The IMF Experience*. Washington, DC: International Monetary Fund.

Dreher, Axel, and Nathan Jensen. 2007. "Independent Actor or Agent? An Empirical Analysis of the Impact of US Interests on IMF Conditions." *Journal of Law and Economics* 50, no. 1: 105–124.

Dreher, Axel, Jan-Egbert Sturm, and James Raymond Vreeland. 2009. "Global Horse Trading: IMF Loans for Votes in the United Nations Security Council." *European Economic Review* 53, no. 7: 742–757.

Dreher, Axel, and Roland Vaubel. 2004. "The Causes and Consequences of IMF Conditionality." *Emerging Markets Finance and Trade* 40, no. 3: 26–54.

Drezner, Daniel. 2010. "Will Currency Follow the Flag?" *International Relations of the Asia-Pacific* 10: 389-414.

Dooley, Michael. 2000. "A Model of Crises in Emerging Markets." *Economic Journal* 110, no. 2: 56–72.

EBD. 1962, October 24. "United States—Adherence to Decision on General Arrangements to Borrow." EBD 62/177. IMF Archives.

EBM. 1961, December 18. "Minutes of Executive Board Meeting 61/55." IMF Archives.

———. 1983a, April 6. "Minutes of the Executive Board Meeting 83/57." IMF Archives.

———. 1983b, April 22. "Minutes of the Executive Board Meeting 83/65." IMF Archives.

———. 1994, October 24. "Minutes of the Executive Board Meeting 94/95." IMF Archives.

———. 1995, February 1. "Minutes of the Executive Board Meeting 95/11." IMF Archives.

———. 1961, December 13. "Letter from Mr. Baumgartner, Minister of Finance, France, to the Other Participants in the Special Borrowing Arrangements with the [IMF]." EBS 61/168. IMF Archives.

Edwards, Jr., Richard W. 1985. *International Monetary Collaboration*. Dobbs Ferry, NY: Transnational Publishers.

Eichengreen, Barry. 1995. "Hegemonic Stability Theories of the International Monetary System." In *International Political Economy*, 3rd edition, edited by Jeffry A. Frieden and David A. Lake, 220–244. New York: St. Martin's.

———. 2000. "From Benign Neglect to Malignant Preoccupation: US Balance-of-Payments Policy in the 1960s." NBER Working Paper 7630. http://www.nber.org/papers/ w7630.pdf. Accessed February 2012.

————. 2004. "A Century of Capital Flows." In *Capital Flows and Crises,* edited by Barry Eichengreen, 13–46. Cambridge, MA: MIT Press.

————. 2011. *Exorbitant Privilege: The Rise and Fall of the Dollar and the Future of the International Monetary System.* New York: Oxford University Press.

Eichengreen, Barry, and Marc Flandreau. 2008. "The Rise and Fall of the Dollar (Or When Did the Dollar Replace Sterling as the Leading Reserve Currency?)" *European Review of Economic History* 13, no. 3: 377–411.

Eichengreen, Barry, and Ricardo Hausmann. 1999. "Exchange Rates and Financial Fragility." *New Challenges for Monetary Policy.* Federal Reserve Bank of Kansas City. http://www.kc.frb.org/publicat/sympos/1999/S99eich.pdf. Accessed January 2011.

————. 2005. *Other People's Money: Debt Denomination and Financial Instability in Emerging Market Economies.* Chicago: University of Chicago Press.

Eichengreen, Barry, and Richard Portes. 1989. "After the Deluge: Default, Negotiation, and Readjustment during the Interwar Years." In *The International Debt Crisis in Historical Perspective,* edited by Barry Eichengreen, 12–47. Cambridge, MA: MIT Press.

————. 1997. "Managing Financial Crises in Emerging Markets." Paper prepared for the Federal Reserve Bank of Kansas City's annual economics conference, Jackson Hole, WY, August 29–30. http://emlab.berkeley.edu/~eichengr/research/jackson.pdf. Accessed August 2013.

Eichengreen, Barry, Andrew K. Rose, Charles Wyplosz, Bernard Dumas, and Axel Weber. "Exchange Market Mayhem: The Antecedents and Aftermath of Speculative Attacks." *Economic Policy* 10: 249–312.

Eldar, Ofer, 2008. "Vote-trading in International Institutions." *European Journal of International Law* 19, no. 1: 3–41.

Erb, Richard D. 1983, April 6. "Statement by Mr. Erb on Fund Policies and External Debt Servicing Problems, Executive Board Meeting 83/57." IMF Archives.

European Council. 2010, December 16–17. "Conclusions." General Secretariat of the Council. http://www.consilium.europa.eu/uedocs/cms_ data/docs/pressdata/en/ec/118578. pdf#page=6. Accessed March 2012.

Farnsworth, Clyde H. 1982, December 14. "Brazil Requests a Further Loan of $1.5 Billion." *New York Times,* Section A, Column 1, p. 1.

Farrell, Diana, Susan Lund, Oskar Skau, Charles Atkins, Jan Philipp Mengeringhaus, and Moira S. Pierce. 2008, October. "Mapping Global Capital Markets: Fifth Annual Report." McKinsey Global Institute.

Felsenthal, Mark, and Glen Somerville. 2010, May 11. "Bernanke Saw Threat to US Banks from Europe: Shelby." *Reuters.* http://mobile.reuters.com/article/idUSTRE647 16U20100511.

Fernandez-Arias, Eduardo, and Eduardo Levy-Yeyati. 2012. "Global Financial Safety Nets: Where Do We Go from Here?" *International Finance* 15, no. 1: 37–68.

Fischer, Stanley. 1999. "On the Need for an International Lender of Last Resort." *Journal of Economic Perspectives* 13, no. 4: 85–104.

Fishlow, Albert. 1986. "The Debt Crisis in Historical Perspective." In *The Politics of International Debt,* edited by Miles Kahler, 37–94. Ithaca, NY: Cornell University Press.

Fitch Ratings. 2007, September 12. "Asset-Backed Commercial Paper and Global Banks Exposure—10 Key Questions." http://www.fitchratings.com/dtp/pdf3-07/babp1209.pdf. Accessed April 2010.

Flemming, Michael J., and Nicholas J. Klagge. 2010. "The Federal Reserve's Foreign Exchange Swap Lines." *Current Issues in Economics and Finance* 16, no. 4: 1–7.

FOMC. 1960, October 4. Meeting of the Federal Open Market Committee, historical minutes. http://www.federalreserve.gov/monetarypolicy/files/fomchistmin 19601004.pdf. Accessed December 2011.

———. 1961a, December 5. Meeting of the Federal Open Market Committee, historical minutes. http://www.federalreserve.gov/monetarypolicy/files/ fomchistmin19611205. pdf. Accessed December 2011.

———. 1961b, December 19. Meeting of the Federal Open Market Committee, historical minutes. http://www.federalreserve.gov/monetarypolicy/files/ fomchistmin19611219.pdf. Accessed December 2011.

———. 1962, February 13. Meeting of the Federal Open Market Committee, historical minutes. http://www.federalreserve.gov/monetarypolicy/files/fomchistmin 19620213.pdf. Accessed December 2011.

———. 1982a, August 24. Meeting of the Federal Open Market Committee, transcript. http://www.federalreserve.gov/monetarypolicy/files/ FOMC19820824meeting. pdf. Accessed July 2013.

———. 1982b, November 16. Meeting of the Federal Open Market Committee, transcript. http://www.federalreserve.gov/monetarypolicy/files/ FOMC19821116   meeting. pdf. Accessed July 2013.

———. 1982c, December 20–21. Meeting of the Federal Open Market Committee, transcript. http://www.federalreserve.gov/monetarypolicy/files/FOMC19821221 meeting.pdf. Accessed July 2013.

———. 1984, March 26–27. Meeting of the Federal Open Market Committee, transcript. http://www.federalreserve.gov/monetarypolicy/files/FOMC19840327   meeting. pdf. Accessed August 2013.

———. 1995, March 28. Meeting of the Federal Open Market Committee, transcript. http://www.federalreserve.gov/monetarypolicy/files/ FOMC19950328meeting. pdf. Accessed August 2013.

———. 1997a, November 12. Meeting of the Federal Open Market Committee, transcript. http://www.federalreserve.gov/monetarypolicy/files/ FOMC19971112   meeting. pdf. Accessed August 2013.

———. 1997b, December 16. Meeting of the Federal Open Market Committee, transcript. http://www.federalreserve.gov/monetarypolicy/files/ FOMC19971216   meeting. pdf. Accessed August 2013.

———. 2007a, August 16. Conference call of the Federal Open Market Committee, transcript. http://www.federalreserve.gov/monetarypolicy/files/   FOMC20070816confcall. pdf. Accessed August 2013.

———. 2007b, September 18. Meeting of the Federal Open Market Committee, transcript. http://www.federalreserve.gov/monetarypolicy/files/   FOMC20070918meeting. pdf. Accessed August 2013.

———. 2007c, December 6. Conference call of the Federal Open Market Committee, transcript. http://www.federalreserve.gov/monetarypolicy/files/ FOMC20071206confcall.pdf. Accessed August 2013.

———. 2007d, December 11. Meeting of the Federal Open Market Committee, transcript. http://www.federalreserve.gov/monetarypolicy/files/   FOMC20071211meeting. pdf. Accessed August 2013.

———. 2008a, January 29–30. Meeting of the Federal Open Market Committee, transcript. http://www.federalreserve.gov/monetarypolicy/files/FOMC20080130   meeting. pdf. Accessed March 2014.

———. 2008b, March 10. Conference call of the Federal Open Market Committee, transcript. http://www.federalreserve.gov/monetarypolicy/files/FOMC20080310confcall. pdf. Accessed March 2014.

———. 2008c, March 18. Meeting of the Federal Open Market Committee, transcript. http://www.federalreserve.gov/monetarypolicy/files/FOMC20080318   meeting. pdf. Accessed March 2014.

———. 2008d, April 29–30. Meeting of the Federal Open Market Committee, transcript. http://www.federalreserve.gov/monetarypolicy/files/FOMC20080430 meeting.pdf. Accessed March 2014.

———. 2008e, August 5. Meeting of the Federal Open Market Committee, transcript. http://www.federalreserve.gov/monetarypolicy/files/FOMC20080805 meeting. pdf. Accessed March 2014.

———. 2008f, September 16. Meeting of the Federal Open Market Committee, transcript. http://www.federalreserve.gov/monetarypolicy/files/FOMC20080916 meeting. pdf. Accessed March 2014.

———. 2008g, September 29. Conference call of the Federal Open Market Committee, transcript. http://www.federalreserve.gov/monetarypolicy/files/FOMC20080929 confcall.pdf. Accessed March 2014.

———. 2008h, October 7. Conference call of the Federal Open Market Committee, transcript. http://www.federalreserve.gov/monetarypolicy/files/FOMC20081007 confcall.pdf. Accessed March 2014.

———. 2008i, October 29. Meeting of the Federal Open Market Committee, transcript. http://www.federalreserve.gov/monetarypolicy/files/FOMC20081029 meeting. pdf. Accessed March 2014.

———. 2008j, December 15–16. Meeting of the Federal Open Market Committee, transcript. http://www.federalreserve.gov/monetarypolicy/files/FOMC20081216 meeting.pdf. Accessed March 2014.

FRBNY. 1983. "Treasury and Federal Reserve Foreign Exchange Operations." *FRBNY Quarterly Review.* Spring.

Freixas, Xavier, Curzio Giannini, Glenn Hoggarth, and Farouk Soussa. 2002. "Lender of Last Resort: A Review of the Literature." In *Crises, Contagion, and the Lender of Last Resort,* edited by Charles A. E. Goodhart and Gerhard Illing, 27–53. New York: Oxford University Press.

Frieden, Jeffry A. 2006. *Global Capitalism: Its Fall and Rise in the Twentieth Century.* New York: W. W. Norton.

G-7. 1997, December 24. "G-7 Statement on Korean Situation." http://www.g8.utoronto. ca/finance/fin_dec2497.htm. Accessed June 2014.

Gartzke, Erik. 1998. "Kant We All Just Get Along? Opportunity, Willingness, and the Origins of the Democratic Peace." *American Journal of Political Science* 42, no. 1: 1–27.

Gelman, Andrew, and Iain Pardoe. 2007. "Average Predictive Comparisons for Models with Nonlinearity, Interactions, and Variance Components." *Sociological Methodology* 37, no. 1: 23–51.

Gerring, John. 2007. *Case Study Research: Principles and Practices.* New York: Cambridge University Press.

Gilpin, Robert. 1975. *US Power and the Multinational Corporation: The Political Economy of Foreign Direct Investment.* New York: Basic Books.

———. 1981. *War and Change in World Politics.* Cambridge, UK: Cambridge University Press.

———. 1987. *The Political Economy of International Relations.* Princeton, NJ: Princeton University Press.

Goldberg, Linda S., Craig Kennedy, and Jason Miu. 2010. "Central Bank Dollar Swap Lines and Overseas Dollar Funding Costs." NBER Working Paper No. 15763. http://www. nber.org/ papers/w15763. Accessed March 2010.

Goldberg, Linda S., and Cedric Tille. 2008. "Vehicle Currency Use in International Trade." *Journal of International Economics* 76, no. 2: 177–192.

Goodhart, Charles A. E. 1985. *The Evolution of Central Banks.* London: London School of Economics and Political Science.

———. 1999. "Myths about the Lender of Last Resort." *International Finance* 2, no. 3: 339–360.

Goodhart, Charles A. E., and Gerhard Illing. 2002. "Introduction." In *Financial Crises, Contagion, and the Lender of Last Resort,* edited by Charles A. E. Goodhart and Gerhard Illing, 2–26. New York: Oxford University Press.

Greenspan, Alan. 2007. *The Age of Turbulence: Adventures in a New World.* New York: Penguin.

Grimes, William M. 2011. "The Asian Monetary Fund Reborn? Implications of Chiang Mai Initiative Multilateralization." *Asian Policy* 11, January: 79–104.

Guitian, Manuel. 1992. "Rules and Discretion in International Economic Policy." Occasional Paper, no. 97. Washington, DC: International Monetary Fund.

———. 1995. "Conditionality: Past, Present, Future." *Staff Papers—International Monetary Fund* 42, no. 4: 792–835.

Halifax. 1995. "The Halifax Summit Review of the International Financial Institutions: Background Documen." Section 5. http://www.g7.utoronto.ca/summit/1995halifax /financial/. Accessed July 2013.

Harrison, David. 2015, November 30. "Fed Adopts Dodd-Frank Bailout Limits." *Wall Street Journal.* http://www.wsj.com/articles/fed-set-to-adopt-final-emergency-lending-rule-1448889633.

Helleiner, Eric. 1994. *States and the Reemergence of Global Finance: From Bretton Woods to the 1990s.* Ithaca, NY: Cornell University Press.

———. 2014. *The Status Quo Crisis: Global Financial Governance after the 2008 Meltdown.* New York: Oxford University Press.

Helleiner, Eric, and Bessma Momani. 2007. "Slipping into Obscurity? Crisis and Reform at the IMF." Centre for International Governance Innovation, Working Paper No. 16. http://papers.ssrn.com/sol3/papers.cfm?abstract_id=964915. Accessed April 2011.

Henning, Randall. 1999. *The Exchange Stabilization Fund: Slush Money or War Chest.* Washington, DC: Peterson Institute for International Economics.

Hilsenrath, Jon. 2010, May 11. "Fed to Defend Loan Program." *Wall Street Journal.* http:// www.wsj.com/articles/SB10001424052748703880304575236290266862342.

The Hindu. 2013, August 27. "Currency Swap Pacts with Key Partners under Study." http:// www.thehindu.com/business/markets/currency-swap-pacts-with-key-partners-under-study/article5065486.ece?homepage=true.

Hiroyuki, Ito, and Cesar Rodriguez. 2015. "Clamoring for Greenbacks: Explaining the Resurgence of the US Dollar in International Debt." RIETI Discussion Paper Series, 15-E-119. http://web.pdx.edu/~ito/Ito-Rodriguez_15e119.pdf. Accessed October 2015.

Howell, Kristin K. 1995. "The Evolution and Goals of Lending to Developing Countries by the Bank for International Settlements." *Journal of Economic Studies* 22, no. 6: 69–80.

Humphrey, Thomas M. 1975. "The Classical Concept of the Lender of Last Resort." Federal Reserve Bank of Richmond. *Economic Review* 61, January/February: 2–9.

———. 1989. "Lender of Last Resort: The Concept in History." Federal Reserve Bank of Richmond. *Economic Review* 75, March/April: 8–16.

Ikenberry, G. John. 2011. Liberal Leviathan: The Origins, Crisis, and Transformation of the American World Order. Princeton, NJ: Princeton University Press.

Imai, Kosuke, Gary King and Olivia Lau. 2007. "Zelig: Everyone's Statistical Software." http://r.iq.harvard.edu/docs/zelig.pdf. Accessed June 2016.

IMF. 1997. "Korea Strengthens Economic Program; IMF to Activate Additional Financial Support." News Brief No. 97/32. http://www.imf.org/external/np/sec/nb/1997/nb9732.htm. Accessed April 2014.

————. 1998. *Annual Report of the Executive Board for the Financial Year Ended April 30, 1998*. Washington, DC: International Monetary Fund. http://www.imf.org/ external/pubs/ft/ar/98/index.htm. Accessed November 2015.

————. 2003. "The IMF and Recent Capital Account Crises: Indonesia, Korea, Brazil." Independent Evaluation Office. http://www.imf.org/external/np/sec/nb/ 1997/ nb9732.htm. Accessed April 2014.

————. 2006. "Article IV of the Fund's Articles of Agreement: An Overview of the Legal Framework." http://www.imf.org/external/np/pp/eng/2006/062806.pdf. Accessed July 2013.

————. 2009a, March 24. "The Help Countries Face Crisis, IMF Revamps Its Lending." *IMF Survey Magazine*. https://www.imf.org/external/pubs/ft/survey/so/2009/ NEW032409A.htm. Accessed January 2016.

————. 2009b. "GRA Lending Toolkit and Conditionality: Reform Proposals." http:// www.imf.org/external/np/pp/eng/2009/031309A.pdf. Accessed November 2015.

————. 2012a. "The IMF's Flexible Credit Line: Factsheet." http://www. imf.org/external/ np/exr/facts/fcl.htm. Accessed September 2012.

————. 2012b. "The IMF's Rapid Credit Facility: Factsheet." http://www.imf.org/exter-nal/np/exr/facts/rcf.htm. Accessed September 2012.

————. 2013, March 31. "IMF Quotas: Factsheet." http://www.imf.org/external/np/exr/ facts/quotas.htm. Accessed July 2013.

It's a Wonderful Life (film). Directed by Frank Capra. Liberty Films. 1939.

Jacobsson, Erin E. 1979. *A Life for Sound Money: Per Jacobsson, His Biography*. Oxford, UK: Clarendon.

James, Harold. 1996. *International Monetary Cooperation since Bretton Woods*. Washington, DC: International Monetary Fund.

Jeanne, Oliver, and Charles Wyplosz. 2001. "The International Lender of Last Resort: How Large Is Large Enough?" NBER Working Paper No. 8381.

Jervis, Robert. 2009. "Unipolarity: A Structural Perspective." *World Politics* 61, no. 1: 188–213.

Miles Kahler. 1992. "The United States and the [IMF]: Declining Influence or Declining Interest?" In *The United States and Multilateral Institutions: Patterns of Changing Instrumentality and Influence*, edited by Margaret P. Karns and Karen A. Mingst, 62– 77. Routledge.

Kaminsky, Graciela L., and Carmen M. Reinhart. 1999. "The Twin Crises: The Causes of Banking and Balance-of-Payments Problems." *American Economic Review* 89: 473–500.

Kaufman, George G. 2002. "Lender of Last Resort: A Contemporary Perspective." In *Crises, Contagion, and the Lender of Last Resort*, edited by Charles A. E. Goodhart and Gerhard Illing, 169–185. New York: Oxford University Press.

Keleher, Robert. 1999, February. "The International Lender of Last Resort, the IMF, and the Federal Reserve." Paper presented to the Joint Economic Committee, United States Congress.

Kenen, Peter B. 2001. *The International Financial Architecture: What's New? What's Missing?* Washington, DC: Peterson Institute for International Economics.

Keohane, Robert. 2006. "The Contingent Legitimacy of Multilateralism." GARNET Working Paper No. 09/06. https://www.researchgate.net/profile/Robert_Keohane/ publication/228621543_The_contingent_legitimacy_of_multilateralism/links/ 00463527298aca9b78000000.pdf. Accessed January 2016.

Kho, Bong-Chan, Dong Lee, and Rene M. Stulz. 2000. "US Banks, Crises, and Bailouts: From Mexico to LTCM." *American Economic Review* 90, no. 2: 28–31.

Kilborn, Peter T. 1984a, April 1. "Regan Says the Loan to the Argentines Is to Avert Crisis." *New York Times*, Section 1, Column 6, p. 1.

——. 1984b, April 3. "Silva: Architect of Debt Plan." *New York Times*, Section D, Column 3, p. 1.

Kindleberger, Charles P. 1973. *The World in Depression, 1929–1939*. Berkeley: University of California Press.

——. 1978. *Manias, Panics, and Crises: A History of Financial Crises*. New York: Basic Books.

——. 1981. "Dominance and Leadership in the International Economy: Exploitation, Public Goods, and Free-Rides." *International Studies Quarterly* 25, no. 2: 242–254.

——. 1983. "Key Currencies and Financial Centers." In *Reflections in a Troubled World Economy: Essays in Honour of Herbert Giersch*, edited by Fritz Machlup, Gerhard Fels, and Hubertus Muller-Groeling. New York: St. Martin's.

——. 1986. "International Public Goods without International Government." *American Economic Review* 76, no. 1: 1–13.

——. 1996. *Manias, Panics, and Crises: A History of Financial Crises*. London: Macmillan.

King, Mervyn. 2006, February 20. "Reform of the International Monetary Fund." http://www.bankofengland.co.uk/publications/speeches/2006/speech267.pdf. Accessed February 2012.

Knight, Malcolm, and Santaella, Julio A. 1997. "Economic Determinants of IMF Financial Arrangements." *Journal of Development Economics*, 54: 405–436.

Knipe, James L. 1965. *The Federal Reserve and the American Dollar: Problems and Policies, 1946–1964*. Chapel Hill: University of North Carolina Press.

Kraft, Joseph. 1984. *The Mexican Rescue*. New York: Group of Thirty.

Kreps, Sarah. 2011. *Coalitions of Convenience: United States Interventions after the Cold War*. New York: Oxford University Press.

Krugman, Paul. 1979. "A Model of Balance-of-Payments Crises." *Journal of Money, Credit and Banking* 11, no. 3: 311–325.

——. 1992. *Currencies and Crises*. Cambridge, MA: MIT Press.

Kuezynski, Pedro-Pablo. 1984. "International Emergency Lending Facilities—Are They Adequate?" Federal Reserve Bank of Boston. http://www.bos.frb.org/economic/conf/ conf28/conf28e.pdf. Accessed April 2010.

Laeven, Luc, and Fabian Valencia. 2008. "Systemic Banking Crises: A New Database." IMF Working Paper. http://www.imf.org/external/pubs/ft/wp/2008/ wp08224.pdf. Accessed July 2010.

Lake, David. 1993. "Leadership, Hegemony, and the International Economy: Naked Emperor or Tattered Monarch with Potential?" *International Studies Quarterly* 37, no. 4: 459–489.

Lau, Sie Ting, and Thomas H. McInish. 2003. "IMF Bailouts, Contagion Effects, and Bank Security Returns." *International Review of Financial Analysis* 12, no. 1: 3–23.

Layne, C., 2012. "This time it's real: The end of unipolarity and the Pax Americana." *International Studies Quarterly* 56, no. 1: 203–213.

Lazarsfeld, Paul. 1959. "Problems in Methodology." In *Sociology Today: Problems and Prospects*, Volume 1, edited by R. K. Merton, L. Broom, and L.S. Cottrell, Jr., 39–71. New York: Basic Books.

Leblang, David. 2003. "To Devalue or to Defend? The Political Economy of Exchange Rate Policy." *International Studies Quarterly* 47, no. 4: 533–560.

Liao, Steven, and Daniel McDowell. 2015. "Redback Rising: China's Bilateral Swap Agreements and Renminbi Internationalization." *International Studies Quarterly* 59, no. 3: 401–422.

Lipton, David. 2014, April 4. Personal interview.

Lombardi, Domenico. 2012. "Strengthening the International Monetary Fund." Brookings. http://www.brookings.edu/research/papers/2012/06/strengthening-imf-lombardi. Accessed January 2016.

Lund, Susan, Toos Daruvala, Richard Dobbs, Philipp Harle, Ju-Hon Kwek, and Ricardo Falcon. 2013. "Financial Globalization: Retreat or Reset?" McKinsey Global Institute. http://www.mckinsey.com/insights/global_capital_markets/financial_globalization. Accessed April 2014.

Mahoney, James, and Gary Goertz. 2004. "The Possibility Principle: Choosing Negative Cases in Comparative Research." *American Political Science Review* 98, no. 4: 653–669.

Martin, Lisa L. 1992. "Interests, Power, and Multilateralism." *International Organization* 46, no. 4: 765–792.

Martin, Philippe, and Hélène Rey. 2002. "Financial Globalization and Emerging Markets: With or Without Crash?" NBER Working Paper No. 9288. http://www.nber.org/papers/w11550.pdf. Accessed February 2011.

McCauley, Robert N., and Patrick McGuire. 2009. "Dollar Appreciation in 2008: Safe Haven, Carry Trades, Dollar Shortage and Overhedging." *BIS Quarterly Review*, December: 85–93.

McDowell, Daniel. 2016. "Need for Speed: The Lending Responsiveness of the International Monetary Fund." *Review of International Organizations*, forthcoming.

McGuire, Patrick, and Gotz von Peter. 2009. "The US Dollar Shortage in Global Banking and the International Policy Response." BIS Working Paper No. 291. http://www.bis.org/publ/ work291.htm. Accessed February 2010.

Meltzer, Allan H. 2000. "Report of the International Financial Institution Advisory Commission." http://www.house.gov/jec/imf/meltzer.htm. Accessed April 2011.

Mishkin, Frederic S. 2000, June 19–20. "The International Lender of Last Resort: What Are the Issues?" Prepared for the Kiel Week Conference, Kiel Institute of World Economics, Kiel, Germany.

Mody, Ashoka, and Diego Saravia. 2013. "The Response Speed of the International Monetary Fund." *International Finance* 16, no. 2: 189–211.

Moser, Christoph, and Jan-Egbert Sturm. 2011. "Explaining IMF Lending Decisions after the Cold War." *Review of International Organizations* 6, nos. 3–4: 307–340.

Munk, Russell. 2010. "Exchange Stabilization Fund Loans to Sovereign Borrowers: 1982–2010." *Law and Contemporary Problems* 73, no. 4: 215–240.

Naftali, Timothy. 2001. *The Presidential Recordings of John F. Kennedy: The Great Crises, Volume One*. New York: W. W. Norton.

National Security Council and Records Management Office. 2016. "Declassified Documents Concerning Tony Blair." *Clinton Digital Library*. http://clinton.presidentiallibraries.us/items/show/48779. Accessed January 2016.

NBER Working Paper No. 16079. http://www.nber.org/papers/w16079. Accessed March 2011.

Nelson, Stephen. 2014. "Playing Favorites: How Shared Beliefs Shape the IMF's Lending Decisions." *International Organization* 68, no. 2: 297–328.

New York Times. 1964, 6 January. "Success of the Federal Reserve's Currency-Swap Program Soothes Fears of Financiers."

Norris, Floyd. 2013, September 19. "Money Funds Are Circling the Wagons on Rules." *New York Times*. http://www.nytimes.com/2013/09/20/business/money-market-funds-circle-the-wagons.html?_r=0.

Oatley, Thomas. 2011. "The Reductionist Gamble: Open Economy Politics in the Global Economy." *International Organization* 65, no. 2: 311–341.

Oatley, Thomas, W. Kindred Winecoff, Andrew Pennock, and Sarah Bauerle Danzman. 2013. "The Political Economy of Global Finance: A Network Model." *Perspectives on Politics* 11, no. 1: 133–153.

Oatley, Thomas, and Jason Yackee. 2004. "American Interests and IMF Lending." *International Politics* 41, no. 3: 415–429.

Oberdorfer, Don. 1983, January 30. "Mexico Crisis Altered US Foreign Loan Views." *Washington Post*, p. A1.

Odell, John S. 1982. *US International Monetary Policy: Markets, Power, and Ideas as Sources of Change*. Princeton, NJ: Princeton University Press.

Oliver, Christian. 2010, March 1. "South Korea Pushes for Global Swaps Regime." *Financial Times*. http://www.ft.com/cms/s/0/b0dc5784-24e6-11df-8be0-00144feab49a.html.

Olson, Mancur. 1965. *The Logic of Collective Action: Public Goods and a Theory of Groups*. Cambridge, MA: Harvard University Press.

Osterberg, William, and James Thompson. 1999. "The Exchange Stabilization Fund: How It Works." Federal Reserve Bank of Cleveland. http://www.clevelandfed.org/research/ commentary/1999/1201.pdf. Accessed March 2011.

Parsons, Christi, and Don Lee. 2011, November 3. "At G-20, US Stays on the Sidelines in Europe Debt Crisis." *Los Angeles Times*. http://articles.latimes.com/2011/nov/03/world/la-fg-obama-g20-20111104.

Parulekar, Rahul, Udairam Bishnoi, Sumeet Kapur, and Tanuj Garg. 2008. "Vicious Cycle: Credit Crunch Could Feedback into Housing as Early as Next Month." Citigroup Global Markets Inc.: ABS & Mortgage Credit Research.

Pastor, Robert A. 2001. *Toward a North American Community: Lessons from the Old World for the New*. Washington, DC: Peterson Institute for International Economics.

Patrick, Stewart. 2002. "Multilateralism and Its Discontents: The Causes and Consequences of US Ambivalence." In *Multilateralism and US Foreign Policy: Ambivalent Engagement*, edited by Patrick Steward and Shepard Forman. Boulder, CO: Lynne Rienner.

Pempel, T. J. 1999. "Conclusion." In *The Politics of the Asian Economic Crisis*, edited by T. J. Pempel, 224–238. Ithaca, NY: Cornell University Press.

Piffaretti, Nadia F. 2009. "Reshaping the International Monetary Architecture: Lessons from Keynes' Plan." World Bank Policy Research Working Paper, 5034. http://papers.ssrn.com/sol3/papers.cfm?abstract_id=1471132. Accessed February 2015.

Prasad, Eswar. 2014. *The Dollar Trap: How the US Dollar Tightened Its Grip on Global Finance*. Princeton, NJ: Princeton University Press.

Prasad, Eswar, Kenneth Rogoff, Shang-Jin Wei, and M. Ayhan Kose. 2003. "Effects of Financial Globalization on Developing Countries." IMF Working Paper.

Prasad, Eswar, and Lei (Sandy) Ye. 2012. "The Renminbi's Role in the Global Monetary System." Global Economy and Development at Brookings. http://www.brookings.edu/~/ media/Files/rc/reports/2012/02_renminbi_monetary_system_prasad/02_renminbi_monetary_system_prasad.pdf. Accessed January 2012.

Rainoni, Antonio. 1973. "Monetary Cooperation in the International Monetary System." In *Monetary Policy in Twelve Industrial Countries*, edited by Karel Holbik, 525–571. Boston: Federal Reserve Bank of Boston.

Ram, Vidya. 2007, August 20. "Sachsen: A Sign of Things to Come?" *Forbes*. http://www.forbes.com/2007/ 08/20/sachsen-german-bank-markets-equity-cx_vr_0820 markets10.html.

Rodrik, Dani, and Andrés Velasco, A. 1999. "Short-term capital flows." NBER Working Paper, 7364.

Roosa, Robert V. 1965. *Monetary Reform for the World Economy*. New York: Harper and Row.

Roubini, Nouriel, and Brad Setser. 2004. *Bailouts or Bail-ins? Responding to Financial Crises in Emerging Markets.* Washington, DC: Council on Foreign Relations.

Rubin, Robert E. 1998. "Address on the Asian Financial Situation to Georgetown University, Washington D.C." http://www.treasury.gov/press-center/press-releases/Pages/rr2168. aspx. Accessed August 2013.

Rubin, Robert E., and Jacob Weisberg. 2003. *In an Uncertain World: Tough Choices from Wall Street to Washington.* New York: Random House.

Ruggie, John G. 1992. "Multilateralism: The Anatomy of an Institution." *International Organization* 46, no. 3: 561–598.

Sachs, Jeffrey. 1995, April 20. "Do We Need an International Lender of Last Resort?" Frank D. Graham Lecture, Princeton University.

Sachs, Jeffrey, and John Williamson. 1986. "Managing the LDC Debt Crisis." Brookings Papers on Economic Activity, no. 2: 397–440.

Sachs, Jeffrey. 1988. "Developing Country Debt." In *International Economic Cooperation,* edited by Martin Feldstein. Cambridge, MA: National Bureau of Economic Research.

Sanger, David E. 1997, August 21. "First Part of Thai Bailout Is Authorized by the I.M.F." *New York Times,* Column 5, p. 2.

Schwartz, Anna J. 1997. "From Obscurity to Notoriety: A Biography of the Exchange Stabilization Fund." *Journal of Money, Credit, and Banking* 29, no. 2: 135–153.

———. 2002. "Earmarks of a Lender of Last Resort." In *Financial Crises, Contagion, and the Lender of Last Resort,* edited by Charles A. E. Goodhart and Gerhard Illing, 449–460. New York: Oxford University Press.

Schwartz, Herman. 2009a. "Origins and Consequences of the US Subprime Crisis." In *The Politics of Housing Booms and Busts,* edited by Herman Schwartz and Leonard Seabrooke. New York: Palgrave Macmillan.

———. 2009b. *Subprime Nation: American Power, Global Capital, and the Housing Bubble.* Ithaca, NY: Cornell University Press.

Schweitzer, Mark, and Guhan Venkatu. 2009. "Adjustable-Rate Mortgages and the Libor Surprise." Federal Reserve Bank of Cleveland. http://www.clevelandfed.org/ research/ commentary/ 2009/012109.cfm. Accessed June 2010.

Seawright, Jason, and John Gerring. 2008. "Case Selection Techniques in Case Study Research." *Political Research Quarterly* 61, no. 2: 294–308.

Serchuk, David. 2009, September 9. "Another Run on Money Market Funds?" *Forbes.* http://www.forbes.com/2009/09/24/money-market-lehman-intelligent-investing-break-buck.html.

Siegman, Charles J. 1994. "The Bank for International Settlements and the Federal Reserve." *Federal Reserve Bulletin,* October: 900–906.

Signorino, Curtis S., and Jeffrey M Ritter. 1999. "Tau-b or Not Tau-b: Measuring the Similarity of Foreign Policy Positions." *International Studies Quarterly* 43, no. 1: 115–144.

Solomon, Robert. 1982. *The International Monetary System, 1945–1981.* New York: Harper and Row.

Stein, Herbert. 1965. "The Evolving International Monetary System and Domestic Economic Policy." *American Economic Review Papers and Proceedings* 55, nos. 1–2: 200–207.

Steinberg, James. 2014, March 18. Personal interview.

Stevenson, Richard W. 1997a, December 2. "Clinton Conditionally Support US Role in Bailout." *New York Times,* Column 3, p. 4.

———. 1997b, December 4. "Washington to Directly Contribute $5 Billion, at the Low End of Expectations." *New York Times,* Column 1, p. 6.

————. 1998, January 13. "White House Bailouts for Asia Draw Fire." *New York Times,* Column 3, p. 3.

Stone, Randall. 2004. "The Political Economy of IMF Lending in Africa." *American Political Science Review* 98, no. 4: 577–591.

————. 2008. "The Scope of IMF Conditionality." *International Organization* 62, no. 4: 589–620.

————. 2011. *Controlling Institutions: International Organizations and the Global Economy.* New York: Cambridge University Press.

Strange, Susan. 1976. *International Monetary Relations.* Oxford: Oxford University Press.

————. (1988) 1994. *States and Markets.* London: Pinter.

Taylor, John B., and John C. Williams. 2008. "A Black Swan in the Money Market." Federal Reserve of San Francisco, Working Series Paper. http://www.frbsf.org/ publications/ economics/papers/2008/wp08-04bk.pdf. Accessed March 2010.

Thacker, Strom C. 1999. "The High Politics of IMF Lending." *World Politics* 52, no. 1: 38–75.

Thornton, Henry. (1802) 2008. *An Enquiry into the Nature and Effects of the Paper Credit of Great Britain.* Whitefish, MT: Kessinger.

Truman, Edwin M. 1996. "The Mexican Peso Crisis: Implications for International Finance." *Federal Reserve Bulletin,* March: 200–209.

Tsebelis, George. 2002. *Veto Players: How Political Institutions Work.* Princeton, NJ: Princeton University Press.

US Congress. 1996. Treasury, Postal Service, and General Government Appropriations Act. One-Hundred Fourth Congress, Second Session.

US Government Accountability Office (GAO). 2011. "Opportunities Exist to Strengthen Policies and Processes for Managing Emergency Assistance." GAO-11-696. http:// www.gao.gov/assets/330/321506.pdf. Accessed July 2013.

US House of Representatives. 1962, February 28. "Statement of William McChesney Martin, Jr., Chairman, Board of Governors of the Federal Reserve System." Committee on Banking and Currency.

————. 1976. Hearing before the Task Force on Tax Expenditures and Off-Budget Agencies of the Committee on the Budget. Ninety-fourth Congress, Second Session.

————. 1984. Hearings before the Subcommittee on International Trade, Investment and Monetary Policy of the Committee on Banking, Finance and Urban Affairs. Exchange Stabilization Fund and Argentina. Ninety-eighth Congress, Second Session.

————. 1989a. Hearings and Markup before the Committee on Foreign Affairs and its Subcommittees on Europe and the Middle East and on International Economic Policy and Trade. United States Economic Programs for Poland and Hungary. One Hundred First Congress, First Session.

————. 1989b, October 19. Congressional Record. One Hundred First Congress, First Session.

————. 1995a. Hearings before the Committee on Banking and Financial Services. US and International Response to the Mexican Financial Crisis. One Hundred Fourth Congress, First Session.

————. 1999, July 15. Committee of the Whole. Limitations on Use of Exchange Stabilization Fund for Foreign Loans and Credits. One Hundred Sixth Congress, First Session.

US Senate. 1934, January 23. Gold Reserve Act of 1934. Seventy-eighth Congress, Second Session.

————. 1976, August 27. Hearing before the Subcommittee on International Finance of the Committee on Banking, Housing and Urban Affairs. Amendments of the Bretton Woods Agreements Act. Ninety-fourth Congress, Second Session.

———. 1977, October 7. Hearing before the Subcommittee on International Finance of the Committee on Banking, Housing and Urban Affairs. Exchange Stabilization Fund. Ninety-fifth Congress, First Session.

———. 1984. Hearing before the Subcommittee on International Finance and Monetary Policy of the Committee on Banking, Housing, and Urban Affairs. The Argentina Debt.

———. 1995. Hearings before the Committee on Banking, Housing, and Urban Affairs. The Mexican Peso Crisis. One Hundred Fourth Congress, First Session. Ninety-eighth Congress, Second Session.

———. 2008. Hearing before the Committee on Banking, Housing, and Urban Affairs. Recent Developments in US Financial Markets and Regulatory Responses to Them. One-hundred tenth Congress, Second Session.

US Treasury. 1994. "Report on the 1994 Benchmark Survey of US Ownership of Foreign Securities." Office of Foreign Investment Studies; Office of the Assistant Secretary, Economic Policy.

Vaubel, Roland. 1986. "A Public Choice Approach to International Organization." *Public Choice* 51, no. 1: 39–57.

———. 1996. "Bureaucracy at the IMF and the World Bank: A Comparison of the Evidence." *World Economy* 19, no. 2: 185–210.

Volcker, Paul, and Toyoo Gyohten. 1992. *Changing Fortunes: The World's Money and the Threat to American Leadership.* New York: Three Rivers.

Vreeland, James R. 1999, April 15–17. "The IMF: Lender of Last Resort or Scapegoat?" Prepared for the Midwest Political Science Association Annual Meeting, Chicago.

———. 2003. *The IMF and Economic Development.* New York: Cambridge University Press.

———. 2007. *The International Monetary Fund: Politics of Conditional Lending.* New York: Routledge.

Wallich, Henry C. 1977. "Central Banks as Regulators and Lenders of Last Resort in an International Context: A View from the United States." *Key Issues in International Banking* 19, October: 91–98.

Weisman, Steven R. 1982, December 2. "President Pledges to Give Brazilians a $1.2 Billion Loan." *New York Times*, Section A, Column 6, p. 1.

Wessel, David. 2009. *In Fed We Trust.* New York: Crown Business.

Whitt, Jr., Joseph A. 1996. "The Mexican Peso Crisis." *Economic Review.* Federal Reserve Bank of Atlanta. http://www.frbatlanta.org/filelegacydocs/j_whi811.pdf. Accessed February 2012.

Willett, Thomas. 2002. "Towards a Broader Public Choice Analysis of the IMF." In *Organizing the World's Money*, edited by David Andrews, Randall Henning, and Louis Pauley. Ithaca, NY: Cornell University Press.

Wilson, Arlene. 1999. "The Exchange Stabilization Fund of the US Treasury Department: Purpose, History, and Legislative Activity." Congressional Research Service paper.

Winecoff, William Kindred. 2015. "Structural Power and the Global Financial Crisis: A Network Analytical Approach." *Business and Politics* 17, no. 3: 495–525.

Wyplosz, Charles. 2001. "How Risky Is Financial Liberalization in the Developing Countries?" G-24 Discussion Paper Series. Available from <http://web.idrc.ca/uploads/user-S/10322098330pogdsmdpbg 24d14.en.pdf> Accessed February 12, 2011.

Zettelmeyer, Jeromin. 2000. "Can Official Crisis Lending Be Counterproductive in the Short Run?" *Economic Notes* 29, no. 1: 12–29.

Zhang, Zhaohui. 2001. "The Impact of IMF Term Loans on US Bank Creditors' Equity Values: An Event Study of South Korea's Case." *Journal of International Financial Markets* 11, nos. 3–4: 363–394.

Zimmerman, Hubert. 2002. *Money and Security: Troops, Monetary Policy, and West Germany's Relations with the United States and Britain, 1950–1971.* New York: Cambridge University Press.

Printed in the USA/Agawam, MA
August 29, 2017

657769.007